PSYCHOLOGICAL DIMENSIONS OF SOCIAL INTERACTION:
Readings and Perspectives

PSYCHOLOGICAL DIMENSIONS OF SOCIAL INTERACTION:
Readings and Perspectives

Edited by
DARWYN E. LINDER
Arizona State University

ADDISON-WESLEY PUBLISHING COMPANY
Reading, Massachusetts
Menlo Park, California · London · Don Mills, Ontario

This book is in the
ADDISON-WESLEY SERIES IN PSYCHOLOGY

DO

To My Parents

Preface

There was a time when science in the academic world that confronted the undergraduate consisted of a set of discrete disciplines. Within each one students were taught as though they intended to become active practitioners and most introductory courses had a distinctly preprofessional emphasis. Those students who did not intend to become members of the profession simply absorbed what they could and were tolerated by their instructors as long as they remained unobtrusive. Introductory textbooks emphasized the theoretical core of the discipline and supplementary readings reinforced that emphasis. Volumes of collected readings almost always consisted of articles that were originally published in the professional journals and were chosen for inclusion according to how well they conveyed information from one professional to another. In psychology, an author who writes for a professional journal can assume that he and his readers will share a great deal of knowledge and that he can use the language, even the jargon, of his special scientific community. He is enabled, then, to present his argument succinctly to those who share his language and are adequately prepared with prior information. In addition, since he is attempting to persuade his audience to accept his conclusions, an author is required to report the most minute details of his procedure and data analysis, and to force his argument through the sieve of a most stringent logic. For the student who will one day become just such an author mastery of this kind of material is essential training, but there are many other kinds of students and they are no longer content to absorb what they can from the preprofessional training directed at others. Enrollments in introductory courses in psychology and sociology have been swelled by students who seek only an amateur's understanding of the disciplines they see as most relevant to the problems of living in modern, western society. For them the jargon and the rigor of scientific communication from one professional to another become barriers to understanding, and it is for them that this book is intended.

A book for such an audience must meet at least two criteria set by its intended readers and at least one that will be set by the instructor who requires them to read it. The students will require that the selections included are well written in language accessible to an intelligent lay public, and that they treat problems and issues deemed important by the students themselves. The instructor will require an honest presentation of material that will contribute to the attainment of the level of intellectual development he has set as a goal for his students. It seemed possible to meet these three criteria with a book of readings and commentary on social interaction. As a teacher of social psychology I wanted students to learn something about the principles that govern different sorts of interactions and about the motivations of the interactors. Also, the study of social interaction provides an opportunity to touch on problems in race relations, friendship and attraction, encounter groups, and a host of topics that are of personal concern to students.

The structure of the book, while simple, is along a theoretical dimension rather than around a set of discrete problems. The first section presents some views on the motivational basis and adaptive functions of human gregariousness. The rest of the book is concerned with the description and analysis of interactions of increasing complexity. Interactions in dyads, small groups, organizations, and, finally, between races, subcultures, generations, and nations are discussed by a distinguished group of social scientists. I have tried to integrate these selections with one another and to place them in some perspective by writing brief introductions and summaries for each section.

One reason for agreeing to edit this book was that I knew of a number of discussions of aspects of social interaction that I had often thought would make excellent reading for beginning students, but were scattered in a wide variety of sources. I also felt that there must be many instances unknown to me in which a sociologist, psychologist, or psychiatrist has tried to communicate his understanding of human interaction to those not initiated into his scientific order. What I started to collect, then, were the more informal writings of scientists whose ideas and empirical contributions I had admired in the professional literature. But in discussing my plans with students and colleagues I found that almost everyone had a favorite selection to recommend, so that I cannot claim to have unearthed the contents of this book singlehandedly.

I suppose that this book could be considered a primer of human social behavior and like any primer it simplifies and omits what many would consider vital. My purpose, however, is not to provide a rigorous introduction to our discipline. A number of textbooks will perform that function for the courses in which I think this book might be a useful supplement. Rather, I hope to engage the student's interest in the psychological dimensions of his interpersonal behavior and, hopefully, to open for him a nascent understanding of the social transactions in which he participates. I think that however well we may teach, we often communicate to students our perception of social psychology as an abstract science. A stunned and incredulous silence often has followed my assertion that the students before me will behave according to the principles I have discussed. In my view, however, one purpose of introductory courses in the behavioral sciences is to demonstrate that much of human behavior is lawful, and to make the further, though obvious, point that the student and those around him, being human, behave according to those very laws. I hope that this book will be useful in providing the student with a personal perspective from which to understand social interaction, as a supplement to, not a substitute for, a more abstract and theoretical approach. One of the musty mottoes of liberal education was that his study of the arts and sciences only prepared the student for a life of continuing education. But an implication of the admonition that we should give psychology to the people, contained in George Miller's American Psychological Association presidential address, is that we should provide students with a psychology they can use and to which they can add as they live their lives. Hopefully, the works presented in this volume will help in the attainment of that goal.

I am grateful to Duke University for supplying facilities, materials, and personnel without which it would have been impossible to begin this project, and for granting me sabbatical leave for the academic year 1971–72 enabling me to complete this work. I also wish to thank Stanford University for being my gracious and supportive host during my sabbatical year. I am grateful for the personal assistance given me by Mrs. Barbara Cameron of Duke University and Mrs. Rosanne Sausotte of Stanford University who helped with the many details of this project. Final work on this book was completed in the winter of 1971–72, while my wife, Marie, and I stayed for several months on the exquisite, winter-bound shore of Lake Tahoe. Marie deserves special thanks from me and from anyone who finds this book useful. Without her assistance in typing the final draft, her patience, and finally her gentle insistence that I finish, it would have been impossible to complete this volume.

Zephyr Cove   D. E. L.
Lake Tahoe, Nevada
February 1972

Contents

Part 1.   Motivational and Functional Bases for Social Interaction

1. The Need for Social Interaction/Darwyn E. Linder 1
2. Affiliation and Isolation/Stanley Schachter 4
3. Preadolescence/Harry S. Sullivan 16
4. People who need people/Darwyn E. Linder 20

Part 2.   Some Dimensions of Dyadic Interaction

1. Attraction in Dyadic Interaction/Darwyn E. Linder 27
2. Some Antecedents of Interpersonal Attraction/
    Elliot Aronson 31
3. Social Class and Campus Dating/Ira L. Reiss 43
4. Conformity as a Tactic of Ingratiation/Edward E. Jones 61
5. Who likes Whom, and Why?/Darwyn E. Linder 78
6. Some Nonverbal Dimensions of Dyadic Interaction/
    Darwyn E. Linder 83
7. Sociology of the Senses: Visual Interaction/Georg Simmel . . . 86
8. Spatial Invasion/Robert Sommer 91
9. Physical Stigma and Nonverbal Cues Emitted in Face-to-face
    Interaction/Robert Kleck 103
10. How Much Do We Say Without Speaking?/
    Darwyn E. Linder 117

11. Interaction in Some Particular Dyads/Darwyn E. Linder 122

12. Some Conditions of Obedience and Disobedience to
    Authority/Stanley Milgram 123

13. Experiments in Dyadic Conflict and Cooperation/
    Anatol Rapoport 151

14. A Conceptual Approach to the Problem of Therapist-Client
    Matching/Robert C. Carson 159

15. Conflict and Accommodation in Dyads/Darwyn E. Linder . . . 167

Part 3.   Interaction in Small Groups

1. An Introduction to Social Interaction in Groups/
   Darwyn E. Linder 173

2. Primary Groups/Charles H. Cooley 177

3. The Nature of Conformity and its Investigation/
   Charles A. Kiesler and Sara B. Kiesler 182

4. Social Determinants of Bystander Intervention in Emergencies/
   Latané Bib and John M. Darley 195

5. The Process of the Basic Encounter Group/Carl R. Rogers . . . 210

6. The Influence of Small Groups on Individual Behavior/
   Darwyn E. Linder 237

Part 4.   Interaction of Groups in Conflict

1. Interaction of Groups in Conflict/Darwyn E. Linder 243

2. Power, Conflict, and Social Change/James H. Laue 246

3. ABM, MIRV, and the Arms Race/Herbert F. York 257

4. Statement on Psychological Aspects of International
   Relations/Jerome D. Frank 266

5. Statement on Psychological Aspects of International
   Relations/Charles E. Osgood 277

6. The Resolution of Intergroup and International
   Conflict/Darwyn E. Linder 286

Index 289

Part 1
Motivational and Functional Bases for Social Interaction

I
The Need for Social Interaction

Darwyn E. Linder

As innumerable observers have noted, people spend a great deal of their time in the company of other people. Explanations for all this gregariousness range from positing a social instinct in man to a functional analysis of the survival value of group membership to the individual. Whether we have an instinctive need to be with others or have learned through experience that people mediate valuable outcomes, social contact becomes for most of us a necessary part of existence. Social contact can even be treated as a reinforcer. Children temporarily deprived of social contact learn a task more quickly once social reinforcement is used than do children who have not been so deprived (Gewirtz and Baer, 1958). But this first section of the book poses the question: What impels people towards social interaction? What are the properties of social interaction that make it a desirable state? Why does social interaction acquire the ability to reinforce other kinds of behavior?

There are, of course, no easy answers to such basic questions. Unlike primary drives that are based on physiological processes, social interaction does not relieve any physical need state. The reinforcing properties of social contact are not tied to the reduction of physical needs in anything like the same way that food and water are tied to the reduction of hunger and thirst. One traditional explanation for the reinforcing properties of social contact is based on the mechanism of secondary reinforcement. A secondary reinforcer is a stimulus configuration that has occurred in temporal or spatial contiguity with a primary reinforcer. A typical example is a colored light presented during the time that a pigeon is feeding. If this light is presented with the onset of access to the feeding box, the pigeon will later learn to emit responses in order to turn on the colored light. The light, then, has acquired reinforcement properties by its association with the primary reinforcement, food. The earliest social interactions experienced by humans have much the same form. The human infant is in social interaction, of a primitive form, with the mother during feeding. Social contact is concommitant with warmth, security, the reduction of hunger and thirst, and the satisfaction of all primary drives that motivate the infant. Thus social contact acquires the ability to reinforce behaviors and becomes a state sought after for its own value.

However, a learning theory explanation, based on the secondary reinforcement properties of social contact, seems to be stretched a little by the persistence of this secondary reinforcer and by the extent to which the secondary reinforcing properties of social contact seem to generalize to all sorts of social stimuli. It could be argued though that a wide variety of other persons provide primary reinforcers for a child as he is growing up, and that it is not generalization but rather a continuous process of acquisition of secondary reinforcers that establishes the reward value of contact with such a wide variety of persons. A learning theory account of man's need to experience social contact may seem cold and barren, nevertheless it is a beginning toward understanding our needs for social interaction.

An alternative to the learning theory account is the hypothesis that man's social behavior is instinctive. An explanation of the human need for social interaction based on instinct must assume that humans through evolutionary processes have developed a pre-programmed response that impels them to associate with other members of the species. It is not difficult to justify the assumption that organisms that could form themselves into tribes or groups were more likely to survive in the primitive environment than organisms that were not capable of social organization. But it is rather a long step to assume that this kind of selection depended upon, or resulted in, a genetic endowment in man for social contact. It seems in many ways more likely that natural selection focused on intelligence rather than on an instinct for social interaction so that more intelligent organisms survived and were able to respond to the primitive environment by learning to organize themselves into tribes or communities having a social structure that enhanced the potential for survival. Furthermore, the data that have accrued over the years on the responses of feral children seem to support a learning hypothesis.

Feral children, abandoned or lost, and deprived of social contact while learning to survive in a wilderness environment have been studied whenever such instances have been authenticated in the past. Perhaps the most famous case is Itard's study of the wild boy of Aveyron (Itard, 1962). In most instances feral children have shown great reluctance to establish social contact, and contact with other human beings has not seemed to provide reinforcement for them, nor has it seemed that they were impelled to seek or maintain social contact once they had been discovered and rescued from their wild environment. If man had a truly instinctive need for social interaction, these feral children might even have been expected to seek out fellow humans, rather than to remain in the wilderness.

Some sort of decision between a learning theory account of man's drive for social interaction and an instinct hypothesis is not easily reached. The work of ethologists, particularly Hess (1959), on imprinting has led to the concept of a critical period. Hess's studies have shown that ducklings will learn to respond to a mother duck as a primary social target only if the mother duck is present during a critical period in which the duckling is imprinted on her, and from that point on follows the mother and seeks social contact with her. Something similar to a critical period may occur in human infants so that children deprived of contact with other humans during the critical period do not imprint on humans as targets for social interaction. Later, when provided the opportunity to experience social contact, they do not respond to it. In much the same way, Hess's ducklings would follow whatever had been the target present during the critical period rather than a more natural social target, the mother duck. It may be, then, that humans do instinctively respond to social interaction with other humans, but only if humans are present during the critical period for imprinting. Of course this is all speculative. To investigate these hypotheses directly would require experiments on human infants that no one would be willing to perform.

But my purpose in this first section of the book is not to provide a definitive answer to the question of why man seems to desire social contact and interaction with others of the species. Rather, the two selections presented in this section are individual attempts to grapple with this problem. Neither of them provides a comprehensive answer to the question we have posed, yet they both seem to capture, sometimes poignantly, sometimes amusingly, something of the quality of our drive for contact with other human beings.

REFERENCES

Gewirtz, J. L. and Baer, D. M., The effect of brief social deprivation on behavior for a social reinforcer. *J. abnorm. soc. Psychol.*, 1958, *56*, 49–56.

Hess, E. H., Imprinting. *Science*, 1959, *130*, 133–141.

Itard, J. M. G., *The Wild Boy of Aveyron*. New York: Appleton-Century-Crofts, 1962. (Translated from *Rapports et memoires sur le sauvage de l'Aveyron*, Paris, 1894).

2
Affiliation and Isolation

Stanley Schachter

Walt Whitman once wrote, "I . . . demand the most copious and close companionship of men." The sentiment is familiar, for most of us have experienced occasional cravings to be with people, sometimes for good reason, frequently for no apparent reason: we seem simply to want to be in the physical presence of others. Whatever the reasons, these desires that draw men together furnish the substance of the social sciences, which in good part are devoted to the study of the process and products of human association.

Despite the importance of the study of the affiliative needs, almost nothing is known of the variables and conditions affecting these needs. We have no precise idea of the circumstances that drive men either to seek one another out or to crave privacy, and we have only the vaguest and most obvious sort of suggestions concerning the kinds of satisfaction that men seek in company. A review of the literature indicates that there has been some psychoanalytic thought on the topic (39); that, at most, there have been two or three immediately relevant experiments; and, most prominently, that there has been a generous amount of common sense, mildly obvious formulation of the fact that people do associate (9, 19).

The gist of what we have called the "common sense" line of thought may be summarized in two propositions:

First, people do mediate goals for one another, and it may be necessary to associate with other people or belong to particular groups in order to obtain specifiable individual goals. For example, to hold a job it may be necessary to join a union; to play bridge it may be necessary to become a member of a bridge club; and so on. Not surprisingly, a number of studies have demonstrated that the attractiveness of the group or of specific individuals will vary with their promised or proven success in facilitating goal attainment (26, 48). Certainly, a large if not major portion of our associational activities can be subsumed in this general class of affiliative behavior. It is a peculiarly asocial sort of affiliation that is under consideration, however, for people qua people may be considered as irrelevant. In these terms, a nonsocial means of goal attainment may be just as satisfactory and attractive as a social means. More cogent to present concerns is the substance of the following proposition.

Second, people, in and of themselves, represent goals for one another; that is, people do have needs which can be satisfied *only* in interpersonal relations. Approval, support, friendship, prestige, and the like have been offered as examples of such needs. There is no doubt that such needs are particularly powerful ones and that association with other people is a necessity for most of us.

The distinction drawn in these two propositions is hardly a sharp one, and one could quibble endlessly as to whether this is a distinction at all. The relative emphasis of the two propositions, however, is clear enough. In the one case, association represents a means to an essentially asocial goal; in the other, the gratifications, whatever they may be, of association itself represent the goal. It is our intention in this volume to concentrate on the latter type of associational activity and to attempt to spell out some of the circumstances and variables affecting the affiliative tendencies.

SOCIAL NEEDS

Perhaps the single study directly concerned with the experimental examination of specific needs which can be satisfied only by means of interpersonal contact is the study of Festinger, Pepitone, and Newcomb (17), where it is suggested that there are two classes of needs which group membership satisfies—needs such as approval, status, and help, which require singling the individual out and necessarily involve high social visibility and individual identifiability; and needs whose satisfaction requires being "submerged in the group," a condition labeled "de-individuation" and described as a state of personal anonymity in which the individual does not feel singled out or identifiable.

It is suggested that there are many kinds of behavior in which the individual would like to engage where activity is prevented by the existence of inner restraints. Instances of such behavior might be acting wildly and boisterously, "talking dirty," expressing hostilities, and so on. Festinger *et al.* suggest that under conditions where the individual is not "individuated" in the group, such restraints will be reduced and individuals will be able to satisfy needs which might otherwise remain unsatisfied. In an ingenious experiment, these authors demonstrate that the state of de-individuation in the group does occur and is accompanied by reduction of the inner restraints of the members of the group. Further, they demonstrate that groups in which such restraints are reduced are more attractive to their members than groups in which restraints are not reduced.

An entirely different set of needs that may be satisfiable only by association with other people is discussed by Festinger (15) in his theoretical paper on social comparison processes. Festinger writes:

> The drive for self evaluation concerning one's opinions and abilities has implications not only for the behavior of persons in groups but also for the processes of formation of groups and changing membership of groups. To the extent that self evaluation can only be accomplished by means of comparison with other persons, the drive for self evaluation is a force acting on persons to belong to groups, to associate with others. And the subjective feelings of correctness in one's opinions and the subjective evaluation of adequacy of one's performance on important abilities are some of the satisfactions that persons attain in the course of these associations with other people. How strong the drives and satisfactions stemming from these sources are compared to the other needs which people satisfy in groups is impossible to say, but it seems clear that the drive for self evaluation is an important factor contributing to making the human being "gregarious." (Pp. 135–136.)

This notion of a "drive for self evaluation" has slowly emerged as the theoretical underpinning for a schema and body of research on social influence. Essentially it has been assumed that, given such a drive, tendencies exist to establish the "rightness" or "wrongness" of an opinion and the "goodness" or "badness" of an ability. If it is possible to check against physical reality or against authoritative sources, such evaluation may be forthright and simple. More often than not, however, such evaluative resources are nonexistent and it is possible to evaluate only by reference to other people. One's ability is good or bad only in comparison with the ability of others; one's opinion may be evaluable as right or wrong only in terms of agreement or disagreement with the opinions held by other people. Such social evaluation is possible, however, only when the comparison points are relatively close to one's own position. A sandlot baseball player learns little about his ability as a batter by comparing himself with Willie Mays; he learns a great deal by comparing himself with his teammates. A Jew does not evaluate the correctness of his opinions of Zionism by comparing them with those of an Arab nationalist. It has been demonstrated (12, 16, 30) that stable evaluation of opinions or abilities is possible chiefly when those with whom comparison is made are quite close to one's own position. The greater the extent to which other people agree with one's opinion, the greater the feeling of correctness and the greater the stability of the opinion. This series of assumptions concerning the evaluation process leads to the expectation that when discrepancies of opinion or ability exist among the members of a group, tendencies will arise to reduce this discrepancy. Spelling out and testing the implications of this expectation, a series of experiments have been conducted in order to examine the conditions under which influence will be exerted by the group (3, 28, 36), influence will be accepted by the individual (3, 20), and deviates rejected by the group (36).

Though the assumption of a drive for evaluation of the opinions and abilities has proven particularly fruitful in generating research tests of its implications, whether or not such a drive is indeed a major source of "gregariousness" is still an open question, for there are, unfortunately, almost no studies bearing directly on the question. The single piece of research that is relevant is the case study by Festinger, Riecken, and Schachter (18) of a millenial group. This group had predicted, for a specific date, the destruction of the world as we know it through a series of earth-shaking cataclysms—a predication which was not confirmed. The effect of this disconfirmation was, of course, to shake all confidence in the belief system which had led to this prediction. The almost immediate reaction to disconfirmation was a frenzy of attempts to convert and proselyte. Prior to disconfirmation, this group had been secretive and inhospitable, avoiding all publicity and contact with outsiders. Following disconfirmation, they exposed themselves to the world, called in newspapers, and worked furiously to convince possible converts—all, presumably, in an attempt to establish a new and firm social basis for their beliefs.

If one broadens this "drive for evaluation of opinions and abilities" into a more general "drive for cognitive clarity," one does find additional evidence for the proposition that evaluative or cognitive needs are an important source of affiliative behavior. There are many thoroughly ambiguous issues that are impossible to clarify by reference either to the physical world or to authoritative sources. For such issues, if one assumes a need for cognitive clarity, it is plausible to assume that attempts to reduce ambiguity will take the direction of intensive social contact and discussion. Evidence that this is indeed the case can be found as a by-product of a study of rumor transmission conducted by Schachter and Burdick (37). This study took place in a girls's school. In a deliberate attempt to create an event that would be mystifying and not readily explainable, the principal of the school went into several classrooms during first-hour classes, pointed at a single girl, and said, "Miss K., get your hat, coat, and books and come with me. You will be gone for the rest of the day." Nothing of this sort had ever occurred before and absolutely no explanation was offered. Not surprisingly, the remaining girls spent almost all of the school day in intensive social contact and communication in an attempt to clear up and understand what had happened.

Such is the research literature that has most immediately stimulated our interest in the topic—a handful of studies suggesting that people will seek one another out when their opinions are shaken; that an otherwise uninterpretable event leads to a search for social reality; and that association may lead to a state of relative anonymity allowing the satisfaction of needs which might otherwise remain unsatisfied. These are intriguing leads, but it is clear that our knowledge of conditions affecting affiliative behavior is still rudimentary.

Many other studies, of course, are tangentially related to present concerns. Atkinson (2) and French (22, 23) and their colleagues have devised measures of a generalized need for affiliation. Their experimental work, however, has been concerned chiefly with a comparison of specific behaviors of those high and low in affiliative needs. They have not as yet published research on the conditions and variables affecting the magnitude of the affiliative need. In addition to studies dealing explicitly with aspects of affiliation, studies of interpersonal communication and rumor spread, studies of panic, and studies of sociometric choice, community studies and analyses of organization behavior almost all rest on implicit assumptions as to the sources of affiliative behavior. However, most of these studies are concerned primarily with the consequences of association rather than with the reasons for association, and we shall not attempt to review studies peripherally related to our central concern.

SOCIAL ISOLATION

If such evidence is needed, an examination of the consequences of social isolation shows convincingly that the social needs are indeed powerful ones. Autobiographical reports of such people as religious hermits, prisoners of war, and castaways make it clear that the effects of isolation can be devastating. For example, a prisoner (52) writes, "Gradually the loneliness closed in. Later on I was to experience situations which amounted almost to physical torture, but even that seemed preferable to absolute isolation." (P. 89.) Such reports are extremely common and seem to be as typical of those who have gone into voluntary isolation as of those forced into solitary confinement. A religious solitary (1) describes the experiences in these words:

> When the great resolution has been taken, to leave all and go in search of God in solitude, there comes that first-hour zest which attends all new undertakings begun with good will. That lasts as long as it ought to last; more shortly for big souls, longer for the lesser— it is the jam to get the powder down. Then begins the first revelation, and a very unpleasant one it is. The solitary begins to see himself as he really is. The meanness, the crookedness of natural character begins to stand out in a strong light; those wounds that disobedience to conscience in the past has left festering, now give forth their poisoned matter. There may be terrible uprisings of lower nature, and more formidable yet, resistance of self-will to the strait-jacket into which he would thrust it. Here you get the reason for what look like eccentricities of asceticism, its bread-and-water fasts, scourges and the rest, even to midnight immersions practiced by Celtic solitaries. It is Master Soul, the rider, whipping Brother Ass, the body, into obedience. This stage may last months or years; how

long, no one can foretell; but while it lasts, solitude is full of strife and pain. (Pp. xv-xvi.)

Aside from these reports of profound disturbance, anxiety, and pain, the condition of absolute social deprivation as described in these autobiographical reminiscences seems responsible for many other dramatic effects. Most prominently, the following three trends characterize many of these reports:

First, the reported "pain" of the isolation experience seems typically to bear a nonmonotonic relationship to time—increasing to a maximum and then, in many cases, decreasing sharply. This decrease in pain is frequently marked by onset of a state of apathy sometimes so severe as to resemble a schizophrenic-like state of withdrawal and detachment, so marked in some cases that prisoners have to be physically removed from their cells (14). Indeed, this condition is so common that the Church recognizes the state of acedia (or sloth, one of the seven deadly sins) as an occupational disease of hermits.

Second, there seems to be a strong tendency for those in isolation to think, dream, and occasionally hallucinate about people. Indeed, comparison of the anchoritic or hermit saints with the cenobitic saints indicates greater frequency of visions and hallucinatory experiences for the religious solitaries.

And third, those isolates who are able to keep themselves occupied with distracting activities appear to suffer less and be less prone to the state of apathy. Those prisoners who are able to invent occupations for themselves and schedule for themselves activities such as doing mental arithmetic or recalling poety seem to bear up better under the experience than those who either think chiefly of their plight or dwell on the outside world. Needless to say, cause and effect are completely confounded in this relationship as stated, but Schönbach (40) in an experimental study addressed directly to this point has demonstrated that a state of deprivation is far more bearable under manipulated conditions of irrelevant and distracting thought than under conditions where thought is concerned almost wholly with the source of deprivation.

Though all of this is of absorbing interest, its interpretation is thoroughly confounded by the multitude of coacting variables and the indistinguishability of cause and effect; proper investigation of these various phenomena demands direct and controlled study. Several years ago, therefore, in a preliminary attempt to examine some of the consequences of social isolation, the author conducted a small series of isolation case studies. Student volunteers, who were paid ten dollars a day, were supplied with food and locked into a windowless room for periods ranging from two to eight days. Their watches and wallets were removed and their pockets emptied. Some subjects were provided with a variety of minor distracting devices, such as metal-link puzzles, dart boards, and so on. Other subjects were left completely to their own devices, and entered a room barren of anything but a bed, a chair, a lamp, a table, and, unknown to the subject, a one-way observation mirror. In no case was a subject permitted books, radio, or any device that could directly serve as a social surrogate. For the period of isolation, all subjects were left completely to their own resources to spend their time as they would and with absolutely no communication with the experimenter or the outside world. In addition to these voluntary isolates, interviews were conducted with a few prisoners who, as punishment, were in solitary confinement cells at the Minnesota State Prison.

After the extremes of the autobiographical reports, this first-hand contact was sobering. The prisoners, who had been in solitary confinement for periods ranging from three to five days, were not particularly troubled by the experience; they were interested chiefly in bumming cigarettes and complaining about the food. As for the students, five subjects were run in the experimental isolation room. One subject broke down after two hours, almost hammering down the door to get out. Of three subjects who remained in isolation for a two-day period, one admitted that he had become quite uneasy and was unwilling to go through the experience again, while the other two subjects seemed quite unaffected by two days of isolation. The fifth subject was isolated for eight days. He admitted that by the end of this eight-day period he was growing uneasy and nervous, and he was certainly delighted to be able to see people again; but one could hardly describe his condition as having grown intolerable.

The results of these few case studies are clearly incompatible with the common report, in the autobiographies analyzed, that isolation is, at some point, an agonizingly painful process. Two explanations come readily to mind: the period of isolation is far longer for real-life isolates than for our subjects; and other variables, most of all fear, account for the extreme suffering of real-life isolates.

Neither of these explanations seems to suffice. Though fear is certainly a reasonable alternative explanation for such isolates as prisoners of war, it can hardly be considered an adequate explanation for the reported sufferings of voluntary isolates such as religious solitaries.

The length of time in isolation does not seem a satisfactory explanation, for in quite a few of these autobiographical reminiscences the reported peak of suffering occurs after only a few hours of isolation and in many of these reports the peak seems to occur within two or three days of isolation. Many other explanations are possible, of course, but the incompatibility of our case studies with the autobiographical reports can most reasonably be explained in terms of the biased sample of documents available for this sort of library survey. Certainly not everyone in isolation suffers so dramatically, and probably only those who have really undergone extreme suffering bother to write about the experience. Also, our own subjects were volunteers, and it is likely that only those who did not anticipate any difficulties would agree to take part in this study.

In any case the fact that we were unable to produce a state of social need or of even mild suffering with any consistency ruled out further research along this line. It had been our intention to conduct an experiment, eventually, in which the social needs would be manipulated by means of social deprivation and the effects of this manipulation noted on a variety of variables, such as influencibility, post-isolation social behavior, and so on. The results of these few cases made it quite clear that this would not be an easy experiment to carry out. It seemed evident that it would require some ten to fourteen days of isolation to produce the state of social need required, that in the process the very best subjects would be lost, and that to complete the multi-condition experiment planned would, with the facilities available, require approximately eleven years.

Needless to say, it was with considerable relief that this particular experiment was abandoned. Happily, however, this was not all wasted effort, for it did lead directly into a more promising line of investigation on the nature of the variables affecting the affiliative tendency.

REFERENCES

1. Anson, P. F., *The Quest of Solitude.* New York: Dutton, 1932.
2. Atkinson, J. W. (ed.), *Motives in Fantasy, Action, and Society.* Princeton: Van Nostrand, 1958.

3. Back, K., Influence through social communication. *J. abnorm. soc. Psychol.*, 1951, *46*, 9–23.

4. Bakan, D., The relationship between alcoholism and birth rank. *Quart. J. Stud. Alc.*, 1949, *10*, 434–40.

5. Baker, H. J., Decker, F. J., and Hill, A. S., A study of juvenile theft. *J. educ. Res.*, 1929, *20*, 81–87.

6. Beller, E. K., Dependence and independence in young children. Doctoral dissertation, State University of Iowa, 1948.

7. Beller, E. K., Dependency and autonomous achievement striving related to orality and anality in early childhood. *Child Developm.*, 1957, *28*, 287–315.

8. Burt, C. *The Young Delinquent.* New York: Appleton, 1925.

9. Cartwright, D., and Zander, A. (eds.), *Group Dynamics: Research and Theory.* Evanston, Ill.: Row, Peterson, 1953.

10. Dean, Daphne A., The relation of ordinal position to personality in young children. Unpublished M. A. dissertation, State University of Iowa, 1947.

11. Draguet, R., *Les pères du désert.* Paris: Plon, 1949.

12. Dreyer, A. S., Aspiration behavior as influenced by expectation and group comparison. *Hum. Relat.*, 1954, *7*, 175–90.

13. Ehrlich, Danuta, Determinants of verbal commonality and influencibility. Unpublished doctoral dissertation, University of Minnesota, 1958.

14. Faris, R. E. L., Cultural isolation and the schizophrenic personality. *Amer. J. Sociol.*, 1934, *40*, 155–64.

15. Festinger, L., A theory of social comparison processes. *Hum. Relat.*, 1954, *7*, 117–40.

16. Festinger, L., Gerard, H., *et al.*, The influence process in the presence of extreme deviates. *Hum. Relat.*, 1952, *5*, 327–46.

17. Festinger, L., Pepitone, A., and Newcomb, T., Some consequences of deindividuation in a group. *J. abnorm. soc. Psychol.*, 1952, *47*, 382–89.

18. Festinger, L., Riecken, H., and Schachter, S., *When Prophecy Fails.* Minneapolis: University of Minnesota Press, 1956.

19. Festinger, L., Schachter, S., and Back, K., *Social Pressures in Informal Groups.* New York: Harper, 1950.

20. Festinger, L., and Thibaut, J., Interpersonal communication in small groups. *J. abnorm. soc. Psychol.*, 1951, *46*, 92–99.

21. Finneran, Mary P., Dependency and self-concept as functions of acceptance and rejection by others. *Amer. Psychol.*, 1958, *13*, 332 (abstract).

22. French, Elizabeth G., Development of a measure of complex motivation. In J. W. Atkinson (ed.), *Motives in Fantasy, Action, and Society*. Princeton: Van Nostrand, 1958, pp. 242–48.

23. French, Elizabeth G., Effects of the interaction of motivation and feedback on task performance. In J. W. Atkinson (ed.), *Motives in Fantasy, Action, and Society*. Princeton: Van Nostrand, 1958.

24. Gewirtz, J. L., Dependent and aggressive interaction in young children. Doctoral dissertation, State University of Iowa, 1948.

25. Gibby, R. G., Stotsky, B. A., Hiler, E. W., and Miller, D. R. Validation of Rorschach criteria for predicting duration of therapy. *J. consult. Psychol.*, 1954, *18*, 185–91.

26. Gilchrist, J. C., The formation of social groups under conditions of success and failure. *J. abnorm. soc. Psychol.*, 1952, *47*, 174–87.

27. Haeberle, Ann, Interactions of sex, birth order and dependency with behavior problems and symptoms in emotionally disturbed preschool children. Paper read at East. Psychol. Assn., Philadelphia, Penn., 1958.

28. Hoffman, P. J., Festinger, L., and Lawrence, D. H., Tendencies toward group comparability in competitive bargaining. *Hum. Relat.*, 1954, *7*, 141–59.

29. Hooker, Helen F., A study of the only child at school. *J. genet. Psychol.*, 1931, *39*, 122–26.

30. Hoppe, F., Erfolg und misserfolg. *Psychol. Forsch.*, 1930, *14*, 1–62.

31. Horwitz, M., Exline, R., Goldman, M., and Lee, F., Motivational effects of alternative decision-making processes in groups. Office of Naval Research Technical Report, June, 1953.

32. Levy, J., A quantitative study of behavior problems in relation to family constellation. *Amer. J. Psychiat.*, 1931, *10*, 637–54.

33. Murphy, G., Murphy, Lois B., and Newcomb, T. M., *Experimental Social Psychology*. New York: Harper, 1937.

34. Rosenow, C., and Whyte, Anne H., The ordinal position of problem children. *Amer. J. Orthopsychiat.*, 1931, *1*, 430–34.

35. Ruchmick, C. A., *The Psychology of Feeling and Emotion*. New York: McGraw-Hill, 1936.

36. Schachter, S., Deviation, rejection and communication. *J. abnorm. soc. Psychol.*, 1951, *46*, 190–207.

37. Schachter, S., and Burdick, H., A field experiment on rumor transmission and distortion. *J. abnorm. soc. Psychol.*, 1955, *50*, 363–71.

38. Schachter, S., and Heinzelmann, F., Cognition, anxiety and time perception. In preparation.

39. Scheidlinger, S., *Psychoanalysis and Group Behavior: A study of Freudian group psychology.* New York: Norton, 1952.

40. Schönbach, P., Need, relevance of ideation, force and time estimation. Doctoral dissertation, University of Minnesota, 1956.

41. Sears, R. R., Ordinal position in the family as a psychological variable. *Amer. sociol. Rev.*, 1950, *15*, 397–401.

42. Sears, R. R., Maccoby, E., and Levin, H., *Patterns of Child Rearing.* Evanston, Ill.: Row, Peterson, 1957.

43. Sears, R. R., Whiting, J. W. M., Nowles, V., and Sears, P. S., Some child-rearing antecedents of aggression and dependency in young children. *Genet. Psychol. Monogr.*, 1953, *47*, 135–236.

44. Slawson, J. *The Delinquent Boy.* Boston: Gorham Press, 1926.

45. Sletto, R. F., Sibling position and juvenile delinquency. *Amer. J. Sociol.*, 1934, *39*, 657–69.

46. Stagner, R., and Katzogg, E. T., Personality as related to birth order and family size. *J. appl. Psychol.*, 1936, *20*, 230–46.

47. Taylor, J. A., A personality scale of manifest anxiety. *J. abnorm. soc. Psychol.*, 1953, *48*, 285–90.

48. Thibaut, J., An experimental study of the cohesiveness of underprivileged groups. *Hum. Relat.*, 1950, *3*, 251–78.

49. Thurstone, L. L., and Thurstone, Thelma G., A neurotic inventory. *J. soc. Psychol.*, 1930, *1*, 3–30.

50. Torrance, E. P., A psychological study of American jet aces. Paper read at West. Psychol. Assn., Long Beach, California, 1954.

51. Torrance, E. P., Survival stresses and food problems. Paper read at the Symposium on Stress as Applied to Food Problems. Quartermaster Research and Development Command, Natick, Mass., 1957.

52. Weissberg, A., *The Accused.* New York: Simon and Schuster, 1951.

53. Whiting, J. W. M., and Child, I. L., *Child Training and Personality.* New Haven: Yale University Press, 1953.

54. Wiener, D. N., and Stieper, D. R., Psychometric prediction of length and outpatient therapy. Monograph in preparation.

55. Witty, P. A., "Only" and "intermediate" children of high school ages. *Psychol. Bull.*, 1934, *31*, 734.

56. Woodworth, R. S., *Experimental Psychology.* New York: Holt, 1938.

57. Woodworth, R. S., and Marquis, D. G., *Psychology*. New York: Holt, 1948.

58. Woodworth, R. S., and Schlosberg, H., *Experimental Psychology*. New York: Holt, 1954.

59. Wrightsman, L., The effects of small-group membership on level of concern. Unpublished doctoral dissertation. University of Minnesota, 1959.

60. Young, P. T., *Emotion in Man and Animal*. New York: Wiley, 1943.

3
Preadolescence

Harry S. Sullivan

NEED FOR INTERPERSONAL INTIMACY

Just as the juvenile era was marked by a significant change—the development of the need for compeers, for playmates rather like oneself—the beginning of preadolescence is equally spectacularly marked in my scheme of development, by the appearance of a new type of interest in another person. These changes are the result of maturation and development, or experience. This new interest in the preadolescent era is not as general as the use of language toward others was in childhood, or the need of similar people as playmates was in the juvenile era. Instead, it is a specific new type of interest in a *particular* member of the same sex who becomes a chum or a close friend. This change represents the beginning of something very like full-blown, psychiatrically defined *love*. In other words, the other fellow takes on a perfectly novel relationship with the person concerned: he becomes of practically equal importance in all fields of value. Nothing remotely like that has ever appeared before. All of you who have children are sure that your children love you; when you say that, you are expressing a pleasant illusion. But if you will look very closely at one of your children when he finally finds a chum—somewhere between eight-and-a-half and ten—you will discover something very different in the relationship—namely, that your child begins to develop a real sensitivity to what matters to another person. And this is not in the sense of "what should I do to get what I want," but instead "what should I do to contribute to the happiness or to support the prestige and feeling of worth-whileness of my chum." So far as I have ever been able to discover nothing remotely like this appears before the age of, say, eight-and-a-half, and sometimes it appears decidedly later.

Thus the developmental epoch of preadolescence is marked by the coming of the integrating tendencies which, when they are completely developed, we call love, or, to say it another way, by the manifestation of the need for interpersonal intimacy. Now even at this late stage in my formulation of these ideas, I still find that some people imagine that intimacy is only a matter of approximating genitals one to another. And so I trust that you will finally and forever grasp that interpersonal intimacy can really consist of a great many things without genital contact; that intimacy in this sense means, just as it always has meant, closeness, without specifying that which is close other than the persons. Intimacy is that type of situation involving two people which permits validation of all components of personal worth. Validation of personal worth requires a type of relationship which I call collaboration, by which I mean clearly formulated adjustments of one's behavior to the expressed needs of the other person in the pursuit of increasingly identical—that is, more and more nearly mutual—satisfactions, and in the maintenance of increasingly similar security operations.[1] Now this preadolescent collaboration is distinctly different from the acquisition, in the juvenile era, of habits of competition, cooperation, and compromise. In preadolescence not only do people occupy themselves in moving toward a common, more-or-less impersonal objective, such as the success of "our team," or the discomfiture of "our teacher," as they might have done in the juvenile era, but they also, specifically and increasingly, move toward supplying each other with satisfactions and taking on each other's successes in the maintenance of prestige, status, and all the things which represent freedom from anxiety, or the diminution of anxiety.[2]

THE EXPERIENCE OF LONELINESS[3]

Before going on, I would like to discuss the developmental history of that motivational system which underlies the experience of loneliness.

Now loneliness is possibly most distinguished, among the experiences of human beings, by the toneless quality of the things which are said about it. While I have tried to impress upon you the extreme undesirability of the experience of anxiety, I, in common apparently with all denizens of the English-speaking world, feel inadequate to communicate a really clear impression of the experience of loneliness in its quintessential force. But I think I can give you some idea of why it is a terribly important component of personality, by tracing the various motivational systems by developmental epochs that enter into the experience of loneliness. Of the components which culminate in the experience of real loneliness, the first, so far as I know, appears in infancy as the need for contact. This is unquestionably composed of the elaborate group of dependencies which characterize infancy, and which can be collected under the need for tenderness. This kind of need extends into childhood. And in childhood we see components of what will ultimately be experienced as loneliness appearing in the need for adult participation in activities. These activities start out perhaps in the form of expressive play in which the very young child has to learn how to express emotions by successes and failures in escaping anxiety or in increasing euphoria; in various kinds of manual play in which one learns coordination, and so on; and finally in verbal play—the pleasure-giving use of the components of verbal speech which gradually move over into the consensual validation of speech. In the juvenile era we see components of what will eventually be loneliness in the need for compeers; and in the later phases of the juvenile era, we see it in what I have not previously mentioned by this name, but what you can all recognize from your remembered past, as the need for acceptance. To put it another way, most of you have had, in the juvenile era, an exceedingly bitter experience with your compeers to which the term "fear of ostracism" might be justifiably applied—the fear of being accepted by no one of those whom one must have as models for learning how to be human.

And in preadolescene we come to the final component of the really intimidating experience of loneliness—the need for intimate exchange with a fellow being, whom we may describe or identify as a chum, a friend, or a loved one—that is, the need for the most intimate type of exchange with respect to satisfactions and security.

Loneliness, as an experience which has been so terrible that it practically baffles clear recall, is a phenomenon ordinarily encountered only in preadolescence and afterward. But by giving this very crude outline of the components that enter into this driving impulsion, I hope I have made it clear why, under continued privation, the driving force of this system may integrate interpersonal situations despite really severe anxiety. Although we have not previously, in the course of this outline of the theory of personality, touched on anything which can brush aside the activity of the self-system, we have now come to it: Under loneliness, people seek companionship even though intensely anxious in the performance. When, because of deprivations of companionship, one does integrate a situation in spite of more or less intense anxiety, one often shows, in the situation, evidences of a serious defect of personal orientation. And remember that I am speaking of orientation in living, not orientation in time and space, as the traditional psychiatrists discuss it. I have already given my conception of orientation in living in discussing the juvenile era. Now this defective orientation may be due, for instance, to a primary lack of experience which is needed for the correct appraisal of the situation with respect to its significance, aside from its significance as a relief of loneliness. There are a good many situations in which lonely people literally lack any experience with things which they encounter. . . .

Loneliness reaches its full significance in the preadolescent era, and goes on relatively unchanged from thenceforth throughout life. Anyone who has experienced loneliness is glad to discuss some vague abstract of this previous experience of loneliness. But it is a very difficult therapeutic performance to get anyone to remember clearly how he felt and what he did when he was horribly lonely. In other words, the fact that loneliness will lead to integrations in the face of severe anxiety automatically means that loneliness in itself is more terrible than anxiety. While we show from the very beginning a curiously clear capacity for fearing that which might be fatally injurious, and from very early in life an incredible sensitivity to significant people, only as we reach the preadolescent stage of development does our profound need for dealings with others reach such proportion that fear and anxiety actually do not have the power to stop the stumbling out of restlessness into situations which constitute, in some measure, a relief from loneliness. This is not manifest in anything like driving force until we arrive at the preadolescent era.

NOTES

1. [*Editors' note:* Sullivan's use of the terms "collaboration" and "cooperation" should be kept in mind throughout this section. By cooperation, he means the usual give-and-take of the juvenile era; by collaboration, he means the feeling of sensitivity to another person which appears in preadolescence. "Collaboration ... is a great step forward from cooperation— *I* play according to the rules of the game, to preserve *my* prestige and feeling of superiority and merit. When we collaborate, it is a matter of *we*." (*Conceptions of Modern Psychiatry*, p. 55.)]

2. [*Editors' note:* Up to this point, this chapter is taken from 1944–1945 lectures, rather than from the series on which this book is primarily based, since this portion is missing in the latter series because of failures of recording equipment. The material corresponds, however, to the outline in Sullivan's Notebook.]

3. [*Editors' note:* Several times, in the series of lectures which has been used as the basis for this book, Sullivan has made reference to a later discussion of loneliness. Yet this discussion does not appear in this particular series, probably through an oversight. We have therefore included here a discussion of loneliness from a 1945 lecture.]

4
"People who need people ...

Darwyn E. Linder

... are the luckiest people in the world." So goes a popular song of several years ago, and yet the fact that we all seem to need contact with other humans provides a necessary condition for the existence of the terrible effects of social isolation. Stanley Schachter attempted to use the effects of social isolation to understand more completely the social needs of humans. He found, however, that he was unable to produce with regularity the effects of social isolation that he required in order to study the impact of that kind of deprivation on subsequent social behavior. But other researchers have found that even brief periods of social deprivation can produce greater responsiveness to social reinforcement. See for example Stevenson (1965). To summarize, social deprivation can cause anxiety in some normal adults, and is often followed by greater responsiveness to social reinforcement. But this still leaves us with the basic question: Why is social interaction a valued state?

While Schachter was dissatisfied with his attempts to use social deprivation to study social motivation in humans, the work to which he refers at the end of the selection presented here dealt with the effects of fear on affiliation tendencies, and established the link between anxiety and affiliation. He found that subjects made fearful by being led to expect a series of painful electric shocks were much more likely to want to affiliate with others than subjects who expected only mild and not at all unpleasant electric shocks. An unexpected finding in this series of experiments was that first born and only children apparently were more strongly motivated to seek affiliation when they had been made anxious. It seems, then, that the social milieu into which the first born child enters provides him with a stronger need to affiliate with people under conditions of stress than does the environment later born children enter at birth. Schachter offers some tantalizing speculations as to the nature of these differences and the mechanisms by which affiliation motivation is affected. For example, it may be that the mother of a first born child is much more attentive to his needs and reinforces his affiliative tendencies to a greater extent than the mother of a later born child who by this time has had experience and is more casual in the amount of attention she pays to the baby's needs. But while birth order has been shown to be related to a number of psychological characteristics (Sampson, 1965), no truly satisfactory explanations have been offered.

Other authors, Berne (1964) and Harlow and Harlow (1962), for example, have placed heavy emphasis on the effects of social conditions during infancy upon later social and sexual functioning. Berne refers to early work by Spitz (1945) and others, indicating that institutionalized children develop various kinds of physical and intellectual deficiencies, and traces these deficiencies to the absence of social stimulation.

The Harlows' experiments, in which infant monkeys experience various kinds of social isolation from birth, have reinforced, as they point out, our faith in the clinical findings relevant to human infants. The complete lack of social responsiveness and the apparent inability to learn to respond to social stimuli shown by the monkeys the Harlows raised in isolation for the first two years of life, indicates that there are irreversible and irremediable deficiencies occasioned by this kind of deprivation. Neither learning theory nor an instinct model of social motivation seems to explain these drastic effects. If social motivation is a learned response, then it should have been possible for these monkeys to learn some social responsiveness. If social motivation is an instinctive part of the animal's behavioral repertoire, then some vestiges of social responsiveness should have survived. Perhaps work by ethologists such as Konrad Lorenz (1952) and Eckard Hess (1959) on imprinting may again be relevant. The concept of critical period mentioned in the introduction to this section may be useful in explaining why these infant monkeys were unable to attain any level of social interaction. If social stimuli were totally absent during the critical period for imprinting, then socially directed responses could never be successfully elicited by subsequent exposure to other members of the species.

One of the fascinating implications of the Harlows' work (Harlow and Harlow, 1962), comes from the evidence gathered from monkeys raised in the absence of real mothers, but in the presence of other infant monkeys. These subjects apparently demonstrated almost completely normal social and sexual development while never experiencing contact with a biological mother. Apparently, infant monkeys can successfully socialize one another in the absence of adults. It is interesting to note that the social behavior of infant monkeys raised only in the presence of other infant monkeys was more fully developed than that of infants who had been raised with their biological mothers, but isolated from other infant monkeys. As the Harlows point out, these infant-infant affectional systems may be very important in establishing the basis for later mature social and sexual behavior. The importance of social relationships with age mates for later integration of personality has been emphasized by Sullivan's description of the need for interpersonal intimacy in the pre-adolescent era of development. Sullivan asserts that this form of intimacy permits the validation of personal worth. Perhaps this is a way of saying that in the more complex motivational system of human beings, intimacy with age mates is as necessary to full development as contact between infant monkeys is to the later development of adequate social and sexual adjustments.

Sullivan and Harlow and Harlow in their different ways emphasize the power of social motivation. Sullivan speaks of the terrible experience of true loneliness. He asserts that it is so terrible because it deprives us of needed contact or the tenderness required during infancy, it deprives us of the acceptance necessary during the juvenile era—acceptance by compeers—and of the intimate exchange necessary for the validation of personal worth during the pre-adolescent era. He goes on to point out that loneliness must be more terrible than anxiety because persons will move into anxiety arousing situations in order to escape from loneliness. Harlow and Harlow, in discussing the behavior of motherless mother monkeys with regard to their own offspring, point out that the offspring of these socially deprived mothers would withstand terrible physical abuse in order to remain in contact with a cruelly unrewarding mother. The persistence of these infants raises some doubt as to the complete malleability of social motivation through mechanisms of punishment and reinforcement. Their determination to remain in contact with the mother in the face of so much punishment looks very much like an instinctive response.

Now we come back to our original question: Is man a social animal by instinct or by conditioning? Do we seek out the company of other humans because of the reinforcements they provide or because in the dim and primitive past only those humans with an instinct for social contact could survive the rigors of the primitive environment? I am certainly not yet ready to answer that question definitively, or even to attempt an answer. Nor, I think, are any of my colleagues ready to make definitive statements about the root causes of human gregariousness. But in this section I have tried to emphasize again the power of the motivation in humans for contact with other humans. We can now move on in the succeeding portions of this book to an examination of what happens when humans do come into contact with one another, confident that, as we knew all along, people do need people.

REFERENCES

Berne, E., *Games People Play*. New York: Grove Press, 1964.

Harlow, H.F., and Harlow, Margaret K., The effect of rearing conditions on behavior. *Bulletin of the Menninger Clinic*, 1962, 26, 213–224.

Hess, E. H., Imprinting. *Science*, 1959, *130*, 133–141.

Lorenz, K., *King Solomon's Ring*. New York: Crowell, 1952.

Sampson, E. E., The study of ordinal position: antecedents and outcomes. In B. A. Maher (ed.), *Progress in Experimental Personality Research*. Vol. 2. New York: Academic Press, 1965, pp. 175–222.

Spitz, R. A., Hospitalism: Genesis of psychiatric conditions in early childhood. *Psychoanalytic Study of the Child*, 1945, *1*, 53–74.

Stevenson, H. W., Social reinforcement of children's behavior. In L. P. Lipset and C. C. Spiker (eds.), *Advances in Child Development*. Vol. 2. New York: Academic Press, 1965, pp. 97–126.

Part 2
Some Dimensions of Dyadic Interaction

I
Attraction in Dyadic Interaction

Darwyn E. Linder

The simplest form of social interaction is the two-person group, or dyad. But even these interactions are incredibly complex, and we shall be able in this book to look only at a few aspects of interaction in dyads before we move on to even more complex social interactions. Perhaps the most basic dimension in dyadic interaction is the attraction of the two members of the dyad for one another. Attraction is most basic because without it the dyad would not form and there would be no interaction to talk about. Cohesiveness, the force that binds individual members to a group (Festinger, 1950), has been defined as the algebraic sum of the forces that pull members toward a group, the group's attractiveness, and those forces that push him away from the group. By definition, then, a person must be more attracted than repelled if he is to remain a group member, and this applies to dyads as well as to larger groups. It is true that some dyads are formed on the basis of necessity and some dyadic interactions occur in competition for scarce resources, but most often dyads are formed only if the two members of the dyad are attracted to one another, only if they like one another.

Despite man's gregariousness, documented in the last section, we are not equally attracted to all other human beings. We exercise selectivity in the choice of partners for dyadic interaction and in our choice of groups for more complex kinds of interactions. There seems little reason to doubt the almost circular statement that we like people who provide positive outcomes for us, but having made such a statement we are still left with the problem of attempting to specify what outcomes are positively valued by what individuals. It is easy to say that if P likes

O, it must be because some of *O*'s behaviors are reinforcing or have some positive value for *P*, but I point out again that this is really a circular statement.

One fascinating area of research in social psychology has been to try to break out of this circularity by specifying the conditions under which some unlikely behaviors, or usually non-reinforcing behaviors, are in fact valued and do lead to increases in liking for the people who emit them. Elliot Aronson, whose article in this section recounts some of his contributions to this research enterprise, has put together a lecture entitled "How to Win Friends and Influence People by Being Hostile, Clumsy and Stupid." Some of his research has been focused on discovering the circumstances in which hostility, clumsiness, and other usually negatively valued characteristics do in fact increase the liking that one has for the person who possesses them. For example, in a study by Aronson, Willerman, and Floyd (1966), an intelligent, graceful, successful person, practically perfect in every way, was better liked if he was perceived to take a clumsy pratfall, spilling coffee all over himself, than when the pratfall was not included in the stimulus tape presented to subjects who judged his attractiveness. Aronson, *et al.*, argued that increased attractiveness following a clumsy pratfall occurs because the clumsiness humanizes an otherwise forbiddingly perfect person, and that this quality of human warmth, clumsiness, allows greater attraction for the stimulus person. This is not to say that the stimulus person who didn't take the pratfall was disliked—he was liked much more than the person whose qualities were less positive. So it is true that we generally like people who have positively valued characteristics, and there is general agreement on what those characteristics are. Nevertheless there are some circumstances in which some unusual, or rather, usually negatively valued characteristics do in fact enhance the attraction we feel for another person.

Another complicating factor in the equations of who likes whom and why, is that each of us has experienced a unique socialization and has through that socialization come to appreciate unique combinations of qualities in other persons. Some of us like artists and some of us like athletes; some of us like tall people and others are attracted to short people. Males simply do not share universal standards in what makes an attractive female figure, and neither do females share universal norms about what is an attractive male. This brings us to one of the most fascinating and at the same time most complex questions in the study of attraction, attraction between the sexes. Basically, I suppose everyone is attracted to attractive members of the opposite sex, even though our agreement on which members of the opposite sex are most attractive is less than perfect. Even so, there just aren't enough attractive women to go around so that every male may have one, nor are there enough attractive men around so that every female may have the ideal romantic partner. Furthermore, it seems that the more attractive an individual is, the more attractiveness he or she demands of potential partners. But this looks like the beginning of an ever-increasing spiral so that everyone is attracted to people who are more attractive and the more attractive people are attracted to people who are still more attractive. And yet somehow we manage to work it out. We find partners with whom we are compatible and share our lives with people that we love. That this is so is perhaps the result of many factors entering into these relationships in addition to attractiveness or the possession of generally highly valued qualities. In his article in this section Ira Reiss describes some factors that influence campus dating, and other writers have suggested a wide variety of determinants of attraction. For example, Winch (1958) has proposed that people are attracted to one another on the basis of need complementarity. That is, a dominant person will find the behavior of a submissive partner more reinforcing than he would the behavior of an equally dominant partner. As with all such intrinsically appealing ideas, there is evidence to support a process of mate selection based in part on need complementarity, but simultaneously there is evidence to demonstrate that we are attracted to people who are similar to us, similar in political ideology, similar in religious beliefs, similar in tastes, ethnic and socioeconomic backgrounds, etc. Research by Donn Byrne and his associates (Byrne, 1969) has documented that the simple knowledge that another person shares some of your attitudes will enhance the attraction you feel for that person. Again, it seems reasonable that one would be more comfortable in a long-term relationship with a person whose political and religious beliefs were similar to your own, with a person who shared your tastes in music and food and lifestyle, but, of course, we find exceptions to these general propositions in many instances.

Still another factor determining how well we like particular individuals may be the extent to which we are committed to interacting with them. An experiment by Darley and Bersheid (1967) has demonstrated that commitment to prolonged interaction with another individual will lead to enhanced attraction for that person. Enhancement can take the form of emphasizing the positive qualities the person does possess and deemphasizing or diminishing the importance of the negative qualities that he may possess. So perhaps our attraction to the partners we find for dyadic interaction is in part determined simply by our commitment to a long-term interaction with those people.

Finally, there is another side to the coin of attraction. Having determined that we are attracted to someone, we then become interested in whether or not that person is attracted to us. Since the positive qualities that we can offer within an interaction are generally determined and not easily manipulated, we may begin to wonder if there are any tactics or strategies that we can employ to enhance the liking for us that a particular person may have. The word that describes these strategies and tactics is ingratiation. The word has some mildly pejorative connotations in that we generally devalue or dislike ingratiators. We think of ingratiation as unauthentic behavior, as dissembling, and disingenuous. But it seems to me that these descriptions, these negative feelings about ingratiation and ingratiators are somewhat misplaced. If I find myself attracted to another person isn't it only honest of me to attempt to win his reciprocal attraction? Do I have to depend solely on his perceptions of me, or can I try to take some steps to insure that he sees the positive qualities I have, and that he is aware of the reinforcements I could provide in an interaction? But whatever the evaluation we place on ingratiation and ingratiators, there are research questions to be asked. What are the conditions under which a person may wish to engage in behaviors designed to make himself more attractive to another. That is, when will people attempt ingratiation? Secondly, what behaviors will they employ, how will they try to win the esteem or affection of a target person? And third, what will be the effect of these behaviors on the target person? Will they have the desired outcome of increasing his esteem for the ingratiator, or will they in some way boomerang, winning for the ingratiator only the disapprobation that is attached to that term? Edward E. Jones had dealt with these questions in a series of experiments that are reported most fully in his book *Ingratiation* (Jones, 1964) but some of his work is summarized in his article presented in this next group of selections.

We will focus, then, on some unusual determinants of attraction, some factors in the selection of romantic partners, and some strategies for winning the esteem of others. The three articles I have selected do not constitute a survey or overview of the literature on social attraction. Rather, they deal with questions that I think are intriguing and important.

REFERENCES

Aronson, E., Willerman, B., and Floyd, J., The effect of a pratfall on increasing interpersonal attractiveness. *Psychonomic Science*, 1966, *4*, 227–228.

Byrne, D., Attitudes and attraction. In L. Berkowitz (ed.), *Advances in Experimental Social Psychology*. New York: Academic Press, 1969.

Darley, J., and Berscheid, E., Increased liking caused by the anticipation of personal contact. *Hum. Relat.* 1967, 20, 29–40.

Festinger, L., Informal social communication. *Psychological Review*, 1950, *57*, 271–282.

Jones, E. E., *Ingratiation*. New York: Appleton-Century-Crofts, 1964.

Winch, R. F., *Mate Selection: A Study of Complementary Needs*. New York: Harper and Row, 1958.

2

Some Antecedents of Interpersonal Attraction[1]

Elliot Aronson

During the past several years, my students and I have been busily and even happily engaged in an investigation of the antecedents of interpersonal attraction. In simple language, our aim is to understand what makes people like one another. Since man *is* a social animal, it seems reasonable to assume that being liked by his fellows would be important to him. Indeed, even a casual observation of human behavior suggests that most people much of the time act in a manner which can be interpreted to mean that they like to be liked. They seek friendships, they try to impress others with their abilities, they entertain guests, they

Reprinted (abridged) from *Nebraska Symposium on Motivation 1969*, W. J. Arnold and D. Levine (eds.). by permission of University of Nebraska Press. Copyright © 1970 by the University of Nebraska Press.

smile a lot, they express pleasure when told someone is fond of them, they give presents, they seem unhappy when someone ignores them or acts unkindly to them, they turn a simple little book called *How to Win Friends and Influence People* into a phenomenal best seller.

What affects interpersonal attraction? If we look at the research literature, several important antecedents emerge:

1. Propinquity—we like people who are close to us better than people who are at a distance from us, all other things being equal (Festinger, Schachter, & Back, 1950; Kendall, 1960; Newcomb, 1961; Gullahorn, 1952).

2. Similarity of values and beliefs—we like people who agree with us better than people who disagree with us (Richardson, 1940; Precker, 1952; Schachter, 1951; Newcomb, 1961; Byrne, 1969).

3. Similarity of personality traits—we like people who are like us (Shapiro, 1953; Secord & Backman, 1964).

4. Complementarity of need systems—under certain conditions we like people whose characteristics make it easy for them to satisfy our needs and whose needs are such that we can easily satisfy them (Winch, 1958).

5. High ability—we like able and competent people better than incompetent people (Stotland & Hillmer, 1962; Iverson, 1964).

6. Pleasant or agreeable characteristics or behavior—we like people who are "nice" or who do "nice things" (Bonney, 1944; Lemann & Solomon, 1952; Jackson, 1959).

7. Being liked—we like people who like us (Backman & Secord, 1959).

All of these antecedents can be loosely summarized under a general reward-cost or exchange kind of theory. It is tempting to encompass all of these phenomena under one blanket (see, for example, Homans, 1961): We like people who bring us maximum gratification at minimum expense; or, more succinctly, we like people most whose overall behavior is most rewarding. Briefly, to go through the list I have just presented, 1) propinquity is more rewarding, all other things being equal, because it costs less in terms of time and effort to receive a given amount of benefit from a person who is physically close to us than one who is at a distance

(Thibaut and Kelley, 1959); 2) people with similar values reward each other through consensual validation (Byrne, 1969); 3) the same would be true for similarity of some personality traits, whereas 4) for some needs, complementarity would be most rewarding—for example, sadism-masochism or nurturance-dependency; 5) people perhaps expect to gain more through association with highly competent people than with people of low or moderate competence. That is, in general, our past histories are such that we have usually been more rewarded by people who knew what they were about than by people who tended to blunder frequently. 6) Obviously, pleasant, agreeable behavior is more rewarding than unpleasant, disagreeable behavior; and 7) being liked can probably be considered a reward in and of itself—in addition, for most people it also entails a similarity of beliefs because most of us think rather highly of ourselves (Byrne & Ramey, 1965).[2]

While the data embodied in these statements are undoubtedly accurate and useful, one may legitimately question the extent to which one can generalize from them. It is tempting to postulate a general reward theory and let it go at that—but perhaps we should resist this temptation. I believe that the major problem with such a general theory is the difficulty of establishing an a priori definition of reward in a complex social situation. In simple situations we have little trouble: For a starving man, food is a clear-cut reward; therefore the person who provides food will probably be liked better than one who withholds food. For someone who is drowning, rescue is a clear-cut reward; therefore a drowning man will like a person who saves his life more than someone who allows him to drown. But many social situations are not that clear. As the situation becomes more complex, the context in which the "reward" is provided can change its meaning and, consequently, have a great effect upon whether or not the "rewarder's" attractiveness is increased. For example, if a person does a fine piece of work and his boss says, "Nice work, Joe," that phrase will function as a reward and Joe's liking for his boss will probably increase. But suppose Joe did a very poor job—and knew it. The boss comes along and emits the exact same phrase in exactly the same tone of voice. Will that phrase function as a reward in this new situation? I am not sure. Joe *may* interpret this statement as the boss's attempt to be encouraging and nice even in the face of a poor performance. Because of this display of considerateness, Joe may come to like the boss even more than in the case where he *had*, in fact, done a good job. On the other hand, Joe may interpret this behavior as being sarcastic, manipulative, dishonest, undiscriminating, patronizing, or stupid—any one of which could reduce Joe's liking for his boss.

The simplicity of a reward theory of liking is appealing, but its usefulness is diminished to the extent that it is difficult to specify the events and situations which are, in fact, rewarding. How might one attempt to specify these events in advance? One reasonable but rather laborious strategy involves the refinement of a definition of reward and requires the following steps: a) searching the literature for instances where an event which would appear to be rewarding does not, indeed, lead to an increase in liking; b) trying to understand the dynamics of this apparent contradiction; and c) testing this interpretation empirically. Although this is a rather painstaking procedure, it can help to clarify what we mean by "reward" and, consequently, it can lead to a greater understanding of the antecedents of attraction. We have been pursuing this strategy for the past few years with some success, but it is not very efficient—it would be extremely tedious to attempt to map out a definition of reward and its relationship to attraction by employing a technique which is almost exclusivey empirical. My inclination is not to produce an encyclopedia of antecedents of liking. A more efficient approach would entail the development and testing of different "mini-theories" of attraction. This could lead to a greater understanding of the antecedents of attraction by helping us to define the limitations of a general reward theory. I have been working on one such "mini-theory" in recent years, and I would like to describe it as well as some of the research it has led to. I call it the gain-loss theory, and I refer to it as a "mini-theory" in order to emphasize the fact that it is not intended to account for all of the data of attraction; rather, it is to be considered useful in helping us understand a smal! sub-set of such data. The simplest way to state it is as follows: Increases in rewarding behavior from another person (P) have more impact on an individual than constant, invariant reward from P. Thus, a person whose esteem for us increases over time will be liked better than one who has always liked us. This would be true even if the number of rewards were greater in the latter case. Similarly, losses in rewarding behavior have more impact than constant punitive behavior on P's part. Thus, a person whose esteem for us decreases over time will be disliked more than someone who has always disliked us—even if the number of punishments were greater in the latter situation. The reasons behind this proposition will be clearer if discussed after a description of the definitional experiment.

Imagine yourself at a cocktail party having a conversation with a person whom you've never met before. After several minutes he excuses himself and drifts into a different conversational group. Later that evening, while standing out of sight behind a potted palm, you happen to overhear this person in conversation—talking about a person he met earlier in the evening; lo and behold, it's you that he's talking about! Suppose that you attend seven consecutive cocktail parties, have a conversation with the same person at each of these parties, and, as luck would have it, chance to overhear him talking about you each time.

There are four outcomes that I find particularly interesting: 1) you overhear the person saying exclusively positive things about you on all seven occasions; 2) you overhear him saying exclusively negative things about you on all seven occasions; 3) his first couple of evaluations are exclusively negative, but they gradually become increasingly positive; 4) his first couple of evaluations are exclusively positive, but they gradually become more negative. Which situations would render him most attractive to you? Our theory would predict that you'd like him best in the "gain" condition and least in the "loss" condition.

In order to test our theory, we needed an experimental analogue of the above situation—but for reasons of control we felt that it would be essential to collapse the above events into a single long session. Moreover, it was essential that, unlike our example, the subject be absolutely certain that his evaluator is totally unaware that he (the evaluator) is being overheard; this would eliminate the possibility of the subject's suspecting that he is being flattered when he is being evaluated positively.

The central problem involved in operationalizing this situation was this: How do we provide a credible situation where, in a relatively brief period of time, the subject a) interacts with a preprogrammed confederate, b) eavesdrops while the preprogrammed confederate evaluates him to a third party, c) engages in another conversation with the confederate, d) eavesdrops again, e) converses again, etc., through several pairs of trials. To provide a sensible cover story would indeed be difficult; to provide a sensible cover story which would prevent subjects from becoming suspicious would seem impossible. We (Aronson & Linder, 1965) solved our problem with the following scenario:

When the subject arrived for the experiment, the experimenter greeted her and led her to an observation room which was connected to the main experimental room by a one-way window and an audio-amplification system. The experimenter told the subject that two girls were scheduled for this hour—one would be the subject and the other would help perform the experiment. He said that since she had arrived first, she would be the helper. The experimenter asked her to wait while he left the room to see if the other girl had arrived yet. A few minutes later, through the one-way window, the subject was able to see the experimenter enter the experimental room with another female student (the paid confederate). The experimenter told the confederate to be seated for a moment and that he would return shortly to explain the experiment to her. He then returned to the observation room and began the instructions to the real subject. The experimenter told her that she was going to assist him in performing a verbal conditioning experiment on the other student. He explained verbal conditioning briefly and went on to say that his particular interest was in the possible generalization of conditioned verbal responses from the person giving the reward to a person who did not reward the operant response. He explained that he would condition the other girl to say plural nouns to him by rewarding her with an "mmm hmmm" every time she said a plural noun. He mentioned that this should increase the rate of plural nouns said to him by the other girl. The subject was then told that her tasks were: 1) to listen in and record the number of plural nouns used by the other girl, and 2) to engage her in a series of conversations (not rewarding plural nouns) so that the experimenter could listen and determine whether generalization occurred. The experimenter told the subject that they would alternate in talking to the girl (first the subject, then the experimenter, then the subject) until each had spent seven sessions with her.

The experimenter made it clear to the subject that the other girl must not know the purpose of the experiment lest the results be contaminated. He explained that, in order to accomplish this, some deception must be used. The experimenter said that as much as he regretted the use of deception, it would be necessary for him to tell the girl that the experiment was about interpersonal attraction. ("Don't laugh, some psychologists are actually interested in that stuff.") He said that the other girl would be told that she was to carry on a series of seven short conversations with the subject and that between each of these conversations both she and the subject would be interviewed, the other girl by the experimenter and the subject by an assistant in another room, to find out what impressions they had formed. The experimenter told the subject that this "cover story" would enable the experimenter and the subject to perform their experiment on verbal behavior since it provided the other girl with a credible explanation for the procedure they would follow.

The independent variable was manipulated during the seven meetings that the experimenter had with the confederate. During their meetings the subject was in the observation room, listening to the conversation and dutifully counting the number of plural nouns used by the confederate. Since she had been led to believe that the confederate thought that the experiment involved impressions of people, it was quite natural for the experimenter to ask the confederate to express her feelings about the subject. Thus, without intending to, the subject heard herself evaluated by a fellow student on seven successive occasions.

Note how, by using a cover story that *contains* a cover story involving interpersonal attraction, we were able to accomplish our aim without arousing suspicion—only 4 of 84 subjects had to be discarded. Again, there were four major experimental conditions: 1) Positive—the successive evaluation of the subject made by the confederate were all highly positive; 2) Negative—the successive evaluations were all very negative; 3) Gain—the first few evaluations were negative but gradually became more positive, reaching an asymptote at a level equal to the level of the positive evaluations in the positive condition 1; 4) Loss—the first few evaluations were positive but gradually became negative, leveling off at a point equal to the negative evaluations in the Negative condition 2. The results confirmed our theoretical position: The subjects in the Gain condition liked the confederate better than the subjects in the Positive condition. It should be noted that if one had simply summed the number of positive (rewarding) statements, one would have been led to the opposite prediction; i.e., the confederate handed out more rewards and fewer punishments in the Positive condition than in the Gain condition. By the same token, the subjects in the Loss condition had a tendency to dislike the confederate more than the subjects in the Negative condition. This latter result did not quite reach an acceptable level of statistical significance. Once again, a theory which merely summed rewards and punishments algebraically would have led to the opposite prediction. In sum, the results are in line with our general theoretical position: A gain has more impact on liking than a set of events that are all good, and a loss tends to have more impact on liking than a set of events that are all nasty. There are probably a great many possible explanations; I will discuss the most plausible ones:

1. Anxiety reduction. When a person expresses negative feelings toward us, we probably experience some negative affect—for example, anxiety, hurt, self-doubt, etc. If the person's behavior gradually becomes more positive, his behavior is not only more rewarding in and of itself, but it also serves to reduce the existing anxiety that he previously aroused. The total reward value of his positive behavior is, therefore, greater. Thus, paradoxically, we will like the person better *because* of his previous negative, punitive behavior. This reasoning is consistent with that of Walters and Ray (1960), who demonstrated that prior anxiety arousal increases the effectiveness of social reinforcement on children's performance. Our "mini-theory" goes a step further—the existence of prior anxiety increases the attractiveness of an individual who has both created and reduced this anxiety. The kind of relationship we have in mind was perhaps best expressed some 300 years ago by Spinoza in Proposition 44 of *The Ethics:*

> Hatred which is completely vanquished by love passes into love, and love is thereupon greater than if hatred had not preceded it. For he who begins to love a thing which he was wont to hate or regard with pain, from the very fact of loving, feels pleasure. To this pleasure involved in love is added the pleasure arising from aid given to the endeavor to remove the pain involved in hatred accompanied by the idea of the former object of hatred as cause.

The same kind of reasoning, in reverse, underlies the loss part of our theory. Here the person tends to like the confederate better when the latter's behavior was invariably negative than if his initial behavior had been positive and gradually became more negative. When negative behavior follows positive behavior, it is not only punishing in its own right, but it also eradicates the positive effect associated with the rewarding nature of the other person's earlier behavior. He showed us how good it could feel to be liked—and then he snatched it away from us. Therefore, we dislike this person more than the entirely negative person, not *in spite* of the fact that he had previously rewarded us, but precisely *because* of the fact that he had previously rewarded us.

2. Competence. A second reason for the gain-loss phenomenon may involve the feeling of competence or effectance (White, 1959). If a person succeeds in changing someone's opinion, he may feel effective. Since this is a positive feeling, it may generalize to its cause. Therefore, the person may like the evaluator better because of his success at converting him. By the same token, if the person likes us initially and then gradually comes to dislike us, we may feel a loss of effectance, and this negative feeling may generalize to the person who is the cause of it.

3. Discernment. The gain-loss phenomenon may also be due to the attributed discerning ability of the evaluator. By changing his opinion about us, *P* forces us to take his evaluation more seriously. If he had expressed a uniformly positive or uniformly negative feeling toward us, we could dismiss this behavior as being a function of his own style of response; that is, we could believe either that *P* likes everybody or that *P* dislikes everybody. But if he begins by evaluating us negatively and then becomes more positive, we must consider the possibility that his evaluations are a function of his perception of us, and not merely a function of his style of responding. Because of this, we are more apt to take his evaluations personally and seriously if he changed his opinion than if his opinion had been invariably positive or invariably negative. In short, *P*'s early negative evaluations force us to take his subsequent positive evaluation more seriously because he is displaying discernment and discrimination. It proves, if nothing else, that he's paying attention to us; that he's neither blind nor bland. This renders his subsequent positive evaluation all the more meaningful and valuable. By the same token, if *P*'s evaluation of us was entirely negative, we may be able to write him off as either a misanthrope or a fool. But if his initial evaluations were positive and then became negative, we are forced to conclude that he can discriminate among people. This adds meaning (and sting) to his subsequent negative evaluation and, consequently, will decrease our liking for him.

4. Contrast. Another conceivable alternative explanation involves the phenomenon of contrast. After a succession of negative statements, a single positive statement may stand out and, therefore, may seem more positive than the same statement preceded by other positive statements. Similarly, a negative evaluation following closely behind several positive evaluations may appear to be more negative than one that forms part of a series of uniformly negative responses. I believe that this explanation is less likely because in our experiment a sharp contrast did not occur between adjacent sessions; rather, the shift from positive to negative and from negative to positive in the behavior of the confederate in this experiment was very gradual—that is, from extremely negative, to negative, to slightly negative, to neutral, to slightly positive, etc. Therefore, it seems unlikely that a contrast effect would be operating during such a gradual transition.

Although these explanations for the gain-loss phenomenon are not necessarily mutually exclusive, it would be helpful if we could determine which, if any, of the processes is involved—and if more than one is involved, which is most powerful. Some evidence concerning necessary preconditions occurs in the Aronson-Linder experiment itself. In this experiment we had a fifth experimental condition not previously described. In this condition, the confederate's initial evaluation of the subject was neutral rather than negative, and then became increasingly positive. Our reasoning behind this condition was that if some sort of anxiety or pain was unnecessary, then it might be the case that the results of the Neutral-Positive condition would be closer to those of the Gain condition than to those of the entirely Positive condition. If this had occurred, then one could conclude that pain or suffering is not necessary. However, in this condition the mean liking for the confederate was almost identical with the mean in the completely Positive condition. The difference between the Neutral-Positive and the Gain condition approaches statistical significance ($p < .07$, two-tailed). Thus, on the basis of these results, we certainly cannot eliminate anxiety reduction as a possible explanation. But, alas, we cannot easily eliminate any of the other explanations either.

GAIN-LOSS THEORY, MARITAL INFIDELITY, AND THE MAINTENANCE OF FRIENDSHIPS

Our theorizing and research leads us to postulate what some of my students have dubbed "Aronson's law of marital infidelity." Let me describe it for you: One of the implications of gain-loss theory is that, in the words of the well-known ballad, "you always hurt the one you love." That is, once we have grown certain of the good will (rewarding behavior) of a person (e.g., a mother, a spouse, a close friend), that person may become less potent as a source of reward than a stranger. Since we have demonstrated that a gain in esteem is a more potent reward than the absolute level of the esteem, then it follows that a close friend (by definition) is operating near ceiling level and, therefore, cannot provide us with a gain. To put it another way, since we have learned to expect love, favors, and praise from a friend, such behavior is not likely to represent a gain in his esteem for us. On the other hand, the constant friend and rewarder has great potential as a punisher. The closer the friend, the greater the past history of invariant esteem and reward, the more devastating is its withdrawal. Such withdrawal, by definition, constitutes a loss of esteem. In effect, then, he has power to hurt the one he loves—but very little power to reward him.

NOTES

1. Supported by a grant from the National Institute of Mental Health (MH 12357) to Elliot Aronson.
2. It should be noted that these seven antecedents of liking do not quite encompass all of the research on attraction. There are some findings that cannot be easily squeezed under the rubric of reward theory. For example, it has been repeatedly shown that people like other people and things for which they have suffered (Aronson & Mills, 1959; Aronson, 1961; Gerard & Mathewson, 1966). These phenomena will not be discussed in this essay.

REFERENCES

Aronson, E. The effect of effort on the attractiveness of rewarded and unrewarded stimuli. *J. abnorm. soc. Psychol.*, 1961, *63*, 375–380.

Aronson, E., and Cope, V. My enemy's enemy is my friend. *J. Pers. soc. Psychol.*, 1968, *8*, 8–12.

Aronson, E., and Linder, D. Gain and loss of esteem as determinants of interpersonal attractiveness. *J. exp. soc. Psychol.*, 1965, *1*, 156–171.

Aronson, E., and Mills, J. The effect of severity of initiation on liking for a group. *J. abnorm. soc. Psychol.*, 1959, *59*, 177–181.

Backman, C. W. and Secord, P. F. The effect of perceived liking on interpersonal attraction. *Human Relat.*, 1959, *12*, 379–384.

Bonney, M. E. Relationships between social success, family size, socioeconomic home background, and intelligence among school children in grades III to V. *Sociometry*, 1944, *7*, 26–39.

Byrne, D. Attitudes and attraction. In L. Berkowitz, *Advances in Experimental Social Psychology*. Vol. 4. New York: Academic Press, 1969. (In press.)

Byrne, D., and Rhamey, R. Magnitude of positive and negative reinforcements as a determinant of attraction. *J. Pers. soc. Psychol.*, 1965, *2*, 884–889.

Festinger, L., Schachter, S., and Back, K., *Social Pressures in Informal Groups: A Study of Human Factors in Housing*. New York: Harper, 1950.

Gerard, H. B., and Mathewson, G. C., The effects of severity of initiation on liking for a group: a replication. *J. exp. soc. Psychol.*, 1966, 2, 278–287.

Gullahorn, J. T., Distance and friendship as factors in the gross interaction matrix. *Sociometry*, 1952, 15, 123–134.

Homans, G., *Social Behavior: Its Elementary Forms*. New York: Harcourt, Brace & World, 1961.

Iverson, M. A., Personality impressions of punitive stimulus persons of differential status. *J. abnorm. soc. Psychol.*, 1964, 68, 617–626.

Jackson, J. M., Reference group processes in a formal organization. *Sociometry*, 1959, 22, 307–327.

Kendall, Patricia, Medical education as social process. Abstract, American Sociological Association, 1960.

Lemann, T. B., and Solomon, R. L., Group characteristics as revealed in sociometric patterns and personality ratings. *Sociometry*, 1952, 15, 7–90.

Newcomb, T. M., *The Acquaintance Process*. New York: Holt, Rinehart & Winston, 1961.

Precker, J. A., Similarity of valuings as a factor in selection of peers and near-authority figures. *J. abnorm. soc. Psychol.*, 1952, 47, 406–414.

Richardson, Helen M., Community of values as a factor in friendships of college and adult women. *J. soc. Psychol.*, 1940, 11, 302–312.

Schachter, S., Deviation, rejection and communication. *J. abnorm. soc. Psychol.*, 1951, 46, 190–207.

Secord, P. F., and Backman, C. W., Interpersonal congruency, perceived similarity and friendship. *Sociometry*, 1964, 27, 115–127.

Shapiro, D., Psychological factors in friendship, choice, and rejection. Unpublished Ph.D. dissertation, Univ. of Michigan, 1953.

Spinoza, B., *The Ethics*. Dover Press.

Stotland, E., and Hillmer, M. L., Jr., Identification, authoritarian defensiveness, and self-esteem. *J. abnorm. soc. Psychol.*, 1962, 64, 334–342.

Thibaut, J., and Kelley, H. H., *The Social Psychology of Groups*. New York: Wiley, 1959.

Walters, R. H., and Ray, E., Anxiety, social isolation, and reinforcer effectiveness. *J. Pers.*, 1960, 28, 258–267.

White, R. W., Motivation reconsidered: the concept of competence. *Psychol. Rev.*, 1959, 66, 297–334.

Winch, R. F., *Mate-selection: A Study of Complementary Needs*. New York: Harper & Row, 1958.

3
Social Class and Campus Dating

Ira L. Reiss

GENERAL BACKGROUND OF THE RESEARCH AREA

About 30 years ago, there began to appear in the sociological literature accounts of dating practices on college campuses. Although earlier writers had mentioned the same phenomenon, it was a 1937 journal article by Willard Waller that has come to epitomize this early literature on campus dating customs.[1] Waller reported that the older accepted code of a courtship system that led to formal engagement and marriage in a predictable fashion had decayed and was being replaced by a thrill seeking and exploitive type of relationship which was not integrated with marriage. This new type of relationship was a dalliance relationship, needed to fill in the time it took to get a college education and establish oneself financially. Connected with this type of dating was the "rating-dating complex" which was a set of customs that established one's prestige on campus and which in turn determined one's dating desirability. The key prestige variables were things like popularity, access to cars and money, and belonging to the best Greek organizations. Serious, marriage-oriented dating did not involve these prestige ratings. Thus, such prestige rating-and-dating was not viewed as "true" courtship. This campus dating system was discerned by Waller at the Pennsylvania State University in the early 1930's and was documented by discussion and interviews with students.

In order to clarify the place of my research, it may be well to recount very briefly a few of the relevant studies that followed the Waller article. In the 1940's Hollingshead brought forth considerable evidence indicating the social behavior of adolescents was functionally related to the social class of their parents.[2] Particularly relevant here was Hollingshead's finding that dating among high school students was heavily controlled by social class background. Then shortly after the war Harold Chris-

This selection is reprinted from: Ira L. Reiss, "Social Class and Campus Dating," *Social Problems*, 1965, *13*, 193–205.

Reprinted with the permission of the author and The Society for the Study of Social Problems.

tensen, Robert Blood, and William Smith, in separate research work, tested college students to see if the sort of rating factors (cars, money, dancing ability, etc.) which Waller found to hold at Penn State would also hold true in their samples.[3] They each found that the students in their sample largely rejected the "competitive-materialistic" items that Waller reported and instead favored "personality" factors such as "sense of humor, cheerful, good sport, natural and considerate."[4] Blood found that the type of value system Waller was speaking of was most likely to be found among the Greeks on campus but that even there it was not supported unanimously by any means. These findings brought into question Waller's own views.[5] Nevertheless, it must be borne in mind that Waller's observations may have been correct for the time and place they were made.

In 1960 Everett Rogers and Eugene Havens published a study done on Iowa State College students.[6] They had 11 judges rank the Greek organizations and the major residence on campus and then, by interviews with a random sample of 725 students and by checking the student newspapers, they gathered evidence regarding the relation of prestige to dating of various types. They found a high probability for people to date those who are ranked similar to themselves. They concluded from this:

> Therefore, Waller's hypothesis that prestige ranking governs casual campus dating but not more serious mate selection is not substantiated to any great degree by present findings. Instead, these findings indicate that students follow prestige lines at all stages of the mate selection process.[7]

A study of fraternity pledging at an Eastern college by Gene Levine and Leila Sussmann lent support to the Rogers and Havens findings on prestige factors in dating.[8] Levine and Sussmann found that it was the wealthier students who more often pledged and who more often were accepted into fraternities and who in addition had the "proper" attitudes toward fraternities. Thus, there seemed to be a class factor not only in campus ratings but in parental background that distinguished the Greek and non-Greek student.

In effect, these findings on campus dating radically revamped much of Waller's position. The "competitive-materialistic" system of values that Waller described seems to be present on college campuses today mainly as a sub-cultural element, most likely to be found among the Greek organizations. But the more recent findings on class prestige factors in dating are even more important theoretically. Waller's view of the prestige system at Penn State was not a view of people of different parental social classes dating along those class lines. Rather, Waller explicitly stated that he did not believe there were any basic social class background differences among the students.

> The students of this college are predominantly taken from the lower half of the middle classes, and constitute a remarkably homogeneous group. Numerous censuses of the occupation of fathers and of living expenses seem to establish this fact definitely.[9]

The prestige that Waller spoke of was obtained by success in dating the highest ranked girls and boys. The rating-dating system was a popularity system in which having a good line, knowing how to dance, dressing nicely, all had a part. It was, to Waller, based predominantly on dating desirability, and social class in any fundamental sense was not the basis of it. The system produced a sort of superficial rating-dating class of its own rather than depending on any more basic class system. Thus, one important question now is, is there a more fundamental class system both on and off campus with which the campus dating system is integrated and which Waller has overlooked? The Levine and Sussmann study of fraternities lends support to a positive answer to this question as does the Rogers and Havens study. Research on social class homogamy in marriage and engagement also strongly supports the view of the importance of social class in mating.[10] Careful research of this sort has not often been done on the college campus. In fact, some writers stress the democratization effects of college life and the homogeneity of social class on campuses.[11] Nevertheless, I am suggesting that the social classes on campus are not simple "popularity" classes but that they are stable class structures based on many campus values and that they reflect parental social class and affect serious as well as casual dating.

THEORY AND HYPOTHESES

In its broadest sense the orientation of my research embodies the well-tested theory that *the dating patterns of a group will follow the social class lines of that group and thereby encourage class endogamous dating and mating.*[12] The implications of this theory have only rarely been tested on college campuses although it is often spoken about.[13] It follows from this theory that one should expect to find a stratified dating system on any campus, except those campuses where, due to extremely small size and homogeneity, there is no class distinction among the students. It also follows from our knowledge that student behavior reflects parental class, that the social class differences among students should reflect class differences among the parental adult population.[14] It is of theoretical value to know not only whether or not the campus is stratified but to know whether the class system tends to reflect in some ways the parental class lines. If it does, then one latent consequence of such a system may be to maintain some remnant of adult control over mating via the promotion of class endogamous marriages which parents generally seem to favor.

The Waller approach to campus dating focused on specific date-rating factors and took them to be the essence of the dating system. It is my contention that the rating factors are merely symptoms of basic campus and parental class distinctions and that the entire system can best be understood from this social class perspective. The rating-dating system of any sort, competitive or personality based, is believed to be a direct reflection of the campus and parental class system and a way of clarifying and identifying class differences. Such clarification is viewed as part of a serious mate-selection system. Thus, Waller's view that rating-dating is a dalliance system and not integrated with serious dating or mating is questioned.

In summary, I am proposing to test two hypotheses related to the basic "class-dating" theory: (1) serious dating on campus will be in line with an existing campus stratification system, and (2) campus dating will reflect the parental class system.

METHODOLOGY

The data on campus dating were gathered at a coeducational liberal arts college in Virginia. The 19 Greek organizations (ten fraternities and nine sororities) had 840 members and 151 pledges out of a total student body of 1800 single students. There were 809 single independent students. There was a relatively even sex ratio in both Greek and independent groupings. It was decided that full information on Greek serious dating practices would be obtained as one test of the stratification-dating theory. If in 19 highly organized fraternities and sororities there was no indication of the relation of social class and serious dating, then the theory and its derivative hypotheses would be brought into question. In addition to the sample of all seriously dating Greeks, I drew a random sample which I could use to rank all campus groups, to obtain information on parental social class, and to further test on a representative sample the relation of campus class to dating patterns in both independent and Greek student groups. The random sample was an important group since it represented the entire campus. The all-Greek sample was used to give a fuller and more detailed picture of the serious dating patterns of the Greeks.

The Greek organizations all met on Monday nights and usually had over 90 percent attendance at meetings. I sent one student assistant to each Greek organization to obtain information regarding all "serious" dating relationships.[15] A serious dating relation was defined as a relatively exclusive dating relation such as going steady, being pinned or engaged. All such relations were reported to my informants together with information on the Greek, independent, or off-campus status of the dating partner. If class-dating were found in these serious relations it would be evidenced that serious dating relationships were not *just* based on "personality factors" but that these very personality factors could possibly be viewed as influenced by stratification factors.[16] Finally, if one wanted to check on the relation of mating to stratification then serious dating and not just casual dating must be checked.

The check of all 19 Greek organizations yielded 133 serious dating relations for sorority girls and 112 such relations for fraternity boys. About 30 percent of the Greek members were involved in serious relations. Sixty-two of these relations were between a sorority girl and a fraternity boy. (These figures are for members only, not pledges. Pledges were also investigated and they will be reported on later.) The 62 couples consisting entirely of Greeks on campus afforded a check on the reliability of our information. If our data were accurate the sororities and fraternities should each report 62 matched serious relations. This was the case.[17]

In addition to this all-Greek sample, a random sample of all single students on the campus was drawn and given a questionnaire. One hundred forty-four questionnaires were obtained.[18] There were 25 non-responses who were mostly students who were not located by my research assistants. Questionnaires were given out and picked up within a few hours by my 19 assistants. The questionnaire asked the respondent to rank each of the ten fraternities as high, medium, or low, and to do the same for the nine sororities, and to give reasons for the rankings assigned. In addition, questions were asked concerning the students' background including income and occupation of father, their own dating behavior, and the relative rank they would give to male and female independents and Greeks.

The all-Greek sample containing all 245 seriously dating Greeks was used as one test of Hypothesis One concerning the congruence of the dating system with the campus class system. The random sample of the campus was used to further check this hypothesis for both Greeks and independents, to rank all campus groups, and also to check the second hypothesis concerning the relation of campus class to parental social class.

THE CAMPUS STRATIFICATION SYSTEM

If the first hypothesis is correct there should be a significant association between the rank of the various campus segments and the serious dating patterns of these groups. Table 1 presents information on all the Greek students who were involved in serious dating. The fraternities and sororities were listed according to the ranking assigned by the random sample of campus students. The majority of students agreed on all rankings, although the rankings on sororities were more unanimous than the rankings on fraternities. The fraternities were divided into five high and five low ranked groups and the sororities into five high and four low ranked groups. It should be noted that many other cuts were tried on these data and the results were the same, i.e., there is a significant and strong relation between one's organizational rank and that of one's serious date. This is particularly true for the high ranked Greeks.

Table 1 also shows that although all Greek organizations have roughly the same percent involved in serious dating, the high ranked Greek organizations (particularly the fraternities) have a significantly higher percent involved in serious dating with members of Greek organizations rather than with off-campus or independents. Serious dating within the Greek system is dominated by the high ranked organizations. The low ranked Greeks, for the most part, obtain their serious dates outside the Greek system. It should be noted here that the Greek dating reported by our random sample was very similar and this is evidence of the representativeness of our random sample.

When we look in Table 1 at the relation of sorority ranking to the choice of dating an off-campus or an independent male, the results are

Table 1. Percentage Distribution of Types of Serious Dating Partners Among Greeks in the All-Greek Sample*

| | Percentage of Each Type of Partner | | | | |
	High ranked Greeks	Low ranked Greeks	Off-campus	Inde-pendent	Number of serious dating relations†
High ranked fraternities	63	12	17	8	(60)
Low ranked fraternities	14	19	23	44	(52)
High ranked sororities	44	8	48	0	(86)
Low ranked sororities	15	21	45	19	(47)

*   Significant differences exist between high and low ranked Greeks in their choice of a Greek dating partner and in the percent dating Greeks and in the percent dating independents. Also, a significant difference exists between fraternities and sororities in percent dating off-campus.

†   The percent of total members involved in serious relations is not significantly different for these four groups. Going from top to bottom of the table the percent is: 31, 27, 32, 25.

rather striking. Of the high ranked sorority girls who are not dating within the Greek system, all of them are dating off-campus and not one is seriously dating an independent male on campus. Whereas, of the low ranked sorority girls, 19 percent seriously date independent males. Since there are an equal supply of Greeks and independents on campus and an equal sex ratio, this pattern seems to imply an avoidance of independents, perhaps due to a low ranking on campus. This avoidance is particularly pronounced for the high ranked sororities.

If we look at fraternity members in Table 1 to see their choice of off-campus or independent dates, we find a pattern somewhat similar to that of the sororities. Table 1 shows that the high ranked fraternity men prefer off-campus dates significantly more than the low ranked fraternity men. In fact, the low ranked fraternity men date independent females more than they date off-campus girls. Here too, then, is evidence that the independents are ranked low particularly by high ranked Greeks, but it would seem that the independent females are not avoided to the extent that the independent males are. Our double standard culture dictates that in a dating relation, if one person is to be higher in status than the other, it should be the male; and perhaps this is why independent females are not avoided as much as independent males.[19]

There is direct evidence of the relative ranking of campus groups from our random sample which can be compared with the above evidence from the Greek sample. We asked the random sample respondents to state their relative ranking of independent males and fraternity males and of independent females and sorority girls. Rankings were asked for in terms of one's personal views and not in terms of what one thought others would generally say. The results indicated that most individuals, except independent males, feel that independent males rank below fraternity males. The independent females were evenly divided regarding their own superiority, and the independent males closely agreed with them. However, most all the Greeks were convinced that sorority girls outranked the independent girls.[20]

It should be noted that this view of the independents is generally shared by both high and low ranked Greeks.[21] Thus, it would seem that when low ranked Greeks date independents, they believe they are dating "down" but are willing to do so for other compensatory reasons or, in the case of males, simply because they don't feel the distance is so great and that it is accepted for males to date down. Perhaps some of the low ranked fraternity males date independent females with sexual goals uppermost in mind. However, in serious dating relationships this is less likely to happen.[22]

Additional evidence on this relative campus ranking comes from a further look at serious dating patterns of the independents in our random sample.[23] If independent males are ranked lower than the independent females, then it follows that the independent females in our random sample should report more serious relations with the upper classes, namely, the Greeks. This was the case—of 19 independent females with serious dates, seven were with fraternity men. It should be noted that five of the seven fraternity men dating independent females were from low ranking fraternities. This, too, would be expected. There were 11 independent males with serious dates, and only one was with a sorority girl and this was with a girl from the lowest ranking sorority on campus. Further, the independent females are more likely to have their serious dates on campus than are the independent males. Only one-third of the serious dates were off campus for independent females, whereas two-thirds of the serious dates of independent males were off campus. Finally, the independent females are involved with fraternity men about as much as the low ranked sorority girls, while the independent males are involved with sorority girls much less than low ranked fraternity males. The evidence on independents here is based on a small number of cases. However, since the results are consistent with several other checks, the confidence in the findings is increased.

In sum then, the stratification system which emerges at this point is one in which the Greeks are clearly at the top, but the low ranked Greeks are more likely to date seriously outside the Greek part of the system. In addition, the independents seem stratified by sex, with females ranked higher than males; and here too it is noted that the females have their serious dates more within the total campus system and the independent males have their serious dates predominantly outside the entire campus system.

Table 2. Percentage of Those Who Date Greeks, Who Are Dating in High Ranked Greek Organizations, in the Random Sample

Group	Percent dating high ranked Greeks
High ranked Greeks	78 (41)*
Low ranked Greeks	54 (24)
Independent females	50 (20)
Independent males	20 (10)

$$X^2 = 8.95$$
$$P < .05$$
$$G = .53†$$

* The number in parentheses is the base for the percentage.

† G = Gamma or Index of Order Association devised by Goodman and Kruskal.

Casual dating was also checked in the random sample and proved to follow stratification lines quite similar to serious dating. Many independents, especially males, do not date at all in Greek organizations. Table 2 shows the distribution of those students who do date Greeks. The same relations among high and low Greeks and male and female independents prevail in casual dating as prevailed in serious dating.[24] It may be argued that if casual dating and serious dating both show a similar relation to the campus rating system, then the rating system is integrated with serious dating and mating and is "true" courtship and not just a dalliance system as Waller contended.

An additional search was made via the questionnaire and campus records to see whether the above noted differences in campus prestige are related to differences in some key characteristics of the students in the four major campus groups. A comparison of age at which dating began among sorority and independent females revealed no significant differences. However, the same comparison of independent males and fraternity males revealed a moderately strong and almost significant difference.[25]

A stronger and a significant difference appeared between the fraternity and independent males when compared on whether they had been in love before. There was no significant difference among females.[26] Thus, it seems the fraternity males started dating earlier and had more love experiences. This "sociability" factor is one that was found to characterize fraternity men in the Levine and Sussmann study referred to above.[27] Such "sociability" background may well represent a social class difference in this sample as it did in the Levine and Sussmann sample.

A check of attitudes toward pre-marital intercourse was also undertaken. The independent males were the most conservative male group. This somewhat fits with their lack of dating and love experience. The low fraternity males were the most liberal group with high fraternity males falling in the middle. All females were about equally conservative.

The reasons for the relative ranking of the fraternities and sororities given by the total random sample were also examined to see if independents and Greeks differed here. All groups agreed that high ranking was given to a Greek organization for things such as sociability, intelligence and maturity, and campus activities. These were the most frequently mentioned ranking factors. There is evidence that these reasons are accurate perceptions of differences among the Greek organizations. A search of school records revealed that the high ranked Greeks control the student assembly and its officers. All but seven of the 125 student assembly members during a three-year period preceding the study were Greeks, and of the 118 Greeks, 87 were from high ranked Greek organizations. Of 63 Greek class officers, 53 were high ranked Greeks. This relation held up for sororities as well as fraternities.

Good looks and good grades were evaluated differently by Greek and independent males. The Greeks stressed good looks and the independents stressed good grades. Available evidence generally fits these rankings.

In the three years preceding this study, 30 beauty queens were chosen. Five of them were low ranked Greeks; 25 were high ranked Greeks; none of the beauty queens were independents. In terms of academic grades, the high ranked sororities outdo the low ranked sororities. However, among males the situation is different and the high ranked fraternities do not outdo the low ranked fraternities in grades. The independent males are better than the fraternity males in grades; but the independent females are poorer than the sorority females. The academic grade records for a ten-year period were checked and verified that this was a stable patterning of grades.

Finally, independent males valued dancing, sports, and parties less than fraternity males. The differences among sorority and independent females in rankings were fewer than those between fraternity and independent males. The sorority females gave more importance to such items as good manners, dress, and dancing ability, but otherwise there was general agreement. So here, too, the independent females are closer to the Greek females than the independent males are to Greek males.

Some of the reasons for ranking Greek organizations are similar to the sort of factors about which Willard Waller wrote. In particular, this is true of such factors as "good dancer," "good dresser," "good looking." These factors were not the most frequently mentioned; nevertheless, here is evidence of the sort of rating-dating that Waller had in mind. However, and this is my major point here, to focus on these factors as the heart of the dating system and to conclude that the system is superficial and unintegrated with marriage is to miss the crux of the matter. I am suggesting that these factors are merely part of the complex of factors which defines what sort of organization the high ranked students on campus achieve. These prestige factors are some of the variables that go with belonging to a certain campus social class and serve to identify that class. They are merely symbols of campus class status, and it is that class status that is crucial, not the symbols.[28]

I should add here that an examination of the dating behavior of the 151 pledges in the Greek organizations revealed a very similar pattern to that of Greek members. This examination involved all pledges from all Greek organizations. Also, a study checking Greek rating and dating was done on this same campus in 1954 with quite similar results.[29] Thus, the stratification we are describing has roots in the past and our examination of pledges indicates that it is being extended into the future.

CAMPUS SOCIAL CLASS AND PARENTAL SOCIAL CLASS

Although other studies have shown that parental social class affects dating and mating, there is very little data on the relation of campus social class to parental social class. Evidence from our own sample is relevant here, although our testing of this hypothesis is nowhere near as thorough as was our testing of Hypothesis One. We have shown above that the fraternity men are more socialized in terms of dating and love experience. There is also evidence showing that Greeks value elements such as dress, parties, dancing, sports, and drinking activities more than independents. Such values are again part of a "socialized" image of man which the Greeks promote and which Levine and Sussmann have identified as part of the middle classes.[30]

In the random sample, I also have information on fathers' income and occupation. Here too some differences appear among the campus strata. As can be seen in Table 3 the overall occupations of Greeks are significantly higher than those of the independents. High status occupation here is defined as executive or professional. There is also a difference in occupation of father between high and low fraternities and high and low sororities. However, these differences are not quite significant. The differences in Table 3 reflect the general rank of each campus group as discussed in this paper.[31]

Table 3 Percentage of Fathers with High Status Occupations for Various Campus Groups in the Random Sample*

Groups	Percent of fathers in high status occupations
High fraternity	69(13)†
Low fraternity	54(13)
High sorority	80(25)
Low sorority	60(10)
Independent female	42(31)
Independent male	41(22)

*   Differences within the three pairs in this table are not significant but the difference between all Greeks and all independents is significant.

†   The number in parentheses is the base for the percentage.

The females in sororities are somewhat higher in class background than the independent females and are also somewhat above the fraternity men. Females in college often come from higher class backgrounds than males. Possibly this is due to females' college attendance being considered of secondary importance to males' college attendance and so those females that do go to college come from wealthier homes.[32] This higher background may further explain the reluctance of sorority girls (particularly high ranked ones) to date independent males.

A check on income revealed one interesting relationship. Although the differences between high and low ranked Greeks and male and female independents were present, the difference between all independent females in particular came out quite high on income. One might interpret these occupational and income results as indicating that although Greeks come from higher social classes as indicated by occupation, they do not come from wealthier homes. Thus, the overall campus class differences between Greeks and independents reflect the style of life of each group as related to occupational background more than income background. It may be argued that the occupation of a father affects male values more than female values. Thus, despite their wealth the independents, particularly the males, lack the values that go with the high occupational groupings and thus are ranked lower on campus. Although this *post factum* explanation does make sense of these findings, it must, of course, be tested in new research.

The question raised in Hypothesis Two asks how parental social class affects the relationship, found in Hypothesis One, between one's own campus rating and the campus class rating of one's date. Unfortunately, the more crucial tests of Hypothesis Two cannot be made with the existing data I have available. Such tests would involve checking the various possible relations between parental social class and campus social class dating more directly. For example it is possible that, even though high campus class individuals are more likely to come from high parental classes (see Table 3), parental social class does not affect the campus class dating system. For example, even though the higher parental class boys join the higher ranking fraternities, the reasons why these boys most often date equally high campus ranked girls may well be fully independent of their parental social class. This possibility does *not* fit with Hypothesis Two. On the other hand, it is possible that parental class would fully explain the tendency of high campus ranked boys to date high campus ranked girls. If so, when one held parental social class constant and looked at only one parental social class at a time, the relation showing high campus ranked boys dating high campus ranked girls would disappear. If this happened, then one could conclude that parental class fully explained why boys and girls dated as they did within the campus class system. This would fit with Hypothesis Two.

Finally, there is another possible way that the parental social class system could influence the campus class dating system. It could be that one's campus social class acts as an intervening variable between one's parental social class and one's choice of a dating partner. Possibly it is because one has high parental social class that one gets involved in high campus class groups and these high campus class groups might develop a style of life which in turn would make one more likely to date others from similar high campus groups. This eventuality would also fit with Hypothesis Two for it would show the influence of parental class on the campus social class dating system. It is hoped that future research will test these several possibilities and thereby afford us a more precise test of Hypothesis Two.[34]

In sum then, this check of Hypothesis Two shows that there is some evidence to support the hypothesis that the stratification system on the college campus reflects the stratification system of the students' parents. However, the evidence is surely more suggestive than conclusive and is not nearly as complete as that supporting Hypothesis One.

CONCLUSIONS

The importance of this theoretical approach is its relevance for much of the past work on campus dating. In part, it tests ideas often verbalized but seldom tested, and tries to organize the many *ad hoc* findings in this area into one theory. The theory bears on Waller's position in that it defines his "materialistic-competitive" system as but one set of rating factors that can be used to symbolize the class differences among students. The rating-dating system (whether "competitive" or "personality" based) doesn't block mating; it is more an indication of the presence of an underlying campus stratification system than it is an indication of a thrill centered, exploitative dating system unintegrated with marriage or social class. As a matter of fact, the rating system operates not only on casual dating but in serious dating also and therefore seems well integrated with marriage. The manifest consequences of this dating system may well be involved with the establishment of one's rating, as Waller suggested, but the latent consequences are the support of campus and parental class endogamy. It may further be hypothesized that since parents usually favor matings within the same social class, then another latent consequence is to aid in achieving such parental goals. Awareness of such latent consequences is crucial to the understanding of the campus dating system. Without this awareness the system may appear to be merely an "irrational" system of dalliance.

There is need for several types of additional research. First it would be important to examine a more representative sample of American college students to see how this theory and its derivative hypotheses fare on different types of campuses. Stratification on campuses without Greek organizations needs investigation. My data indicate that independents do indeed have hierarchical divisions just as Greeks do, but more investigation is needed. Testing this theory on various size campuses with differing proportions of Greeks would also be valuable. In addition, how individual choice operates within the limits of a stratification system should be conceptualized more clearly. There is the important problem of how such factors as propinquity, ideal mate image, parental images, basic values, and other variables operate in relation to social class and in relation to mate selection in general. Finally, the relation of other institutions such as the political, economic, and religious to campus dating and campus class should be explored.

It is particularly important in the analysis of a "free dating system," such as we possess, to keep in mind the ways in which the system is structured and the controls of a socio-cultural nature that are operative. It is all too easy to believe the cultural ideology that we have a "free" system. The theory put forth in this paper keeps the socio-cultural limitations of our dating system in the foreground. It is by focusing on such socio-cultural factors that we may obtain insight into the functional relations of mate-selection to the overall institutional structure of our society.

NOTES

1. Willard Waller, "The Rating and Dating Complex," *American Sociological Review*, October, 1937, 2, 727–734. Joseph K. Folsom was one of the sociologists who presented similar ideas before Waller's article.

2. August B. Hollingshead, *Elmtown's Youth* (New York: John Wiley and Sons, Inc., 1949).

3. Harold T. Christensen, *Marriage Analysis* (New York: Ronald Press, 1958), 2nd edition, esp. 235–243, 261–264; Robert O. Blood, Jr., "A Retest of Waller's Rating Complex," *Marriage and Family Living*, February, 1955, *17*, 41–47; William M. Smith, Jr., "'Rating and Dating: A Restudy," *Marriage and Family Living*, November, 1952, *14*, 312–317.

4. See in particular Robert O. Blood, Jr., "Uniformities and Diversities in Campus Dating Preferences," *Marriage and Family Living*, February, 1956, *18*, 37–45. An interesting report of a similar research project on a Negro campus can be found in Charles S. Anderson and Joseph S. Himes, "'Dating Values and Norms on a Negro College Campus," *Marriage and Family Living*, August, 1959, *21*, 227–229.

5. At about this same time an article by Samuel H. Lowrie had questioned Waller's characterization of campus dating. See "Dating Theories and Student Responses," *American Sociological Review*, June, 1951, *16*, 334–340. A more recent discussion of this point can be found in Jack Delora, "Social Systems of Dating on a College Campus," *Marriage and Family Living*, February, 1963, *25*, 81–84.

6. Everett M. Rogers and A. Eugene Havens, "Prestige Rating and Mate Selection on a College Campus," *Marriage and Family Living*, February, 1960, *22*, 55–59.

7. Rogers and Havens, *ibid.*, 59.

8. Gene N. Levine and Leila A. Sussmann, "Social Change and Sociability in Fraternity Pledging," *The American Journal of Sociology*, January, 1960, *65*, 391–399.

9. Waller, *op. cit.*, 729.

10. The classic study establishing homogamy in mating is Ernest W. Burgess and Paul Wallin, *Engagement and Marriage*, (New York: Lippincott, 1953). There is an excellent account of the relation of parental class and student dating in Winston W. Ehrmann, *Premarital Dating Behavior* (New York: Holt, Rinehart & Winston, Inc., 1959), 144–169. For interesting evidence that sorority and fraternity people marry each other, see A. Philip Sundal and Thomas C. McCormic, "Age at Marriage and Mate Selection: Madison, Wisconsin, 1937–1943," *American Sociological Review*, February, 1951, *16*, 37–48, esp. p. 47. Sixty-one percent of the sorority girls married fraternity boys. A recent study reporting class homogamy in campus marriages and showing parental influence is Robert H. Coombs, "Reinforcement of Values in the Parental Home as a Factor in Mate Selection," *Marriage and Family Living*, May 1962, *24*, 155–157. For a much older

statement along these lines see Alan Bates, "Parental Roles in Courtship," *Social Forces*, May, 1942, *20*, 483–486. For evidence on the continued importance of social class in mate selection in general, see Simon Dinitz, Franklin Banks, and Benjamin Pasamanick, "Mate Selection and Social Class: Changes During the Past Quarter Century," *Marriage and Family Living*, November, 1960, *22*, 348–351; J. Daniel Ray, "Dating Behavior as Related to Organizational Prestige," (M.A. Thesis), Indiana University, 1942; Ernest A. Smith, "Dating and Courtship at Pioneer College," *Sociology and Social Research*, 1955, *40*, 92–98. Marvin Sussman has shown the ways parents control marriage in a New Haven study: Parental Participation in Mate Selection and Its Effect Upon Family Continuity," *Social Forces*, October, 1953, *32*, 76–81.

11. Listed below is one such study that tested for class homogamy in campus marriages and found little evidence of it. These authors believe that the campus is a democratizing influence which *reduces* class endogamy. Clark R. Leslie and Arthur H. Richardson, "Family Versus Campus influences in Relation to Mate Selection," *Social Problems*, October, 1956, *4*, 117–121. The literature on intermarriage also mentions that the campus breaks through traditional barriers. See Albert I. Gordon, *Intermarriage* (Boston, Beacon Press, 1964). However, there could be a democratization concerning interfaith marriage, without affecting class endogamy.

12. The references in footnote 10 are relevant here. Also, the role of stratification in love relations has been dealt with in William J. Goode, "The Theoretical Importance of Love," *American Sociological Review*, February, 1959, *24*, 38–47.

13. For a relatively early statement in this area and an interesting test of courtship among college men see Robert F. Winch, "Interrelations Between Certain Social Backgrounds and Parent-Son Factors in A Study of Courtship Among College Men," *American Sociological Review*, June, 1946, *11*, 333–341, esp. p. 338. For a study showing similarities and changes in basic values see Robert McGinnis, "Campus Views in Mate Selection: A Repeat Study," *Social Forces*, May, 1958, *36*, 368–373.

14. Hollingshead had found considerable evidence that the social class of one's parent was a good predictor of adolescent behavior. Hollingshead, *op. cit.*

15. The student assistants went back two more times to verify and check all information they had received the first time.

16. Blood, *op. cit.*, Smith, *op. cit.*; both stress personality factors as crucial in dating.

17. One additional couple broke up due to differences in the definition of their relationship that came to the foreground during the research.

18. There were 16 pledges and 5 No Answers on organizational membership which were not included in the general analysis of Greeks and independents in this paper. This left 123 respondents to be used in the general analysis. The pledges were analyzed separately.

19. For evidence and elaboration on the double standard see Ira L. Reiss, *Premarital Sexual Standards in America* (New York: The Free Press, 1960), esp. ch. 4.

20. Eighty percent of the independent males thought they ranked higher than fraternity men but all other groups had over 80 percent who said the opposite. Fifty percent of the independent females felt they ranked higher than sorority girls. Although the independent males agreed, over 80 percent of the Greeks disagreed.

21. Low fraternity as compared to high fraternity men are somewhat kinder in their ratings of independents whereas low sorority girls are almost unanimous in giving low rank to independents. These differences were not quite significant.

22. For data on this see Winston W. Ehrmann, *op. cit.*, chs. 4 and 5.

23. The independent females reported the largest group of friends from the other three campus groups, thereby further showing their pivotal positions and their tendencies to date both independent and Greek boys.

24. Table 2 is composed of answers from those who do date in Greek organizations to the question, "In which Greek organizations have you dated the most?" Some respondents will include serious dating as well as casual. However, the bulk of the dating reported is casual. Further, when known serious dating is eliminated, the relationship still holds up the same as reported although a little weaker. Actually, the relation is understated since about 35 percent of the independent females and almost 60 percent of the independent males do not date Greeks at all. This fact supports the relation of social class and dating but is not presented in the table.

25. Sorority girls had 74 percent who started dating by age 16 to the independent girls 66 percent. The percentages for fraternity and independent males were 65 and 41 respectively.

26. Sorority girls had 84 percent who had been in love to the independent girls 94 percent. The percentages for fraternity and independent males were 96 and 60 respectively.

27. Levine and Sussmann, *op. cit.*

28. For a discussion of how fashion in dress symbolizes status see Bernard Barber and Lyle S. Lobel, "Fashion in Women's Clothes and the American Social System," *Social Forces*, December, 1952, *31*, 124–131.

29. This unpublished study was done by two students: Withers Davis and Penny Hutchinson.

30. Levine and Sussman, *op. cit.* Religious differences were also checked and the only religious difference discovered was that low fraternity men were highest on Catholic and Baptist members.

31. An unpublished study by two of my students (Rusty Dietrich and Barbara Clarke) at this same college did show that, among freshmen, independent females as compared to sorority girls had lower income, less church attendance, and fewer parents who had been in sororities. No test of males was done in this study.

32. Recent evidence of females' higher status on other specific campuses can be found in Leslie Richardson, *op. cit.*, p. 120, and Robert P. Bell and Leonard Blumberg, "Courtship Intimacy and Religious Background," *Marriage and Family Living*, November, 1959, 21, 356–360, esp. p. 357.

33. The mean income based on questionnaire response of the random sample is estimated to be: High fraternity, \$12,400; Low fraternity, \$9,400; High sorority, \$12,600; Low sorority, \$11,100; Independent females, \$13,000; and Independent males, \$12,400.

34. I did ask each person in the random student sample to give me information on his or her parental social class. However, in order to make the checks suggested it would be necessary to have parental social class information on *both* the boy and the girl involved in a dating relationship. My random sample consisted mostly of students who were seriously dating someone else *not* included in the sample and this left us with a lack of knowledge about the parental class of their dates. Because of this we could only perform the partial testing of Hypothesis Two which appears in the text and in Table 3.

4
Conformity as a Tactic of Ingratiation

Edward E. Jones

There seems to be much promise in looking at social interaction with an eye to the unfolding of strategies designed to gain or maintain personal power. There is nothing novel in the suggestion that there is a strategic side to social behavior—that people try to calculate ways to

Reprinted by permission from *Science*, July 9, 1965, Vol. 149, No. 3680, pages 144–150. Copyright 1965 by the American Association for the Advancement of Science.

make the most of a particular relationship—but the attempt to study such strategies by laboratory experimentation is a recent development. Here I shall review several studies which especially concern ingratiation, or "strategic behaviors . . . designed to influence a particular other person concerning the attractiveness of one's personal qualities."[1] I hope, in the process, not only to present results relevant to a developing theory of strategic overtures, but also to illustrate a form of experimental research which seems to show promise of unraveling the subtleties of social behavior.

All interpersonal relationships involve mutual dependence; this is the equivalent of saying that each party to a social interchange has potential influence over certain rewards available to and costs incurred by the other. If the dependences of one on the other are not only mutual but approximately equal, then there is a balance of power in which each can enforce a certain minimal receipt of rewards through his capacity to enact or fail to enact the responses sought by the other. When the power in a two-person relationship is asymmetrical, however, the more dependent person is somewhat at the mercy of the more powerful one. In any event, we can well understand why the more dependent person is concerned about his poor position and, under most circumstances, tries in various ways to improve it.

When we look at the strategic alternatives available to the more dependent person, it appears that some of these strategies guarantee him at least a certain minimum of rewards but do so at the expense of confirming or strengthening the power asymmetry which defines his dependence. Other strategies, however, may be effective in modifying the asymmetry itself so that the dependent person's power is, in the long run, increased. Compliance is an example of one kind of dependence-confirming tactic. The dependent person may, through overt obedience, avoid punishment and secure the rewards available to him, but such compliance tends to perpetuate the power differential to which it is a response. For example, the more reliable the worker becomes in meeting the supervisor's demands, the more confident the supervisor will be that these demands are reasonable, and that the worker is happy with the "bargain" symbolized by the difference in their power. In contrast to compliance, we may view ingratiation as power-enhancing or dependence-reducing. By making himself attractive to the more powerful person, the more dependent person increases the value of his own sanctioning responses at the same time that he make it more difficult for the powerful person to apply the full range of sanctions that were initially part of his repertory. In other words, as the dependent person becomes more attractive, the powerful person cannot punish him without greater cost to himself. This, in effect, means that his power has been reduced.

By what specific tactical means may the dependent person increase his attractiveness? Such tactics are undoubtedly as various as social behavior itself—there is an appealing and an unappealing way of doing almost everything. But I have found it particularly useful to consider three main classes of tactics available to the "ingratiator": compliments, agreement, and presentation of oneself in a favorable light. We may support and flatter others, convince them that we share their views, or present our characteristics in terms that they can appreciate. In this article, I single out agreement, or conformity of opinion, as the dependent variable of particular interest. The experiments reviewed all show how persons modify their publicly expressed opinions as a way of coping with a condition of social dependence.

First, however, it is appropriate to comment on some of the moral issues involved in the behavior we are studying. *Ingratiation*, like its sister term, *flattery*, is at least mildly pejorative in everyday usage. The word has connotations of dissimulation and deceit in social communication. Am I suggesting, then, that most of us are so concerned with the effects of our behavior on others that we deliberately engage in manipulative and deceitful tactics in order to gain their esteem? I do not know how one could ever obtain actuarial figures on this point, but I would argue—without great alarm—that all of us under appropriate circumstances do shape our social responses to increase our attractiveness to particular people. The scientific student of such response-shaping is unlikely to make much progress by interviews or naturalistic observation. In this particular area, I have learned through research experience that people are extremely likely to deceive themselves. Not only do they want to avoid publicizing the extent to which their responses to others are conditioned by approval-seeking motives, they work busily to protect themselves from awareness of the link between wanting to be liked and modifying one's behavior to this end. It is my current belief that only by comparing appropriate experimental and control treatments can we begin to explore the conditions favorable to the tactics of ingratiation and thus begin to specify the variables essential to construction of a theory concerning it. Questions of the frequency of occurrence and the extent of such behavior in the natural environment, and questions concerning individual differences, are not considered here.

THE INGRATIATOR'S DILEMMA

Much of the fascination in studying ingratiation comes from the fact that the same situational factors that increase one person's desire to be found attractive by another alert the other (the "target" person) to the likelihood of tactical behavior. Thus, the dependent person will be strongly motivated to be ingratiating, but the fact that his dependence stands revealed reduces the likelihood that his overtures will be effective. His dilemma is magnified further by his natural reluctance to see himself as deceitful or manipulative. Thus, the more dependent he is on another, the more he will be forced to justify to himself any actions conceivably designed to curry favor with the other. These two factors—the target person's alertness to overtures from a dependent person and the dependent person's reluctance to see himself as one who uses manipulative social tactics—would seem almost to rule out ingratiating tactics in those very situations where it is important to be liked. Indeed, there is fairly good evidence that such tactics can boomerang; especially when the "actor" is highly dependent on the target person, the latter is apt to be more attracted to him if he shows some restraint in his praise or in the degree of his agreement. The results of three studies[2,3] show that, in the ambiguous area of social responses that may or may not make one seem attractive to another person, the role relation between the ingratiator and the target person is a critical factor which affects the latter's judgments of manipulative intentions or ulterior motivation.

To some extent, however, the ingratiator is protected by the vanity of the target person from having such judgments go against him. Each of us likes to believe the best about himself, and many of us must be exposed to the most blatant praise before we begin to suspect that we are the targets of manipulative intentions. Often, no doubt, the ingratiator joins his target in what might be called an autistic conspiracy, since, for understandable psychological reasons, both the ingratiator and the target person are anxious to believe that the latter is better than he is.

I now feel that this autistic conspiracy may be maintained by the most intricate interpersonal tactics—tactics designed to conceal from both the "tactician" and the target person the former's underlying intentions. Since I believe that not many of us deliberately and consciously calculate such tactical maneuvers, I am suggesting that, from well-learned orientations toward those more powerful than ourselves, we develop patterns of social behavior unwittingly designed to attract, while avoiding the extremes of sycophancy. Such extremes would reveal to both parties the true nature of the autistic conspiracy.

Let us turn now to four illustrative studies which involve agreement as the dependent variable, and which show a few of the subtleties of behavior whereby the ingratiator tries to resolve his dilemma.

ISSUE RELEVANCE AND AGREEMENT

My central thesis thus far has been that dependence increases the motivation to make oneself seem attractive, but public knowledge of this dependence makes it more difficult to gain esteem through such simple stratagems as slavish agreement or effusive compliments. In order to be successful, the ingratiator must complicate his tactics and inject some subtlety. One obvious way to increase subtlety is to convey the impression of agreeing in a discerning way. The ingratiator must steer between the Scylla of errant disagreement and the Charybdis of blatant conformity, conveying minor disagreement within the context of a general similarity of position. Beyond this, if we know something about the social context in which opinions are being exchanged, it may be possible to specify the issues on which agreement is most likely and the issues on which moderate disagreement may be expected.

One important aspect of the social context is the relative difference in status between the two persons involved in the interchange. Status differences usually imply asymmetrical power, which is one of the preconditions for ingratiation tactics, as noted above. Jones, Gergen, and Jones[3] conducted an experiment in which freshmen and upper classmen were used as subjects. Moreover, these subjects were recruited through a campus ROTC unit, and it was emphasized that their participation in the experiment was relevant to an investigation of leadership in the Navy. Thus the status differences already implied by differences in undergraduate class were reinforced by systematic reference to status differences within the ROTC unit itself; throughout the experiment, to remove any final doubt about the status discrepancy, the freshman was called "subordinate" and the upperclassman was called "commander."

After initial instructions, summarized below, members of each pair of high- and low-status subjects purportedly exchanged written messages concerning their opinions on a variety of issues. Each subject was seated in a private booth, and it was possible to intercept all outgoing communications and to control the information received by the subject. Each "message" the subject received was allegedly from the partner of different status, but in fact all subjects received the same written statements of opinion. Twelve such "messages" were received by each subject. He was asked to indicate, on the same message form, his own opinion on the issue in question, in the belief that the message form would then be "returned" to the partner. Nine of the twelve statements received were expressions of opinions highly discrepant from norms which had been established earlier in questioning an equivalent population. Our measure of conformity was the degree of discrepancy between the subject's "opinion," as recorded on the message form, and the class norm on that issue, if this discrepancy was in the direction of the opinion received. (It was assumed that the subject would have scored at or near his class norm in the absence of any social-influence pressures within the experiment.)

Crucial for our study is the fact that the 12 statements of opinion ("items") concerned three classes of subject matter, varying in their relevance to the basis of the hierarchy relating the high- and low-status partners. Three of the items concerned highly relevant Navy matters, such as whether Annapolis graduates should be given positions of authority over ROTC graduates of comparable seniority; three items concerned issues of intermediate relevance to the hierarchy—college courses, fraternities, and so on; a final set of items concerned miscellaneous general issues quite unrelated to the specific basis for the status differential. Thus, in applying the measure of conformity it was possible to gauge the degree of agreement between the received statement and the subject's expressed opinion in each of these three content areas.

Different pairs of subjects "exchanged messages" under different instructions, this difference being a major variable in the experiment. Members of some of the pairs were urged not to mislead each other and were told that the experiment was being conducted primarily to find whether people of different status could form accurate impressions of each other. (This instruction established the "control" condition.) The experimenter told subjects in the remaining pairs that the study was concerned with testing leadership potential. These subjects were told that attempts to develop leadership tests in real-life settings had foundered because commanders and subordinates had not always been initially compatible, and that the purpose of the study was to find whether "compatible groups provide a better setting in which to test leadership potential than do incompatible groups." (This instruction established the "ingratiation" condition.) The subjects were told that leadership tests would be given during drill periods later in the year. The purpose of the experimental session, they were told, was to determine the degree of compatibility of each pair of subjects of different status; each was told that his partner had expressed an initial preference for him, and he was urged by the experimenter to make a special effort to gain the liking and respect of the partner.

Now let us consider the psychological positions of the high- and low-status persons, especially in the ingratiation condition. Here, presumably, each would like to make himself attractive to the other, if only to avoid the embarrassment of ending up as a member of an incompatible pair. We would expect this desire to reflect itself in greater agreement in the ingratiation (as opposed to the control) condition. As Fig. 1 shows, this greater agreement was found: the level of conformity of opinion was significantly higher in the ingratiation condition for subjects in both low- and high-status groupings (for the moment I am disregarding the matter of item relevance). But it would be wrong to assume that the amount of agreement approached complete similarity

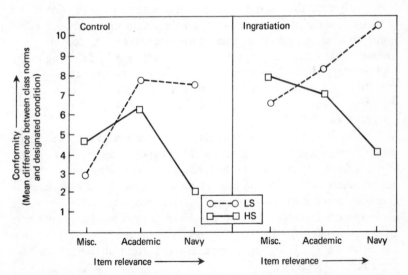

Fig. 1 Conformity as a function of status, experimental dependence, and issue relevance. *LS*, low status; *HS*, high status.

of views, even in the ingratiation condition. The average subject typically moved about halfway between his initial ratings and the ratings on the bogus messages transmitted to him.

It is obvious from Fig. 1 that the issue under consideration and its relevance to the basis of the status hierarchy is an important determinant of the degree of conformity. Furthermore, it is clear that relevance has different effects on the responses of high- and low-status subjects. This difference may be plausibly related to the difference in their psychological positions. In our study, the high-status person is in the position of wanting to maintain his status, while at the same time showing the freshman that he is "approachable." It is not surprising that he resists changing his opinions on matters having to do with the Navy; after all, his higher relative status, emphasized by the experimental arrangements, is especially based on his more advanced standing in the ROTC. His rather high degree of agreement on the items not relevant to the hierarchy may be viewed as an overture manifesting his approachability. In fact the high-status subjects show more conformity on the items relating to miscellaneous matters than the low-status subjects do, although the difference is not significant.

The position of the low-status subject is different. He must make it perfectly clear that he has no intention of usurping the position of the potential leader, but he must also avoid slavish agreement, in view of his highly dependent position and the suspicions that such agreement might arouse. What better way to solve this problem than by deferring to the high-status person's "expertise" on the Navy items and showing some spark of independence on the miscellaneous items? The result, in the ingratiation condition, is a pair of functions that are almost mirror images of each other.

This interpretation of the relation between relevance and social status is plausible and is in line with preexperimental prediction, but it is not forced upon us by the data; obviously, something approximating this relation obtains in the control condition too. It may be that differential conformity as a function of relevance and status has to do entirely with differences in experience or expertise between the partners of different status, and that the special pressures in the ingratiation condition do not bring out this particular pattern in response to strategic requirements.

Only future research can resolve this ambiguity, but certain conclusions relevant to our general proposition may be stated. If we assume that dependence is a function both of the ingratiation instructions and of the built-in differences in status, the subjects who are highest in dependence are those low-status subjects in the ingratiation condition, whereas the high-status subjects in the control condition are lowest in dependence. The former subjects are the most conforming, in general, and the latter subjects are least conforming. This is exactly what we would expect. But even the subjects who show the most conformity do not show uniform shifts from their initial opinions towards agreement with the received items; thus, whether intentionally or not, the variations from issue to issue must help protect the ingratiator from revealing his ulterior designs.

OPTIMUM CONFORMITY

A similar point is made by Jones and Jones.[4] In their study, dependence was varied by fairly elaborate experimental staging, although in this instance the subjects were status peers. Here again, each subject, isolated in a private booth, ostensibly exchanged written opinions with another subject, and here again his responses were intercepted and a prepared set of opinions was delivered to him. These opinions, allegedly from the other subject (the "target" person), bore a systematic relation to prior opinion ratings made by the first subject in the classroom several weeks before the experiment began. In one condition (hereinafter called the "same" condition) the messages were so arranged that the subject's classroom opinions were "preempted" by the incoming statement; that is, the opinions expressed in the statements received from the target person were identical with those expressed several weeks earlier by the subject. In the second variation (the "discrepant" condition), the incoming statements expressed opinions 4 points removed, on a 12-point scale, from the subject's earlier opinion ratings. This means that, if all subjects held to their originally stated opinions, those in the "same" condition would present themselves as behaviorally conforming, while those in the "discrepant" condition would appear distinctly independent. The "same"-"discrepant" variation was cross-cut by the aforementioned variation in how much the subject was made to feel dependent on the target person.

In planning the experiment we reasoned that in the "discrepant" condition the subjects would show greater conformity in a relationship of high dependence than in one of low dependence—that in the low-dependence relation the subject would try to ingratiate himself through the tactic of agreeing without agreeing completely, thus avoiding the risk of being judged a manipulative conformist. Our prediction was confirmed; in the "discrepant" condition the highly dependent subjects ended up expressing views significantly closer to the opinions in the received statements than the less dependent subjects did. We also reasoned that in the "same" condition the highly dependent subjects would show less conformity than the less-dependent subjects in order to avoid the appearance of slavish agreement. We were thus reaching for a paradoxical effect of approval-seeking, expecting to find that highly dependent subjects in the "same" condition would depart from their previously expressed views to avoid the appearance of conformity. Unfortunately, we did not find this; under the "same" condition, neither the average highly dependent subject nor the less-dependent subject changed his expressed views to any marked degree.

However, there is some interesting evidence indicating that in the "same" condition the highly dependent subjects were in something of a dilemma. The average mentioned above in fact reflected the ratings of some subjects who conformed slavishly and of others who were quite independent. Thus, the variability of conformity scores was significantly higher, in the "same" condition, for highly dependent than for less-dependent subjects. Furthermore, those highly dependent subjects in the "same" condition who showed the greatest desire to be respected (as revealed in replies to a questionnaire after the experiment) tended to avoid the extremes of great conformity and nonconformity in favor of moderate agreement. A third finding was that highly dependent subjects in the "same" condition expressed more confidence in their opinions than was found for any other combination of dependence and discrepancy. Also, only for the highly dependent subjects in the "same" condition was there a striking tendency for those who expressed agreement with the received statement to express greater confidence in the validity of their opinions than did those who indicated greater disagreement.

Thus it appears that subjects who were dependent on the target person, needing his approval, and whose own opinions were preempted by the incoming statements supposedly from the target person, showed evidence of conflict and attempted to find ways of convincing the target person of their sincere agreement with his views. In part they tried to accomplish this by striking for optimum conformity with his opinions. In part they tried to resolve the conflict by making adroit use of the opportunity to rate the degree of confidence they felt in their own opinions. A plausible interpretation of the correlation between high conformity and the subject's professed high confidence in his opinions (a correlation found only for highly dependent subjects under the "same" condition) is that subjects who are concerned that they may have shown too much agreement can attempt, through professing high confidence in their opinions, to convince the target person of their autonomy in the agreement process. Those who are concerned that they may have shown too much disagreement can soften the impact of this disagreement by professing little confidence in the validity of their opinions. There was also evidence (not discussed, because of limitations of space) that, in the "same" condition, the highly dependent subjects tried to find ways to avoid any awareness that they had agreed with the partner from any motive of wishing to gain approval.

SELF-PROTECTIVE CONFORMITY

The two studies discussed have shown, then, that the highly dependent person will try to complicate his conformity of expressed opinion in order to conceal any underlying intent to be ingratiating. Another form of complication is clearly revealed in a recent study by Davis and Florquist.[5] These investigators were especially interested in studying the possibilities of conformity as a response to a threatening target person. The experiment was set in the context of a training experience. Each subject (all were female undergraduates) appeared for the experiment and saw that another subject was also there. Each was informed that she would be given extra credit in her psychology course for assisting in the preparation and analysis of data from a large experiment. As part of her assistantship duties she was to learn how to operate certain IBM equipment under the tutelage of the experimenter. When the supervisor-experimenter took the two subjects into a room containing an IBM key punch, one of the subjects was selected to undergo training first, while the other was given an elementary board-wiring task. Actually, the subject selected for keypunch training was an accomplice of the supervisor, and both had been carefully trained to play standardized roles during the "training session." Since the subject's task required little concentration, she could readily observe the "training" across the room. As the training of the accomplice proceeded, the supervisor played one of two roles: either he was irascible, supercilious, and contemptuous of the accomplice, criticizing her errors in an emotional manner (the "emotional" condition), or he was relatively helpful and matter-of-fact (the "stable" condition).

As in the experiments previously discussed, this comparison was crosscut by another variation in the degree to which the subject was dependent on the supervisor. In the "high-dependence" condition, it was stressed that the subject would be expected to return for two additional training and data-analysis sessions, and the supervisor made it clear that he himself was going to rate the quality of her performance, a rating which would constitute 15 percent of her course grade. In the "no-dependence" condition the original supervisor was called away after training the accomplice and stating his opinions (see below), and it was made clear that the subject would be working with another supervisor.[6]

Now, we may ask, how was conformity of opinion measured in this situation? After the accomplice had received her training (under the "emotional" or the "stable" supervisor) it was clearly pointed out to the subject that she would be trained in the use of the key punch during the next session. The supervisor then gave each girl a copy of a 20-item opinion questionnaire that was supposedly in use on the project for which she was being trained. He suggested that she fill out the questionnaire in order to become familiar with it. Before she began, however, he commented, "As you can see, there is only one sensible answer for some questions; for others, there is more room for disagreement." He then read the first five items and gave his alleged opinion, backed up with brief arguments. On three of these items he clearly deviated from college norms. On each of the three items, furthermore, he presented certain arguments supporting his opinions. Three of the remaining 15 items were clearly related to the arguments expressed by the supervisor. Thus it was possible to derive two different measures of conformity: one, a direct measure of agreement on opinions explicitly endorsed by the supervisor; the other, a more indirect measure of agreement with certain arguments or premises which had formed a part of his supporting statements.

In planning the experiment, Davis and Florquist had reasoned that the threatening or emotional manner of the supervisor would have radically different implications for conformity, as a function of the degree to which the subject was dependent on him. Specifically, they predicted that highly dependent subjects would agree more with the emotional than with the stable supervisor, and that independent subjects would agree more with the stable than with the emotional supervisor. The highly dependent subject would agree with the emotional person in the interest of self-protection, to decrease the likelihood that she would later be ridiculed and embarrassed by the supervisor. In the "no-dependence" condition, the investigators reasoned, agreement would be prompted by belief in the credibility of the information source and would be professed as a protective maneuver. The stable supervisor was in fact seen as more able and intelligent and as less dogmatic and opinionated than the emotional supervisor.

Direct measures of agreement with the supervisor on the five items referred to above showed no important variations that could be attributed to the experimental conditions. On the other hand, the predictions were rather well supported when the second, more indirect, measure of conformity was used. These results are presented in Table 1. When dependence is high there is more agreement with the implied views of the emotional supervisor than with those of the stable supervisor. When dependence is low, the converse is true.

It is interesting to speculate on why the results confirmed the predictions only for the indirect measure of conformity. Davis and Florquist feel (and this is quite in line with my present argument) that tactical conformity shows itself only in the indirect measure because agreeing with someone's premises while disagreeing moderately with his conclusions is a more subtle form of ingratiation than slavishly endorsing the conclusions he directly advocates. In addition, the subject's own picture of himself should again be considered. Presumably, if he resists the inclination to agree on issues on which he is openly invited to conform, he may continue to see himself as autonomous and able to resist the self-protective urge to curry favor by agreeing with a threatening target person.

VULNERABILITY OF THE TARGET PERSON

Another way to phrase the central argument of this article is to say that the tendency to try to be ingratiating is a function both of the incentive (that is, of the degree of the "actor's" dependence on the target person) and of the probability that the attempt will be successful. In the last study to be discussed, my colleagues and I[7] attempted to vary the perceived likelihood of success by varying the alleged personal characteristics of the target person. We predicted that tactics of agreeing would be tried only when the ingratiator had something to gain from the target

Table 1 (Scores means and standard deviations) showing degree of indirect conformity on 3 items (see text). The higher the score, the greater the agreement with the supervisor's arguments. Interaction $t = 3.67$, $p. < .001$.

Dependence	Subjects (No.)	Mean score	Standard deviation
	"Stable" supervisor		
None	6	19.83	5.71
High	12	16.42	4.34
	"Emotional" supervisor		
None	6	14.50	6.57
High	10	23.30	2.54

person and at least a fair prospect of gaining it through agreement. If the target person allegedly places high value on agreement and cooperation, this should serve as an "invitation" to conformity, since he is unlikely to interpret agreement as stemming from manipulative intentions.

In this study[8] male college students were invited to participate in a "business game" in which they were to serve as subordinates to a supervisor presented to them as a graduate student in business administration. The supervisor would decide the correctness of the subject's solutions (thereby determining how much money the subject would win or lose), but he had varying degrees of freedom in reaching this decision. In one experimental condition it was clear that the supervisor was "closed-to-influence"—he had worked out the problem solutions in advance and would be simply matching the subject's attempts at solution against the predetermined "correct" answer. In the experimental condition for the remaining subjects, the supervisor was much more "open-to-influence"—he was free to determine, from problem to problem, whether the subject was correct, and had not worked out the solutions beforehand. Before the game was actually played, the subject was asked to work some practice problems to get the "feel" of the task confronting him. By rigging the results, the experimenter made it clear to each subject that he had done very poorly, promoting the inference that he would probably do quite poorly at the game itself (where monetary stakes and his prestige were involved).

Table 2 Degree of conformity of opinion: scores indicating change of opinion toward the alleged position of the supervisor: the higher the score, the greater the tendency to agree with the supervisor. For each subject, each of 20 items was scored + 1 when the subject moved from his original position toward the "position" of the supervisor, and zero when he did not. Interaction $t = 2.25$, $p < .05$. S, "solidarity"; P, "productivity."

Supervisor	Subjects (No.)	Mean score	Standard deviation
"Open-to-influence"			
S	9	8.9	1.6
P	10	6.7	1.9
"Closed-to-influence"			
S	10	6.9	2.0
P	10	7.6	2.4

After the practice game, the experimenter proposed that the subject and the supervisor communicate with each other in order to get acquainted before the real game began. (This, it was suggested, would make the game more realistic, since workers and supervisors do interact over coffee, in the lunch room, and so on.) During this get-acquainted session, a second independent variable was introduced, and our measure of conformity was obtained. The subject and the supervisor were stationed in separate rooms during the crucial interchange. Through a speaker in his room the subject "overheard" the experimenter interview the supervisor. What he heard was in fact one of two standardized tape recordings. On one recording, played to approximately half the subjects, the supervisor presented himself as especially interested in the "human" side of business. In his comments he stressed such factors as the spirit of cooperation, the importance of getting along with others, considerateness, and understanding; we shall call him supervisor S (for solidarity). On the other recording, the supervisor emphasized quality and quantity of job performance above all else; we shall call him supervisor P (for productivity). Our intent was to vary the alleged characteristics of the target person in such a way that the tactical use of agreement would be invited (supervisor S) or discouraged (supervisor P) in the "open-to-influence" condition. We expected this variation to have little or no impact in the "closed-to-influence" condition.

Conformity was measured by the now-familiar method of a bogus "exchange of notes." After listening to the supervisor being interviewed, the subject "exchanged views" with the supervisor on a variety of issues. Before expressing an opinion, the subject always received the corresponding "opinion" of the supervisor; through careful arrangement the received statements differed systematically from the opinions initially expressed by the subject on a classroom questionnaire. The degree of conformity was scored by noting, for each item on which there was a planned discrepancy, whether or not the subject had moved from his initial position toward the alleged position of the supervisor. If he had, a score of 1 was assigned for that item; otherwise no score was assigned. When these values were summed across items for each subject, the results came out as shown in Table 2. Here it may be seen that our theoretical predictions were quite nicely confirmed: conformity is greatest when it is at least possible to affect the target person's disposition to reward or punish by currying favor with him, and when he seems to value accommodation and agreement in general.

Another aspect of these results deserves comment. While, with the "open-to-influence" condition, subjects tend to agree more with S than with P, as predicted, with the "closed-to-influence" condition there is a smaller, reverse difference: subjects tend to agree more with P that with S. This is reminiscent of the results obtained by Davis and Florquist (see Table 1) who predicted and obtained more conformity with the "opinions" of the stable supervisor than with those of the emotional supervisor in the "no-dependence" condition. The emotional supervisor perhaps is analogous o S in the experiment just discussed, because his credibility as an informed communicator is relatively low. Therefore, when there is no prospect of influencing the supervisor (the "closed-to-influence" conditions), and, when the subject has no reason for agreeing with the supervisor other than that he respects his judgment, he tends to agree more with P than with S. This parallels the subject's tendency to agree more with the stable supervisor than with the emotional supervisor in the "no-dependence" condition of the Davis and Florquist experiment. The major finding, however, is that in both experiments the subject expresses most agreement with the (presumably) least-respected supervisor—the most feared or the most gullible— when the incentives for trying to win approval are high.

SUMMARY

I have discussed four experiments concerned with the use of agreement as a tactic of ingratiation—as a means of currying favor with a more powerful individual. These experiments show that the subtleties of human interaction are amenable to controlled experimental research, and they reveal some of the specific tactical maneuvers likely to be employed by those in a position of contrived social dependence. I have emphasized the "ingratiator's" dilemma, pointing out that dependence makes ingratiation tactics less likely to succeed. In each of the four experiments, it can be argued, this dilemma is resolved by some mixture of agreement and disagreement, a mixture designed to reduce the target person's suspicions and to protect the "actor" from acknowledging his tactics to himself.

In the first experiment, agreement was seen to be a joint function of the status of the subject and the relevance of the issue to the status hierarchy. Agreement was neither uniform nor slavish, but high-status subjects conformed more on irrelevant items and low-status subjects conformed more on relevant ones. In the second experiment, the subject reduced the danger of being judged an opportunistic conformist by a tactical rating of his confidence in the validity of his own opinions. His disagreements with the supposed views of the target person were softened by public expressions of low confidence in his own views when he was highly dependent on a target individual whose alleged opinions were very close to his own. In a third experiment, dependent subjects avoided conformity on issues openly endorsed by a threatening target person but tended to agree with the latter's supporting arguments. In the last experiment reported, subtlety was reflected in the decision to conform only when the target person seemed likely to appreciate agreement. The research reported is obviously no more than a first step toward understanding the complexities of strategy in interpersonal behavior.

REFERENCES AND NOTES

1. Jones, E. E., *Ingratiation*, Appleton-Century-Crofts, New York, 1964, p. 11.
2. Jones, E. E., Jones, R. G., and Gergen, K. J., *J. Personality*, 1963, *31*, 436; Dickoff, H., Thesis, Duke University, 1961.
3. Jones, E. E., Gergin, K. J., and Jones, R. G., *Psychol. Monographs*, 1963, *77*, No. 566.

4. Jones, R. G., and Jones, E. E., *J. Personality*, 1964, 32, 436.

5. Davis, K. E., and Florquist, C. C., *J. exp. soc. Psychol.*, in press.

6. In the original experiment a third condition of moderate dependence was also included. Consideration of this condition is omitted here because of space limitations.

7. Jones, E. E., Gergen, K. J., Gumpert, P., and Thibaut, J. W., *J. Personality soc. Psychol.*, in press.

8. Most of this work was supported by a NSF grant.

5
Who Likes Whom and Why?

Darwyn E. Linder

Whenever two people encounter one another, perhaps the most basic question to ask is how much are they attracted to each other. Attraction seems to be the most central or most important dimension of dyadic interaction. Knowing the level of attraction between two individuals, one can make fairly accurate predictions concerning how much influence they will have on one another (Back, 1950), the extent to which their beliefs and opinions will come to be similar (Newcomb, 1961), and a host of other behaviors. One very critical determinant of the attraction individuals hold for one another is the extent to which they mediate positive outcomes for each other. An extensive and detailed analysis of the manner in which individuals provide positive outcomes for one another and the way in which they coordinate the achievement of positive outcomes has been provided by Thibaut and Kelley (1959). In their model, each sequence of behavior emitted by a member of the dyad is paired with a sequence of behavior emitted in response or simultaneously by the other member of the dyad. Each sequence of behavior is emitted at some cost to the actor and perhaps provides some intrinsic positive reinforcement for him, but the response of the other person provides reinforcements to the recipient of that act and may exact some cost from the recipient. Thus, at the end of the behavior set, each member of the dyad can take account of his costs and rewards and determine the extent of the positive outcomes the behavior sequence has provided him. Using a model like this, Thibaut and Kelley describe the process by which persons become acquainted with one another as a series of samples taken from the matrix of possible combinations of behavior sequences. A person will be attracted to the other person in the dyad to the extent that the positive outcomes he receives are greater than those that are available elsewhere. Thus, in this model of dyadic interaction, the first experiences one has with another person would be very important in determining whether or not the interaction will continue.

This analysis may seem at first to be somewhat in contrast to the findings described by Elliot Aronson concerning the gain-loss phenomenon (Aronson and Linder, 1965) in which a person experiencing a gain of esteem from another will finally be more attracted to that person than if he had received constant high esteem. But one crucial difference between the gain-loss experiment described by Aronson and the Thibaut and Kelley model is that in the gain-loss experiments subjects were constrained to stay in the interaction and experience the full gain sequence, even though their inclination after experiencing the first negative evaluations may have been to leave the interaction. The gain-loss model, then, may apply if a person is compelled to remain in interaction, but an individual experiencing negative outcomes at the beginning of an interaction in a natural setting may well terminate it and never experience the entire gain sequence. Thus, adopting the gain-loss notion as a tactic for enhancing your attractiveness to others might, in most circumstances, be a disastrous mistake. In fact, providing an initial positive experience for the other person might be very crucial to the continuation of the interaction.

Observers of the social scene, whether they be social psychologists or college students, often poke fun at what has been called the American greeting ritual—the "hi, what's your name?—where're you from?—what's your major?"—sequence of questions that are almost stereotypically repeated by students encountering one another for the first time. And yet the greeting ritual is probably an effective way of finding out what to expect from an interaction. It is quite clear that a person with similar background and interests is more likely to provide positive outcomes than a person with very different opinions, beliefs, and values, unless, of course, one is looking for a challenge or new experience. In this light it is not at all surprising that Ira Reiss has found a campus dating system in which people with similar backgrounds and similar status tend to date one another.

Also, when we consider that the first few moments of an interaction are crucial in determining what level of reinforcement one is
likely to experience, it is not surprising that physical attractiveness
is important in determining liking. Physical attractiveness is, after
all, rewarding in and of itself to those who observe it. That's what
we mean when we say that someone is attractive—that one experiences
a positive outcome simply by looking at an attractive person. In describing the results of their study of attraction on first dates, Berscheid and
Walster (1969) indicate surprise at how important physical attractiveness
seems to be in determining romantic attraction. They found that ratings
of a date's physical attractiveness were the only measures that correlated
significantly with ratings of romantic attraction. But the attractive
person provides a relatively invariant source of positive outcome. One
need only be in the presence of an attractive other in order to experience
this kind of reinforcement. Furthermore, that reinforcement does not
depend upon any elaborate sequence of behavior. It is available immediately upon encountering the attractive person.

We like people who provide positive outcomes for us. That statement
probably summarizes what is known about the determinants of attraction
and yet in many ways it says very little, because each person, on the
basis of his unique experiences, has a different way of evaluating the
actions of other persons, and different things provide positive experiences
for him. "Different strokes for different folks" means that we are not
all attracted to the same people; it means that social interaction is not
a dull and predictable sequence of seeking out those who are generally
attractive while those who are unable to provide these generally valued
outcomes are ignored. We can all recall instances in which we have been
puzzled by the apparent attraction of one person to another whom we
would judge to be unworthy of that level of esteem. Indeed, these puzzles
and the dynamics that underlie and explain them form the basis of some
of the best of our literature and drama. Thus, a critical thing to remember when considering the reward and cost analysis of attraction is that
the way an individual experiences the behaviors of others is unique to
him and is a function of his entire previous experience and training.
Just as we all develop a unique set of preferences for foods, for clothes,
for cars, we also develop a unique set of preferences for the ways in which
we interact with other individuals. That uniqueness on the part of each
one of us makes the study of the ways in which we are attracted to one
another much more complicated and yet much more fascinating. We

can answer the question, "Who Likes Whom and Why?" with the statement, "people like those who provide positive outcomes for them," and yet leave ourselves lacking a sufficient understanding for a great number of real instances of attraction between members of dyads.

Of course, the study of the determinants of attraction is at the same time a study of the ways in which we might make ourselves attractive to other persons. Edward E. Jones has described a series of experiments in which subjects have attempted to ingratiate themselves with more powerful others by conforming to the opinions of those others. It must follow, then, that these subjects guessed that opinion conformity would be a positive outcome for the target of their ingratiation attempts. But this is just a special case of the more general way in which we make ourselves attractive to other individuals. If the main determinant of attraction is the amount, quality, or number of rewarding outcomes that one can provide, then ingratiation is simply the process of providing positive outcomes for those we want to be attracted to us. I think that basically there is nothing dishonest about this process. If we are attracted to another person, we wish to maintain contact so as to continue to experience those positive outcomes. The best way to do that would be to ensure that the other person is attracted to us. And that attraction can be ensured or enhanced by providing rewarding experiences. Of course, this provides an opportunity for dissembling and for misrepresenting one's own characteristics. Yet at the same time one can view it as a process of caring about the other, wanting to provide positive outcomes for the other. The ability to provide positive outcomes for another person implies the power to withhold those outcomes and perhaps, therefore, in some ways to control the behavior of the other person. If power and control are the reasons one wishes to make himself attractive to another then the pejorative connotations of the term ingratiation indeed apply. But if one wishes to make himself attractive to another person because he is attracted to that person, it seems to me only honest to attempt to be as rewarding as possible, to provide as many positive outcomes for that person as you are able. The ways in which one does that depend very much on judgments about what will be pleasing to the other person and the success of that attempt depends very much on the unique needs and dynamics of that person.

Liking and being liked, attraction, esteem, love, these things concern us almost continually from the days of childhood playmates through the rest of our lives. In some ways it is saddening that we so complicate our relationships that social scientists need to ask who likes whom, and why. I think that we complicate our relationships primarily by not being able to express and receive affection in an open and honest manner. Even if we could do so, I suppose that understanding the determinants of attraction would still be a complex problem for social psychology. But as participants in this matrix of interactions perhaps we would be able to function with less uncertainty and to achieve greater depth and meaning in our encounters with each other. Yet, for many of us honesty is frightening because it leaves one so vulnerable. To express openly your affection for another is to invite reciprocation, but also to allow the possibility of a painful rebuff or costly exploitation. It is impossible to be honest only about positive feelings, for any dishonesty about our negative reactions necessarily dilutes the meaning of an expression of affection, or esteem, or love. So we cannot have candor without accepting its costs, the uncomfortable process of communicating and receiving negative reactions and emotions. It appears that for many people those costs are prohibitive and they choose to interact with most others according to the rules of polite social encounter in which strong feelings are not directly expressed. But is complete candor desirable for all interactions? I think not. Many times an encounter can be conducted politely and efficiently without doing the hard work of being completely honest. Often there is no purpose to be served by being painfully candid. A relationship can proceed at a superficial level, not involving either person deeply, and still be useful in many ways. The danger, however, is that one can lose the ability to relate to others honestly and deeply, and become unable to sustain a more meaningful relationship.

How do we find our way through this barrage of daily encounters and find those people with whom we establish real friendship or love. I think that we usually follow a pattern from polite encounter to deeper engagement. We explore the possibility of deepening the meaning of a relationship by making a series of small overtures and assessing the reaction they evoke. Simultaneously we are responding to the attempts of the other to assess the potential of a continuing interaction. If one of these small, subtle overtures is rebuffed, the encounter is terminated or stabilized at a given level of intimacy and since no truly overt declarations have been made, there is no public embarrassment. Of course, the excessive caution of this process probably means that we do not enjoy as many close relationships as we might, and that because it is easy to misread subtle signals we do not experience the full potential for human contact that may be available in many of our encounters. I can find no general rules for the resolution of this dilemma. It seems that each of us balances his fear of rejection against his need for social contact and achieves a unique if not always satisfying solution. This is one more way in which we differ from one another, our willingness to be engaged by others in meaningful ways.

While each of us tries in his own way to deal with the problems of liking and being liked, loving and being loved, social psychologists are beginning to unravel some of the determinants and consequences of attraction between persons. But until we have much more satisfying answers to questions about who likes whom and why, the puzzles inherent in these questions will continue to baffle, frustrate, and delight each of us, individually.

REFERENCES

Aronson, E., and Linder, D., Gain and loss of esteem as determinants of interpersonal attractiveness. *J. exp. soc. Psychol.*, 1965, *1*, 156–172.

Back, K. W., Influence through social communication. *J. abn. soc. Psychol.*, 1951, *46*, 9–23.

Berscheid, E., and Walster, E. *Interpersonal Attraction*. Reading, Mass.; Addison-Wesley, 1969.

Newcomb, T. M., *The Acquaintance Process*. New York: Holt, Rinehart and Winston, 1961.

Thibaut, J. W., and Kelley, H. H., *The Social Psychology of Groups*. New York: Wiley, 1959.

6
Some Nonverbal Dimensions of Dyadic Interaction

Darwyn E. Linder

Western European and North American cultures, it seems to me, have placed a particularly heavy emphasis on verbal communication. All cultures have, of course, developed languages and most cultures have developed written forms of language for communication and for preserving cultural material in some archival form. Yet, the thrust of technological development in western society has made verbal communication of primary importance in the Western European/North American cultural sphere. The printing press, the typewriter, the radio, are all western technological advances that have served to raise the importance of verbal communication. No one can deny that verbal communication is an efficient and extremely important way of transmitting and preserving information. Yet, when two individuals are present to one another in Goffman's (1959) sense, in addition to the noises they make at each other they emit an astonishing variety of other behaviors—many of which we are just now learning are also important ways of communicating.

Language is essential for the communication of abstract ideas and of conceptual formulations, but it may be that other behaviors are more important for the communication of emotions and attitudes. In face-to-face communication, we can divide the process of communication into two channels—the verbal and the nonverbal. When two people are present to one another, any behaviors in addition to the spoken language can be considered nonverbal communication. While people have always been attuned to nonverbal forms of communication, the scientific study of nonverbal behavior and communication has grown only very slowly, until in recent years it has experienced a large jump in popularity in the scientific community. Earlier, of course, the techniques of the actor and of the mime were all aspects of nonverbal communication but were practiced as arts rather than studied as the subject matter for a scientific discipline. However, a number of men toiled quietly through the years of the 1950's and 1960's to lay the groundwork for what has now become a large movement of behavioral scientists to the study of nonverbal behavior. Ray Birdwhistell has perhaps been the seminal contributor to the study of kinesic behavior, the significance of movements and postures (Birdwhistell, 1952). Additional work has been done by Paul Eckman who has studied the significance of facial expressions (Eckman and Friessen, 1968). E. T. Hall, an anthropologist, studied the spacing behaviors of individuals, the distances that people maintain from one another during various kinds of interactions (Hall, 1966). The more experimental study of interaction distance, called proxemics by Hall, has been conducted principally by Robert Sommer and his students (Sommer, 1969). Other people have contributed significantly to the study of additional aspects of nonverbal behavior, notably Ralph Exline in the study of eye contact (Exline and Winters, 1965) and Michael Argyle and his coworkers in the study of nonverbal behavior in social interaction (Argyle and Dean, 1965).

The study of voice quality and speech habits is an interesting borderline case between verbal and nonverbal communication. The seminal contributor to the study of paralinguistic behavior has been George Trager (1958). In this section of our book we will consider only kinesic and expressive behaviors and interaction distance and we will not be able to present a selection that deals with the study of paralinguistic behavior, although it is no doubt a very important part of the communication process.

There is probably no single or simple explanation for the almost sudden popularity of the study of nonverbal behavior. The significance of the work that had accumulated over a period of time was recognized by behavioral scientists who were able to see the importance of considering nonverbal as well as verbal behaviors in social interaction (Duncan, 1969). At the same time the public, or at least certain segments of the population, became more aware of movement and expression and became more attuned to senses other than those involved in verbal communication. The encounter group movement, sensitivity groups, Gestalt therapy, all emphasized a reawakening of senses and emphasized the use and understanding of nonverbal communication. Now, of course, nonverbal communication has become popularized. We have books for the layman, such as *Body Language* (Fast, 1970). Authors and researchers in nonverbal communication appear on television interview shows. We find ourselves much more aware of the actions that other people emit while they are engaging in conversation or in verbal communication. In a way it will perhaps rob nonverbal communication of its impact when all of us are so aware of the form and meaning of various nonverbal behaviors.

E. T. Hall has commented that we treat space in much the same way as we used to treat sex. We are involved with it all the time but we don't talk about it. This may well be the case with other forms of nonverbal communication and perhaps like sex, nonverbal communication will lose some of its mystery and its power once it becomes an everyday topic or a familiar concept. Nevertheless, the student of social interaction can no longer afford to ignore the importance of nonverbal communication, and I have included three selections that will be but the briefest introduction to some aspects of nonverbal communication in dyadic interaction.

REFERENCES

Argyle, M., and Dean, J., Eye contact, distance, and affiliation. *Sociometry*, 1965, *28*, 289–304.

Birdwhistell, R. L., *Introduction to Kinesics*. Louisville: University of Louisville Press, 1952.

Duncan, S., Nonverbal communication. *Psychological Bulletin*, 1969, *72*, 118–137.

Eckman, P., and Friessen, W. V., Nonverbal behavior in psychotherapy research. In J. Shlien (ed.), *Research in Psychotherapy*, Vol. 3, Washington, D. C.: American Psychological Association, 1968.

Exline, R. V., and Winters, L. C., Affective relations and mutual glances in dyads. In S. S. Tompkins and C. E. Izard (eds.), *Affect, Cognition, and Personality*. New York: Springer, 1965.

Fast, J., *Body Language*. New York: Evans, 1970.

Goffman, E., *The Presentation of Self in Everyday Life*. Garden City, N.Y.; Doubleday Anchor, 1959.

Hall, E. T., *The Hidden Dimension*. Garden City: Doubleday, 1966.

Sommer, R., *Personal Space: The Behavioral Basis of Design*. Englewood Cliffs, N.J.: Prentice-Hall, 1969.

Trager, G. L., Paralanguage: A first approximation. *Studies in Linguistics*, 1958, *13*, 1–12.

7
Sociology of the Senses: Visual Interaction

Georg Simmel

It is through the medium of the senses that we perceive our fellow-men. This fact has two aspects of fundamental sociological significance: (*a*) that of appreciation, and (*b*) that of comprehension.

a) Appreciation.   Sense-impressions may induce in us affective responses of pleasure or pain, of excitement or calm, of tension or relaxation, produced by the features of a person, or by the tone of his voice, or by his mere physical presence in the same room. These affective responses, however, do not enable us to understand or to define the other person. Our emotional response to the sense-image of the other leaves his real self outside.

Translated and adapted from Georg Simmel, *Soziologie*, pp. 646–51. (Leipzig: Duncker und Humblot, 1908.) In Park, R. E., and Burgess, E. W. (eds.), *Introduction to the Science of Sociology*, 3rd edition revised. University of Chicago Press, 1969. Reprinted by permission.

b) Comprehension.   The sense-impression of the other person may develop in the opposite direction when it becomes the medium for understanding the other. What I see, hear, feel of him is only the bridge over which I reach his real self. The sound of the voice and its meaning, perhaps, present the clearest illustration. The speech, quite as much as the appearance, of a person, may be immediately either attractive or repulsive. On the other hand, what he says enables us to understand not only his momentary thoughts but also his inner self. The same principle applies to all sense-impressions.

The sense-impressions of any object produce in us not only emotional and aesthetic attitudes toward it but also an understanding of it. In the case of reaction to non-human objects, these two responses are, in general, widely separated. We may appreciate the emotional value of any sense-impression of an object. The fragrance of a rose, the charm of a tone, the grace of a bough swaying in the wind, is experienced as a joy engendered within the soul. On the other hand, we may desire to understand and to comprehend the rose, or the tone, or the bough. In the latter case we respond in an entirely different way, often with conscious endeavor. These two diverse reactions which are independent of each other are with human beings generally integrated into a unified response. Theoretically, our sense-impressions of a person may be directed on the one hand to an appreciation of his emotional value, or on the other to an impulsive or deliberate understanding of him. Actually, these two reactions are coexistent and inextricably interwoven as the basis of our relation to him. Of course, appreciation and comprehension develop in quite different degrees. These two diverse responses—to the tone of voice and to the meaning of the utterance; to the appearance of a person and to his individuality; to the attraction or repulsion of his personality and to the impulsive judgment upon his character as well as many times upon his grade of culture—are present in any perception in very different degrees and combinations.

Of the special sense-organs, the eye has a uniquely sociological function. The union and interaction of individuals is based upon mutual glances. This is perhaps the most direct and purest reciprocity which exists anywhere. This highest psychic reaction, however, in which the glances of eye to eye unite men, crystallizes into no objective structure; the unity which momentarily arises between two persons is present in the occasion and is dissolved in the function. So tenacious and subtle is this union that it can only be maintained by the shortest and straightest line between the eyes, and the smallest deviation from it, the slightest glance aside, completely destroys the unique character of this union. No objective trace of this relationship is left behind, as is universally found, directly or indirectly, in all other types of associations between men, as, for example, in interchange of words. The interaction of eye and eye dies in the moment in which the directness of the function is lost. But the totality of social relations of human beings, their self-assertion and self-abnegation, their intimacies and estrangements, would be changed in unpredictable ways if there occurred no glance of eye to eye. This mutual glance between persons, in distinction from the simple sight or observation of the other, signifies a wholly new and unique union between them.

The limits of this relation are to be determined by the significant fact that the glance by which the one seeks to perceive the other is itself expressive. By the glance which reveals the other, one discloses himself. By the same act in which the observer seeks to know the observed, he surrenders himself to be understood by the observer. The eye cannot take unless at the same time it gives. The eye of a person discloses his own soul when he seeks to uncover that of another. What occurs in this direct mutual glance represents the most perfect reciprocity in the entire field of human relationships.

Shame causes a person to look at the ground to avoid the glance of the other. The reason for this is certainly not only because he is thus spared the visible evidence of the way in which the other regards his painful situation, but the deeper reason is that the lowering of his glance to a certain degree prevents the other from comprehending the extent of his confusion. The glance in the eye of the other serves not only for me to know the other but also enables him to know me. Upon the line which unites the two eyes, it conveys to the other the real personality, the real attitude, and the real impulse. The "ostrich policy" has in this explanation a real justification: who does not see the other actually conceals himself in part from the observer. A person is not at all completely present to another, when the latter sees him, but only when he also sees the other.

The sociological significance of the eye has special reference to the expression of the face as the first object of vision between man and man. It is seldom clearly understood to what an extent even our practical relations depend upon mutual recognition, not only in the sense of all external characteristics, as the momentary appearance and attitude of the other, but what we know or intuitively perceive of his life, of his inner nature, of the immutability of his being, all of which colors unavoidably both our transient and our permanent relations with him. The face is the geometric chart of all these experiences. It is the symbol of all that which the individual has brought with him as the pre-condition of his life. In the face is deposited what has been precipitated from past experience as the substratum of his life, which has become crystallized into the permanent features of his face. To the extent to which we thus perceive the face of a person, there enters into social relations, in so far as it serves practical purposes, a super-practical element. It follows that a man is first known by his countenance, not by his acts. The face as a medium of expression is entirely a theoretical organ; it does not act, as the hand, the foot, the whole body; it transacts none of the internal or practical relations of the man, it only tells about him. The peculiar and important sociological art of "knowing" transmitted by the eye is determined by the fact that the countenance is the essential object of the inter-individual sight. This knowing is still somewhat different from understanding. To a certain extent, and in a highly variable degree, we know at first glance with whom we have to do. Our unconsciousness of this knowledge and its fundamental significance lies in the fact that we direct our attention from this self-evident intuition to an understanding of special features which determine our practical relations to a particular individual. But if we become conscious of this self-evident fact, then we are amazed how much we know about a person in the first glance at him. We do not obtain meaning from his expression, susceptible to analysis into individual traits. We cannot unqualifiedly say whether he is clever or stupid, good- or ill-natured, temperamental or phlegmatic. All these traits are general characteristics which he shares with unnumbered others. But what this first glance at him transmits to us cannot be analyzed or appraised into any such conceptual and expressive elements. Yet our initial impression remains ever the keynote of all later knowledge of him; it is the direct perception of his individuality which his appearance, and especially his face, discloses to our glance.

The sociological attitude of the blind is entirely different from that of the deaf-mute. For the blind, the other person is actually present only in the alternating periods of his utterance. The expression of the anxiety and unrest, the traces of all past events, exposed to view in the faces of men, escape the blind, and that may be the reason for the peaceful and calm disposition, and the unconcern toward their surroundings, which is so often observed in the blind. Indeed, the majority of the stimuli which the face presents are often puzzling; in general, what we see of a man will be interpreted by what we hear from him, while the opposite is more unusual. Therefore the one who sees, without hearing, is much more perplexed, puzzled, and worried, than the one who hears without seeing. This principle is of great importance in understanding the sociology of the modern city.

Social life in the large city as compared with the towns shows a great preponderance of occasions to *see* rather than to *hear* people. One explanation lies in the fact that the person in the town is acquainted with nearly all the people he meets. With these he exchanges a word or a glance, and their countenance represents to him not merely the visible but indeed the entire personality. Another reason of especial significance is the development of public means of transportation. Before the appearance of omnibuses, railroads, and street cars in the nineteenth century, men were not in a situation where for periods of minutes or hours they could or must look at each other without talking to one another. Modern social life increases in ever growing degree the role of mere visual impression which always characterizes the preponderant part of all sense relationship between man and man, and must place social attitudes and feelings upon an entirely changed basis. The greater perplexity which characterizes the person who only sees, as contrasted with the one who only hears, brings us to the problems of the emotions of modern life: the lack of orientation in the collective life, the sense of utter lonesomeness, and the feeling that the individual is surrounded on all sides by closed doors.

8
Spatial Invasion

Robert Sommer

The best way to learn the location of invisible boundaries is to keep walking until somebody complains. Personal space refers to an area with invisible boundaries surrounding a person's body into which intruders may not come. Like the porcupines in Schopenhauer's fable, people like to be close enough to obtain warmth and comradeship but far enough away to avoid pricking one another. Personal space is not necessarily spherical in shape, nor does it extend equally in all directions. (People are able to tolerate closer presence of a stranger at their sides than directly in front.) It has been likened to a snail shell, a soap bubble, an aura, and "breathing room." There are major differences between cultures in the distances that people maintain—Englishmen keep further apart than Frenchmen or South Americans. Reports from Hong Kong where three million people are crowded into 12 square miles indicate that the population has adapted to the crowding reasonably well. The Hong Kong Housing Authority, now in its tenth year of operation, builds and manages low-cost apartments for families that provide approximately 35 square feet per person for living-sleeping accommodations. When the construction supervisor of one Hong Kong project was asked what the effects of doubling the amount of floor area would be upon the living patterns, he replied, "With 60 square feet per person, the tenants would sublet!"[1]

Although some people claim to see a characteristic aura around human bodies and are able to describe its color, luminosity, and dimensions, most observers cannot confirm these reports and must evolve a concept of personal space from interpersonal transactions. There is a considerable similarity between personal space and *individual distance*, or the characteristic spacing of species members. Individual distance exists only when two or more members of the same species are present and is greatly affected by population density and territorial behavior. Individual distance and personal space interact to affect the distribution of persons. The violation of individual distance is the violation of society's expectations; the invasion of personal space is an intrusion into a person's self-boundaries. Individual distance may be outside the area of personal space—conversation between two chairs across the room exceeds the boundaries of personal space, or individual distance may be less than the boundaries of personal space—sitting next to someone on a piano bench is within the expected distance but also within the bounds of personal space and may cause discomfort to the player. If there is only one individual present, there is infinite individual distance, which is why it is useful to maintain a concept of personal space, which has also been described as a *portable territory*, since the individual carries it with him wherever he goes although it disappears under certain conditions, such as crowding.

There is a formula of obscure origin that a man in a crowd requires at least two square feet. This is an absolute minimum and applies, according to one authority, to a thin man in a subway. A fat man would require twice as much space or more. Journalist Herbert Jacobs became interested in spatial behavior when he was a reporter covering political rallies. Jacobs found that estimates of crowd size varied with the observer's politics. Some estimates by police and politicians were shown to be twenty times larger than the crowd size derived from head count or aerial photographs. Jacobs found a fertile field for his research on the Berkeley campus where outdoor rallies are frequent throughout the year. He concluded that people in dense crowds have six to eight square feet each, while in loose crowds, with people moving in and out, there is an average of ten square feet per person, Jacobs' formula is that crowd size equals length × width of the crowd divided by the appropriate correction factor depending upon whether the crowd is dense or loose. On the Berkeley campus this produced estimates reasonably close to those obtained from aerial photographs.[2]

Hospital patients complain not only that their personal space and their very bodies are continually violated by nurses, interns, and physicians who do not bother to introduce themselves or explain their activities, but that their territories are violated by well-meaning visitors who will ignore "No Visitors" signs. Frequently patients are too sick or too sensitive to repel intruders. Once surgery is finished or the medical treatment has been instituted, the patient is left to his own devices to find peace and privacy. John Lear, the science editor of the *Saturday Review*, noticed an interesting hospital game he called, "Never Close the

Door," when he was a surgery patient. Although his physician wanted him protected against outside noises and distractions, the door opened at intervals, people peered in, sometimes entered, but no one ever closed the door. When Lear protested, he was met by hostile looks and indignant remarks such as, "I'm only trying to do my job, Mister." It was never clear to Lear why the job—whatever it was—required the intruder to leave the door ajar afterwards.[3]

Spatial invasions are not uncommon during police interrogations. One police textbook recommends that the interrogator should sit close to the suspect, with no table or desk between them, since "an obstruction of any sort affords the subject a certain degree of relief and confidence not otherwise obtainable."[4] At the beginning of the session, the officer's chair may be two or three feet away, "but after the interrogation is under way the interrogator should move his chair in closer so that ultimately one of the subject's knees is just about in between the interrogator's two knees."[5]

Lovers pressed together close their eyes when they kiss. On intimate occasions the lights are typically dim to reduce not only the distracting external cues but also to permit two people to remain close together. Personal space is a culturally acquired daylight phenomenon. Strangers are affected differently than friends by a loss of personal space. During rush hour, subway riders lower their eyes and sometimes "freeze" or become rigid as a form of minimizing unwanted social intercourse. Boy-meets-girl on a crowded rush hour train would be a logical plot for an American theater based largely in New York City, but it is rarely used. The idea of meeting someone under conditions where privacy, dignity, and individuality are so reduced is difficult to accept.

A driver can make another exceedingly nervous by tailgating. High-way authorities recommend a "space cushion" of at least one car length for every ten miles per hour of speed. You can buy a bumper sticker or a lapel button with the message "If you can read this, you're too close." A perceptive suburban theater owner noticed the way crowds arranged themselves in his lobby for different pictures. His lobby was designed to hold approximately 200 customers who would wait behind a roped area for the theater to clear.

When we play a [family picture like] *Mary Poppins, Born Free*, or *The Cardinal*, we can line up only about 100 to 125 people. These patrons stand about a foot apart and don't touch the person next to them. But when we play a [sex comedy like] *Tom Jones* or *Irma la Douce*, we can get 300 to 350 in the same space. These people stand so close to each other you'd think they were all going to the same home at the end of the show![6]

Animal studies indicate that individual distance is learned during the early years. At some stage early in his life the individual learns how far he must stay from species members. When he is deprived of contact with his own kind, as in isolation studies, he cannot learn proper spacing, which sets him up as a failure in subsequent social intercourse—he comes too close and evokes threat displays or stays too far away to be considered a member of the group. Newborn of many species can be induced to follow novel stimuli in place of their parents. If a newly hatched chicken is separated from his mother and shown a flashing light instead, on subsequent occasions he will follow the flashing light rather than his mother. The distance he remains behind the object is a function of its size; young chicks will remain further behind a large object than a small one.[7]

Probably the most feasible method for exploring individual distance and personal space with their invisible boundaries is to approach people and observe their reactions. Individual distance is not an absolute figure but varies with the relationship between the individuals, the distance at which others in the situation are placed, and the bodily orientations of the individuals one to another. The most systematic work along these lines has been undertaken by the anthropologist Ray Birdwhistell who records a person's response with zoom lenses and is able to detect even minute eye movements and hand tremors as the invader approaches the emotionally egotistic zone around the victim.[8]

One of the earliest attempts to invade personal space on a systematic basis was undertaken by Williams, who wanted to learn how different people would react to excessive closeness. Classifying students as introverts or extroverts on the basis of their scores on a personality test, he placed each individual in an experimental room and then walked toward the person, telling him to speak out as soon as he (Williams) came too close. Afterward he used the reverse condition, starting at a point very close and moving away until the person reported that he was too far away for comfortable conversation. His results showed that introverts kept people at a greater conversational distance than extroverts.[9]

The same conclusion was reached by Leipold, who studied the distance at which introverted and extroverted college students placed themselves in relation to an interviewer in either a stress or a nonstress situation. When the student entered the experimental room, he was given either the stress, praise, or neutral instructions. The stress instructions were, "We feel that your course grade is quite poor and that you have not tried your best. Please take a seat in the next room and Mr. Leipold will be in shortly to discuss this with you." The neutral control instructions read, "Mr. Leipold is interested in your feelings about the introductory course. Would you please take a seat in the next room." After the student had entered and seated himself, Mr. Leipold came in, recorded the student's seating position, and conducted the interview. The results showed that students given praise sat closest to Leipold's chair, followed by those in the neutral condition, with students given the stress instructions maintaining the most distance from Leipold's chair behind the desk. It was also found that introverted and anxious individuals sat further away from him than did extroverted students with a lower anxiety level.[10]

Glen McBride has done some excellent work on the spatial behaviors of fowl, not only in captivity but in their feral state on islands off the Australian coast. He has recently turned his attention to human spatial behavior using the galvanic skin response (GSR) as an index of emotionality. The GSR picks up changes in skin conductivity that relate to stress and emotional behavior. The same principle underlies what is popularly known as the lie detector test. McBride placed college students in a chair from which they were approached by both male and female experimenters as well as by paper figures and nonhuman objects. It was found that GSR was greatest (skin resistance was least) when a person was approached frontally, whereas a side approach yielded a greater response than a rear approach. The students reacted more strongly to the approach of someone of the opposite sex than to someone of the same sex. Being touched by an object produced less of a GSR than being touched by a person.[11]

A similar procedure without the GSR apparatus was used by Argyle and Dean, who invited their subjects to participate in a perceptual experiment in which they were to "stand as close as comfortable to see well" to a book, a plaster head, and a cut-out life-size photograph with his eyes open. Among other results, it was found that the subjects placed themselves closer to the eyes-closed photograph than the eyes-open photograph.[12] Horowitz, Duff, and Stratton used a similar procedure with schizophrenic and nonschizophrenic mental patients. Each individual was instructed to walk over to a person, or in another condition a hatrack, and the distance between the goal and his stopping place was measured. It was found that most people came closer to the hatrack than they did to another person. Each tended to have a characteristic individual distance that was relatively stable from one situation to another, but was shorter for inanimate objects than for people. Schizophrenics generally kept greater distance between themselves and others than did nonpatients.[13] The last finding is based on average distance values, which could be somewhat inflated by a few schizophrenics who maintain a large individual distance. Another study showed that some schizophrenic patients sat "too close" and made other people nervous by doing this. However, it was more often the case that schizophrenics maintained excessive physical distance to reduce the prospects of unwanted social intercourse.[14]

In order to explore personal space using the invasion technique, but to avoid the usual connotations surrounding forced close proximity to strangers, my own method was to undertake the invasion in a place where the usual sanctions of the outside world did not apply. Deliberate invasions of personal space seem more feasible and appropriate inside a mental hospital than outside. Afterward, it became apparent that this method could be adapted for use in other settings such as the library in which Nancy Russo spent many hours sitting too close to other girls.

The first study took place at a 1500-bed mental institution situated in parklike surroundings in northern California. Most wards were unlocked, and patients spent considerable time out of doors. In wooded areas it was common to see patients seated under the trees, one to a bench or knoll. The wards within the buildings were relatively empty during the day because of the number of patients outside as well as those who worked in hospital industry. This made it possible for patients to isolate themselves from others by finding a deserted area on the grounds or remaining in an almost empty building. At the outset I spent considerable time observing how patients isolated themselves from one another. One man typically sat at the base of a fire escape so he was protected by the bushes on one side and the railing on the other. Others would lie on benches in remote areas and feign sleep if approached. On the wards a patient might sit in a corner and place magazines or his coat on adjacent seats to protect the space. The use of belongings to indicate possession is very common in bus stations, cafeterias, waiting rooms, but the mental patient is limited in using this method since he lacks possessions. Were he to own a magazine or book, which is unlikely, and left it on an empty chair, it would quickly vanish.

Prospective victims had to meet three criteria—male, sitting alone and not engaged in any definite activity such as reading or playing cards. When a patient fitting these criteria was located, I walked over and sat beside him without saying a word. If the patient moved his chair or slid further down the bench, I moved a like distance to keep the space between us to about six inches. In all sessions I jiggled my key ring a few times to assert my dominance, the key being a mark of status in a mental hospital. It can be noted that these sessions not only invaded the patient's personal space but also the nurse's territory. It bothered the nurses to see a high status person (jacket, white shirt, tie, and the title "Doctor") entering their wards and sitting among the patients. The dayroom was the patients' territory vis-à-vis the nurses, but it was the nurses' territory vis-à-vis the medical staff. Control subjects were selected from other patients who were seated some distance away but whose actions could be observed.

Within two minutes, all of the control subjects remained but one-third of the invasion victims had been driven away. Within nine minutes, fully half of the victims had departed compared with only 8 percent of the controls (see Fig. 1). Flight was a gross reaction to the intrusion; there were many more subtle indications of the patient's discomfort. The typical sequence was for the victim to face away immediately, pull in his shoulders, and place his elbows at his sides. Facing away was an almost universal reaction among the victims, often coupled with hands placed against the chin as a buffer. Records obtained during the notetaking sessions illustrate this defensive pattern.

Example A

10:00 Seat myself next to a patient, about sixty years of age; he is smoking and possibly watching TV.

10:04 Patient rubs his face briefly with the back of his hand.

10:05 Patient breathes heavily, still smoking, and puts his ashes into a tin can. He looks at his watch occasionally.

10:06 He puts out his cigarette, rubs his face with the back of his hand. Still watching TV.

10:12 Patient glances at his watch, flexes his fingers.

10:13 Patient rises, walks over and sits at a seat several chairs over. Observation ended.

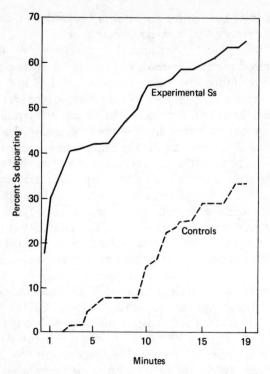

Fig. 1 Cumulative Percentage of Patients Departing
at Each One-Minute Interval.

Example B

8:46 Seat myself next to a 60-year-old man who looks up as I enter the
room. As I sit down, he begins talking to himself, snuffs out his
cigarette, rises, and walks across the room. He asks a patient on
the other side of the room, "You want me to sit here?" He starts
arranging the chairs against the opposite wall and finally sits down.

Ethologist Ewan Grant has made a detailed analysis of the patient's
micro behaviors drawing much inspiration from the work of Tinbergen[15]
as well as his own previous studies with colonies of monkeys and rats.
Among a group of confined mental patients he determined a relatively
straightforward dominance hierarchy based on aggression-flight encounters between individuals. Aggressive acts included threat gestures

("a direct look plus a sharp movement of the head towards the other person"), frowns, and hand-raising. Flight behaviors included retreat, bodily evasions, closed eyes, withdrawing the chin into the chest, hunching, and crouching. These defensive behaviors occurred when a dominant individual sat too close to a subordinate. This could be preceded by some overt sign of tension such as rocking, leg swinging, or tapping. Grant describes one such encounter: "A lower ranking member of the group is sitting in a chair; a dominant approaches and sits near her. The first patient begins to rock and then frequently, on one of the forward movements, she gets up and moves away."[16]

In seventeen British old folks homes Lipman found that most of the patients had favorite chairs that they considered "theirs." Their title to these chairs was supported by the behavior of both patients and staff. A newly admitted inmate had great difficulty in finding a chair that was not owned by anyone. Typically he occupied one seat and then another until he found one that was "unowned." When he sat in someone else's chair, he was told to move away in no uncertain terms.[17] Accidental invasions were an accepted fact of life in these old folks homes. It is possible to view them as a hazing or initiation ceremony for new residents to teach them the informal institutional rules and understandings. Such situations illustrate the importance of knowing not only how people mark out and personalize spaces, but how they respond to intrusions.

We come now to the sessions Nancy Russo conducted in the study hall of a college library, a large high-ceilinged room with book-lined walls. Because this is a study area, students typically try to space themselves as far as possible from one another. Systematic observations over a two-year period disclosed that the first occupants of the room generally sat one to a table at end chairs. Her victims were all females sitting alone with at least one book in front of them and empty chairs on either side and across. In other words, the prospective victim was sitting in an area surrounded by empty chairs, which indicated something about her preference for solitude as well as making an invasion relatively easy. The second female to meet these criteria in each session and who was visible to Mrs. Russo served as a control. Each control subject was observed from a distance and no invasion was attempted. There were five different approaches used in the invasions—sometimes Mrs. Russo would sit alongside the subject, other times directly across from her, and so forth. All of these were violations of the typical seating norms in the library, which required a newcomer to sit at a considerable distance from those already seated unless the room was crowded.

Occupying the adjacent chair and moving it closer to the victim, produced the quickest departures, and there was a slight but also significant difference between the other invasion locations and the control condition. There were wide individual differences in the ways the victims reacted—there is no single reaction to someone's sitting too close; there are defensive gestures, shifts in posture, and attempts to move away. If these fail or are ignored by the invader, or he shifts position too, the victim eventually takes to flight. Crook measured spacing of birds in three ways: *arrival distance* or how far from settled birds a newcomer will land, *settled distance* or the resultant distance after adjustments have occurred, and the *distance after departure* or how far apart birds remain after intermediate birds have left.[18] The methods employed in the mental hospital and portions of the library study when the invader shifted his position if the victim moved, maintained the *arrival distance* and did not permit the victim to achieve a comfortable *settled distance*. It is noteworthy that the preponderance of flight reactions occurred under these conditions. There was a dearth of direct verbal responses to the invasions. Only two of the 69 mental patients and one of the 80 students asked the invader to move over. This provides support for Edward Hall's view that "we treat space somewhat as we treat sex. It is there, but we don't talk about it."[19]

Architecture students on the Berkeley campus now undertake behavioral studies as part of their training. One team noted the reactions of students on outdoor benches when an experimenter joined them on the same bench. The occupant shifted position more frequently in a specified time-frame and left the bench earlier than control subjects who were alone. A second team was interested in individual distance on ten-foot benches. When the experimenter seated himself one foot from the end of the bench, three-quarters of the next occupants sat six to eight feet away, and almost half placed books or coats as barriers between themselves and the experimenter. Another two students studied eyeblink and shifts in body position as related to whether a stranger sat facing someone or sat facing away. Observations were made by a second experimenter using binoculars from a distance. A male stranger directly facing a female markedly increased her eyeblink rate as well as body movements but had no discernible effect on male subjects.[20]

The different ways in which victims react to invasions may also be due to variations in the perception of the expected distance or in the ability to concentrate. It has been demonstrated that the individual distance between birds is reduced when one bird's attention is riveted to some activity.[21] The invasions can also be looked at as nonverbal communication with the victims receiving messages ranging from "This girl considers me a nonperson" to "This girl is making a sexual advance." The fact that regressed and "burnt out" patients can be moved from their places by sheer propinquity is of theoretical and practical importance. In view of the difficulty that nurses and others have in obtaining any response at all from these patients, it is noteworthy that an emotion sufficient to generate flight can be produced simply by sitting alongside them. More recently we have been experimenting with visual invasions, or attempts to dislodge someone from his place by staring directly at him. In the library at least, the evil eye seems less effective than a spatial invasion since the victims are able to lose themselves in their books. If they could not escape eye contact so easily, this method might be more effective. Mrs. Russo was sensitive to her own feelings during these sessions and described how she "lost her cool" when a victim looked directly toward her. Eye contact produced a sudden realization that "this is a human being," which subsided when the victim turned away. Civil rights demonstrators attempt to preserve their human dignity by maintaining eye contact with their adversaries.

There are other sorts of invasions—auditory assaults in which strangers press personal narratives on hapless seatmates on airplanes and buses, and olfactory invasions long celebrated in television commercials. Another interesting situation is the two-person invasion. On the basis of animal work, particularly on chickens crowded in coops, it was discovered that when a subordinate encounters a dominant at very close quarters where flight is difficult or impossible, the subordinate is likely to freeze in his tracks until the dominant departs or at least looks away. Two faculty members sitting on either side of a student or two physicians on either side of a patient's bed would probably produce this type of freezing. The victim would be unlikely to move until he had some sign that the dominants had their attention elsewhere.

The library studies made clear that an important consideration in defining a spatial invasion is whether the parties involved perceive one another as persons. A nonperson cannot invade someone's personal space any more than a tree or chair can. It is common under certain conditions for one person to react to another as an object or part of the background. Examples would be the hospital nurses who discuss a patient's condition at his bedside, seemingly oblivious to his presence, the Negro maid in the white home who serves dinner while the husband and wife discuss the race question, and the janitor who enters an office without knocking to empty the wastebaskets while the occupant is making an important phone call. Many subway riders who have adjusted to crowding through psychological withdrawal prefer to treat other riders as nonpersons and keenly resent situations, such as a stop so abrupt that the person alongside pushes into them *and then apologizes*, when the other rider becomes a person. There are also riders who dislike the lonely alienated condition of subway travel and look forward to emergency situations in which people become real. When a lost child is looking for his mother, a person has been hurt, or a car is stalled down the tracks, strangers are allowed to talk to one another.

NOTES

1. American Institute of Planners Newsletter, January 1967, p. 2.

2. H. Jacobs, "How Big Was the Crowd?" Talk given at California Journalism Conference, Sacramento, February 24–25, 1967.

3. John Lear, "What's Wrong with American Hospitals?" *Saturday Review* (February 4, 1967), pp. 59–60.

4. F. E. Inbau and J. E. Reid, *Criminal Interrogation and Confessions* (Toronto: Burns and MacEachern, 1963).

5. Inbau and Reid, *op. cit.*

6. Bob Ellison, "If the Movie Is Comic, Sex Is OK, in Suburbia," *Chicago Sun Times*, Jan. 15, 1967, Section 3, p. 4.

7. Peter H. Klopfer and J. P. Hailman, *An Introduction to Animal Behavior* (Englewood Cliffs, N.J.: Prentice-Hall, Inc., 1967).

8. R. L. Birdwhistell, *Introduction to Kinesics* (Washington: Foreign Service Institute, 1952).

9. John L. Williams, "Personal Space and its Relation to Extroversion-Introversion" (Master's thesis, University of Alberta, 1963).

10. William E. Leipold, "Psychological Distance in a Dyadic Interview" (Ph.D. thesis, University of North Dakota, 1963).

11. Glen McBride, M. G. King, and J. W. James, "Social Proximity Effects on GSR in Adult Humans," *Journal of Psychology*, LXI (1965), 153–57.

12. Michael Argyle and Janet Dean, "Eye Contact, Distance, and Affiliation," *Sociometry*, XXVIII (1965), 289–304.

13. Mardi J. Horowitz, D. F. Duff, and L. O. Stratton, "Body-Buffer Zone," *Archives of General Psychiatry*, XI (1964), 651–56.

14. Robert Sommer, "Studies in Personal Space," *Sociometry*, XXII (1959), 247–60.

15. N. Tinbergen, *Social Behavior in Animals* (London: Methuen & Co. Ltd., 1953).

16. Grant, *op. cit.*

17. Alan Lipman, "Building Design and Social Interaction," *The Architects Journal*, CXLVII (1968), 23–30.

18. J. H. Crook, "The Basis of Flock Organization in Birds," in *Current Problems in Animal Behavior*, eds. W. H. Thorpe and O. L. Zangwill (London: Cambridge University Press, 1961).

19. Edward T. Hall, *The Silent Language* (Garden City, New York: Doubleday & Company, Inc., 1959).

20. These were term projects in Architecture 140 taught by Professor Richard Seaton. They are available on microfilm from the Dept. of Architecture, University of California, Berkeley 94704.

21. Crook, *op. cit.*

9
Physical Stigma and Nonverbal Cues Emitted in Face-to-face Interaction[1]

Robert Kleck

There seems to be little question that the physical characteristics of a person are important determinants of the behavior he elicits from others in face-to-face interactions. Relatively little attention has been devoted, however, to an experimental analysis of this issue. Recently several authors (e.g. Goffman, 1963) have suggested that physical characteristics which have a strong negative valuation, i.e., physical stigma, may be a particularly important set of "behavior elicitors" in interpersonal encounters. Their importance lies in the suggestion that the physically

From *Human Relations*, 1968, Vol. 21, pages 19–28. Reprinted by permission of Plenum Publishing Co. Ltd. London.

stigmatized person is in a distinctly disadvantageous position *vis-a-vis* the representativeness of behavioral outcomes which he typically experiences from others (Kelley, Hastorf, Jones, Thibaut and Usdane, 1960). There are several reasons for entertaining this expectation. In the first place the physically normal person often reports that he is uncomfortable and uncertain when interacting with a physically disabled person (Richardson, Hastorf, Goodman and Dornbusch, 1961; Davis, 1961; Kleck, 1966). This felt uncertainty and emotional arousal may well serve to reduce the spontaneity of behavior. In the second place, clearly defined norms can operate as a constraint upon behavioral output by delineating the behaviors appropriate to a given interaction context. When the context is defined by the presence of a physically disabled person, strong norms to be kind and considerate may be evoked. Finally, Goffman (1963) argues that a physical disability is typically deeply discrediting to its possessor, and as is the case with other types of stigma, not only will the stigmatized person be discredited in the eyes of others but so will any persons who tend to associate closely with him. The physically normal person can, therefore, be expected to avoid any long-term relationship with the physically handicapped.

These factors, taken together, suggest that the physically stigmatized person will elicit from the social environment behaviors which are consistently stereotyped, inhibited, and overcontrolled. A bias toward behaviors of this sort, if it operates pervasively, will tend to be incompatible with the development on the part of the stigmatized person of sensitivity to others and skill in human relationships.

Recent empirical data suggesting the presence of such a bias comes from a series of studies conducted by Kleck, Ono and Hastorf (1966). In these studies it was found that subjects interacting with a physically disabled person, as compared to subjects interacting with a physically normal person, (a) terminated the interaction sooner, (b) demonstrated less variability in their verbal behavior, and (c) expressed opinions which were less representative of their actual beliefs. While the differences in verbal behavior were striking and consistent with our expectations, the experimenters had a strong impression that the observed inhibition and constraint of behavioral output was also present in the nonverbal aspects of the interaction. Unfortunately the design of the study did not permit a careful analysis of nonverbal cues. The experiment reported below is an attempt to explore this aspect of the interaction and to test several related hypotheses under controlled conditions.

In the analysis of nonverbal communication, considerable recent attention has focused on the mutual glance or 'eye contact' as a salient cue in interpersonal interactions. While eye contact is affected by many variables (Argyle and Dean, 1965), of primary interest here is its relationship to the affective nature of the interpersonal relationship. Exline and Winters (1965) have demonstrated that eye contact is positively correlated with felt affect in a dyad. That is, the more attracted to or the more positively one feels toward another person the more likely it is that one will look directly at this person when interacting with him. At the same time Goffman (1963) has argued that eye contact may be negatively correlated with the degree of tension in a relationship. We know from previous studies (Kleck *et al.*, 1966) that physically normal high school students show greater emotional arousal (as measured by GSR) when interacting with a physically normal peer. Finally, the observation has been made by Goffman (1963) that normals tend to avoid interpersonal involvement with the disabled. On these grounds we are led to hypothesize that the physically normal person will demonstrate less eye contact when interacting with a physically disabled person than with a physically normal person.

The only specific nonverbal cue discussed thus far is associated with the face. Ekman (1964) has demonstrated that the face and body may carry quite different nonverbal informational value and need to be analyzed separately. Specifically which body cues carry what information is an important question and several investigators, particularly Ekman, have made significant gains towards a solution of this problem. In the current case, however, we were not interested in the presence or absence of specific body acts. It was our feeling that the primary nonverbal difference observed in the earlier study was a quite general inhibition of motor movement rather than a selective monitoring of cues on the part of the person. The second specific hypothesis to be explored, therefore, is that in normal-disabled interactions persons will demonstrate less motoric activity than in normal-normal interactions.

In addition to exploring several of the nonverbal differences which are elicited by physical disability the present design also permitted the exploration, under well controlled conditions, of an observation which has been made by several investigators (Barker *et al.*, 1953; Ray, 1946). This is the observation that when persons are asked to form impressions of disabled and nondisabled persons they tend to consistently report a more favorable impression of the former. In the study described below the same person played the role of both a physically normal and a physically disabled stimulus person. It was possible, therefore, to assess the impact of disability on impression formation independent of other stimulus differences. On the basis of the observation previously made by Barker *et al.* (1953) and Ray (1946) we expected our stimulus persons to elicit more favorable impressions when they were disabled than when they were nondisabled.

Finally, the design permitted the partial replication of one of the more important findings of the previous studies, i.e., the finding that persons, when expressing an opinion to a disabled stimulus person distorted their opinion in a direction which would serve to minimize the anxiety in the situation. When describing their own attitude toward sports, in the presence of a disabled person for example they tended to give a less positive reply than when responding to the same question anonymously. In the present study attitudes toward sports and academic achievement were employed as stimulus questions. For the academic achievements question we expected distortion in the direction of increased importance since Ray (1946) had previously found that part of the stereotype of disabled persons is that they have a strong academic achievement orientation.

METHOD

Overview

The interaction situation used in this experiment was a highly structured one in which the subject and a confederate of the experimenter's exchanged information concerning certain of their attitudes. Each subject interacted with one confederate at a time on two separate occasions. The confederates took turns playing the normal and physically disabled roles and their order of appearance in the interactions was balanced across conditions. As in the previous study in this series (Kleck *et al.*, 1966) the disability role assumed by the confederate was that of a left leg amputee and was achieved through the use of a specially designed wheel chair. The primary data collected were 16 mm sound motion pictures of the subject.

Subjects

Fifteen male junior and senior high school students were recruited from history classes to participate in a study of "physiological responses during social interaction." They attended two, one-hour experimental sessions and were paid for their participation.

Procedure

Immediately upon arrival for the first experimental session the S was shown into a 12 ft by 16 ft room containing two arm chairs separated by a distance of 10 ft. The walls immediately behind each chair contained small openings through which wires were supposedly connected to physiological recording equipment. The opening in the wall facing S was used as a camera port for a 16 mm motion picture camera. It was explained to the S that the experimenter was interested in physiological responses during the interaction and electrodes were placed on his nonpreferred hand. The E explained the electrodes as a method of monitoring physiological arousal during interactions. After five minutes confederate A was shown into the room, introduced to the subject, briefed on the supposed nature of the study, and had electrodes attached to his nonpreferred hand. In one half of the cases for Session I the confederate entered as a left leg amputee in a wheel chair and in the other half as a physically normal person. The confederates were age peers of the subjects and underwent ten one-hour training sessions prior to the start of the experiment.

At this point E made a check of the physiological recording equipment and, reported that S's was not working properly. His electrodes were removed but E indicated the experiment could continue because the other subject's (Confederates) were operative. The rationale for focusing expressed experimental interest on physiological responses rather than on verbal behavior was that this might be expected to reduce the impact of the experimental situation *per se* on S's behavior. In earlier exploratory studies conducted by the present author, this rationale was strongly supported. The reason for removing S's electrodes was to obviate the restriction they would place on his bodily movement and associated nonverbal cues and to further reinforce the notion that his behavior was not under surveilance by the experimenter. The E then reiterated that his interest was in physiological responses and explained that to standardize the interaction situation across subjects he had decided to have them exchange information concerning certain of their attitudes. The E stepped behind the wall in back of the confederate to purportedly monitor the physiological recording equipment and from this position operated the motion picture camera and read the interaction questions, first to *S* and then to the confederate. Two minutes was adopted as the amount of time the *S* would be allotted to respond to each question both because of film limitations and because earlier work has suggested this was considerably under the median spontaneous response length for questions of the type employed. The confederate always gave the same carefully rehearsed reply. The questions required the *S* and the confederate to (a) describe themselves briefly, (b) indicate their attitude toward participation in sports in high school, and (c) indicate their opinion toward the importance of academic achievement.

It was during the replies to these questions that the film data were collected. The camera port was located in the wall behind and to the immediate left of the confederate and was positioned such as to get face on, body-length pictures of the subject. It should be noted that no subject was ever aware that pictures were being taken but all were informed of this fact at the completion of the study. The 12-minute film segment covered the time period during which the subject was responding to the three questions as well as while he was listening to the confederate respond to questions (b) and (c).

When the confederate completed his response to the final question an impression scale composed of seven polar adjective pairs separated by a seven-point scale was distributed. The adjective pairs were friendly-unfriendly, unintelligent-intelligent, sincere-insincere, irresponsible-responsible, likeable-unlikeable, unattractive-attractive, and warm-cold. This was followed by a second form of the same impression scale but this time with the instructions to predict "how the other person in the group perceived you". As soon as the questionnaires were complete *E* arranged a second session for the subject three days hence.

Session II was exactly like Session I except that the subject was confronted by a different confederate in a different role. That is, if the first confederate was physically normal the second played the part of a left leg amputee. Again it was stressed that the experimenter was interested in the physiological responses of the participants and both had palm electrodes placed on their nonpreferred hands. In this session, as in the first, the equipment used to monitor the subject's responses was reported to be inoperative and his electrodes were removed. The same questions were used in the same order and motion pictures were again taken. Upon completion of the impression questionnaires the subject was interviewed concerning his reactions to the experimental sessions and to the confederates. The experiment was explained to him in detail and he was asked not to discuss it with others who might be participating. His permission to use the film and questionnaire data for the analysis reported below was requested and was in all cases granted.

RESULTS[2]

Effectiveness of Experimental Manipulations

The attempt to simulate a severe physical disability was, as in the previous studies in this series, highly effective. No subject at anytime, as indicated either by observation of his behavior or by his self report at the conclusion of the experiment suspected the confederate playing the role of the disabled person was not disabled or that he was in fact a confederate of the experimenter. In the first part of the post-experimental interview each subject was asked to state the purpose of the experiment as he interpreted it. All subjects gave the explanation that had been given by the experimenter in the first session, i.e., that the purpose was the measurement of physiological responses during interaction.

Since our interpretation of the results assumes that any differences between the normal-normal and normal-disabled interactions were generated by the disability it was essential that the confederates' behavior be identical in both roles. To facilitate this stimulus similarity the responses the confederate made in the situation were carefully structured and memorized. The confederates each underwent a series of ten, one-hour training sessions in which two observers carefully scrutinized their behavior for stimulus differences. Halfway through the experiment a check for differences was again made without the confederates' knowledge and no differences were found. Finally, the confederates were not informed of the experimental hypotheses until the conclusion of the study.

Eye Contact

It was postulated that normal-disabled interactions would result in less eye contact than normal-normal interactions. Since eye contact implies mutual looking Exline's method was used in which the confederate gazed continually at the Subject. Any time the S returns the glance is therefore eye contact. Exline, *et al.*, (1965) and Argyle and Dean (1965) report high judge agreement ($r = \cdot 98$) when eye contact is judged in a live situation. The reliability and particularly the accuracy of these judgements should be even higher when the subject is filmed and his behavior analyzed on a frame by frame basis as in the present study.

The results relevant to the hypothesis on eye contact are presented in Table I for both talking and listening behavior.[3] The data were analyzed in terms of the percentage of film frames on which S had eye contact with the confederate. The hypothesis is not supported and there is a tendency, which does not reach significance, for the data to go in the reverse direction. As is obvious from Table I, the largest difference occurs during listening behavior ($t = 1.87$, $df = 14$, $p < .10$). Consistent with the results obtained in previous studies by Exline and others there are large differences in percent of eye contact while listening compared to talking ($t = 6.84$, $df = 14$, $p < .001$ in the normal-normal interaction and $t = 7.20$, $df = 14$, $p < .001$ in the normal-disabled interaction).

Table 1 Mean Percentage of Eye Contact

Interaction	Talking	Listening
Disabled	19.3	70.5
Normal	17.3	60.0

The average duration of eye contact was computed for each subject by dividing the number of mutual glances into the total frames of eye contact. These data are presented in Table 2 and again are broken down into talking and listening behavior. While in both cases the average length of eye contact is greater in the normal-disabled interactions this effect reaches significance only in the case of listening behavior ($t = 2.71$, $df = 14$, $p < .02$).

One additional result on eye contact is relevant at this point. In the analysis of eye movements an index of ocular activity was devised by dividing the visual space of the subject into quadrants, the apex of which was formed by the confederate's eyes. A score of one was assigned to the S each time his eyes crossed from one quadrant into the next or went from one of the quadrants to eye contact or vice versa. As before it is in the listening phase of the interaction that a significant difference occurs ($t = 2.30$, $df = 14$, $p < .05$) although the difference is in the same direction for talking. The mean score for the disabled condition was 28 while that for the normal condition was 41·9 which indicates greater ocular activity in the latter condition.

Table 2 Mean Duration, in Seconds, of Eye Contact Per Glance

Interaction	Talking	Listening
Disabled	1·54	16·98
Normal	1·22	7·65

Motoric Activity

To facilitate measurement of motoric activity the wall behind the subject was painted in a checkerboard pattern with six-inch squares. In analyzing motor movement any time a body part moved 6 inches it was scored as a movement of 1. A head turn of 45 degrees was also scored as 1. The mean scores for motoric activity are shown in Table 3 and are reported separately for the talking and listening phases of the interaction. Recall that we expected greater motoric inhibition when the Ss were interacting with the disabled confederate than when they were interacting with the able-bodied confederate. This hypothesis is strongly supported for the overall comparison between normal-normal and normal-disabled interactions ($t = 2·91$, $df = 14$, $p < ·02$). A separate analysis of the talking and listening phases of the interactions indicates that the difference when the subject is listening to the confederate is significant ($t = 3·99$, $df = 14$, $p < ·01$) but when the subject is himself talking it is not ($t = 1·43$, $df = 14$, ns). As might be expected there is a great deal less movement in general when listening than when talking ($t = 7·01$, $df = 14$, $p < ·001$ for normal-normal interactions; $t = 6·71$, $df = 14$, $p < ·001$ for normal-disabled interactions).[4]

Table 3 Mean Amount of Motoric Activity

Interaction	Talking	Listening
Disabled	243·5	14·7
Normal	268·9	41·6

Impression Formation

Previous studies have suggested that a positive bias is present in the impressions people report forming of physically stigmatized persons. The present study permitted a careful test of this notion under controlled conditions in which the same stimulus persons played both the disabled and normal roles. Any consistent differences in impressions under these circumstances could be attributed only to the presence of a disability. The positivity of the impression was taken as the total score summed across the seven separate adjective pairs which S responded to immediately following interaction with each of the confederates. The index could range from 0 to 49 with the latter representing the most positive impression. The mean for the impression formed of the disabled confederate was 43·6 and the mean for the normal was 40·7 ($t = 2·82$, $df = 14$, $p < ·02$). While the absolute differences are small they are highly consistent and involve but a single subject reversal. An inspection of the separate adjective pairs reveals that their contribution to the overall mean differences was approximately equivalent.

We were also interested in exploring the impressions which our subjects expected the disabled and nondisabled confederate to form of them. When these predictions are examined there is a tendency for subjects to expect receipt of a less positive impression from the disabled than from the nondisabled confederate. This effect does not reach an acceptable level of significance.

Opinion Distortion

As part of the present experiment it was possible to attempt a partial replication of the opinion distortion results obtained in an earlier study (Kleck *et al.*, 1966). The two opinion items employed were attitudes towards sports and academic achievement. In the previous study we have found that Ss interacting with a disabled confederate tended to represent their opinions as more anti-sport and more pro-academic achievement than they actually were as measured by a supposedly anonymous questionnaire a month later. This distortion did not characterize a matched group of subjects who interacted with a physically normal confederate under the same conditions. One difficulty with that study was that it had to depend upon matched groups. In the present study the subject served as his own control and it was possible to compare directly the opinions he expressed when inter-acting with the disabled confederate with those he expressed while interacting with the normal confederate. It should be noted that the pressures toward consistency in this case are fairly strong since even though the subject is talking to a different confederate the experimenter was always present and could hear what S was saying. The answers to the two questions were compared in the following way: The two responses generated by each subject for each question was transcribed, duplicated, and presented to a group of 15 judges (male college students) with the instructions that each pair came from a single person but were expected to differ in their degree of favorability toward the attitude object. The judges' task was to select the member of each pair which represented the more favorable attitude toward sports in the first case or academic achievement in the second. The judges were not informed of the stimulus conditions under which the subjects had given the responses and which member of the pair the judge read first was randomly determined. In the analysis each subject response which received the higher rating from 8 or more of the 15 judges was taken as the stronger statement. For the sports question the results strongly support our hypothesis in that the subjects are judged to make stronger pro-sports statements when interacting with the normal confederate ($x^2 = 8 \cdot 06$, $df = 1$, $p < \cdot 01$). Reversals occur for the responses generated by only two of the fifteen subjects. The results for responses to the academic achievement question are in the right direction (subjects are judged to make stronger pro-achievement responses when interacting with the physically disabled confederate) but do not reach an acceptable level of significance.

DISCUSSION

The results strongly reinforce the notion that a physical stigma does have an impact upon the behavior elicited from others. The one hypothesis not confirmed in the present study concerns eye contact. A possible explanation for this rests with what Argyle and Dean (1965) label the "information seeking" function of eye contact. They argue that the face of a listener provides the most important feedback concerning how that person is reacting to us. When involved in an interaction with a physically disabled person the need for information of this sort may be particularly acute and may overcome any eye avoidance tendencies present. In any case the results do suggest that the tension and uncomfortableness present in the normal-disabled interactions were not the primary determinants of looking behavior and that other dynamics were operative.

The most striking difference in nonverbal behavior is the observed motoric inhibition in the normal-disabled interactions. Only one subject showed a reversal on this variable and he is noteworthy for his general lack of movement in the interaction situation. This result fits an earlier finding that Ss are more emotionally aroused and the arousal may serve to inhibit movement, particularly when the arousal may be generated by uncertainty as to how to interact. An interesting question which needs to be investigated further concerns the relationship of the motoric inhibition to the type of disability. That is, the observed inhibition may be a function of the fact that the disability in the present case was motoric rather than cosmetic. A partial test of this notion yielded no results in that leg movements were no less frequent in the disabled interaction than in the normal.

One of the general tendencies observed in the present experiment with regard to differences in nonverbal behavior is that these differences appear more strikingly during listening behavior. This may rest with the fact that the person is more able to monitor the nonverbal aspects of his behavior during this time. This has an important implication in that it is precisely while listening that the behavior of the subject may be expected to have the greatest impact upon the other person. That is to say, a person's behavior while listening to us is used by us as feedback regarding his evaluation of our own behavior, while when he is talking this tends not to be the case.

The impression formation results are consistent with the previous observations made by Ray (1946) and Barker *et al.* (1953) and are impressive in their consistency across subjects. The source of this bias is difficult to determine but may depend upon a general norm in American culture to be kind to disadvantaged persons (Ono, 1963). It is also possible that the inflation of impression is a function of the expectation that physically stigmatized persons will show serious deficits in functioning. In the experiment reported here this expectation is contradicted when the disabled performs as well as the normal. To the extent that this positive bias present in impression formation characterizes other types of evaluation of the disabled it will make it difficult for the disable person to acquire accurate feedback from his environment. This is perhaps particularly true regarding task related behavior and studies now in the planning stage will attempt to explore it in this context. The impression bias results are highly consistent with the opinion distortion findings and essentially the same dynamics may be operative. In any case it again means that the stigmatized person is not getting accurate information from his environment.

An important point to be made concerning the results is that they characterize initial interactions with physically stigmatized persons. To what extent subsequent interaction results in the modification of these tendencies is an empirical question that needs to be investigated. Goffman (1963) has suggested that long-term interactions with stigmatized persons may become more rather than less stereotyped.

This study continues an earlier focus upon the behavioral output of persons involved in interactions with the physically stigmatized. The approach assumes that a point of departure in the analysis of how the stigmatized person perceives himself and others in a careful mapping of the information input which is made available to him. Studies now in progress are attempting to assess the impact of the observed cue differences on the responses the stigmatized person makes to his environment.

SUMMARY

A study of interactions between physically stigmatized and physically normal persons was conducted to explore several non-verbal dimensions of the interaction as well as to test hypotheses related to impression formation. As in a series of previous studies the physical stigma simulated was that of a left leg amputation and was achieved through the use of a specially designed wheel chair. Contrary to expectations the level of eye contact in the disabled normal interactions was not lower than that for normal-normal interactions. Consistent with expectations subjects interacting with a confederate playing the role of a left leg amputee as compared to the same subjects interacting with a physically normal confederate (1) demonstrated greater motoric inhibition, (2) formed a more positive impression of the confederate, and (3) distorted their opinions in the direction of making them more consistent with those assumed to be held by disabled persons. Several suggestions for futher research in this area were made.

NOTES

1. This study was supported by a grant from the Association for the Aid of Crippled Children and by Research Grant MH 12508–01 from the National Institute of Mental Health, United States Public Health Service.
2. The author would like to express his appreciation to Judith Armstrong and Carolyn Lyons who analyzed the film data.
3. It should be noted that the persons conducting the analysis of the film data were blind with regard to the condition (disabled or nondisabled) from which the film came.
4. The t tests were computed for the average movement per minute in the talking and listening conditions since these differed in total length.

REFERENCES

Argyle, M., and Dean, Janet, Eye contact, distance and affiliation. *Sociometry*, 1965, 28, 289–304.

Barker, R. G., Wright, Beatrice, Meyerson, L., and Gonick, Mollie, *Adjustment to physical handicap and illness: a survey of the social psychology of physique and disability* (rev. ed.). New York: Social Science Research Council, Bull. No. 55 (1953).

Davis, F., Deviance disavowal: the management of strained interaction by the visibly handicapped. *Social Problems*, 1961, 9, 120–32.

Ekman, P., A comparison of the information communicated by head and body cues. Paper read at American Psychological Convention, 1964.

Exline, R. V., and Winters, L. C., Affective relations and mutual glances in dyads. In S. S. Tomkins and C. E. Izard (eds.) *Affect, Cognition, and Personality*. New York: Springer, 1965.

Goffman, E., *Stigma: Notes on the Management of Spoiled Identity*. Englewood Cliffs, N. J.: Prentice-Hall, 1963.

Kelley, H. H., Hastorf, A. H., Jones, E. E., Thibaut, J. W., and Usdane, W. M., Some implications of social-psychological theory for research on the handicapped. In *Psychological Research and Rehabilitation*. Miami Conf. Report: Amer. Psychol. Assoc., 1960.

Kleck, R., Emotional arousal in interactions with stigmatized persons. *Psychol. Rep.*, 1966, 19, 1226.

Kleck, R., Ono, H., and Hastorf, A. H., The effects of physical deviance upon face-to-face interaction. *Hum. Relat.*, 1966, 19, 425–36.

Ono, H. (1963). Unpublished data.

Ray, M. H., (1946), The effect of crippled appearance on personality judgments. Unpublished Master's thesis, Stanford University.

Richardson, S. A., Hastorf, A. H., Goodman, N., and Dornbusch, S. M., Cultural uniformity in reaction to physical disabilities. *Amer. sociol. Rev.*, 1961, 26, 241–7.

10
How Much Do We Say Without Speaking?

Darwyn E. Linder

Nonverbal behavior was not really just discovered in 1970 as some might be led to believe by the recent burst of popularity that the study of body language, spacing behavior, and eye contact has now received. People have been emitting nonverbal behaviors since they become people, and our primate ancestors employed nonverbal behavior in communication, so we know that it has a very long history. However, concern with nonverbal behavior by social scientists has been greatest in the last 15 to 20 years. Nevertheless, many theorists, like Simmel, were concerned with explaining the function of various sorts of nonverbal behavior in the very early stages of the social science disciplines. Note the 1908 date on the selection of Simmel's work that was presented. But Simmel's analysis of nonverbal behavior and especially of eye contact was not empirical. What he reports are his insights about the communicative functions of eye contact, the language of glances.

The wonderful array of expressions that were attributed to the eyes have now been shown by empirical work to depend really upon the expression of the entire face, or at least of the portions of the face nearest to the eyes. Ray Birdwhistell (1970) has analyzed the possibilities for movement in the face of North Americans. He has found that people ordinarily use four different movements of the eyebrows, lifted brow, lowered brow, knit brow, and single brow movement, and four different degrees of eyelid closure: over-open, slit, closed, and squeezed. These different movements in the immediate area of the eye no doubt combine with movements of the nose and mouth and cheek portions of the face to give us the wide variety of expressions that we label as different kinds of glances. The eyeball itself is relatively incapable of movement or expressive movement. It moves to focus on new objects so that one can look from the corner of his eye or look straight ahead. The pupils also dilate and contract. Aside from these special cases the eyeball is not capable in and of itself of the wide variety of expressions, the cold stare, the warm, come hither look, that have been called meaningful glances. These are combinations of looking directly at a person or making eye contact with him and at the same time expressing emotion with the remainder of the face.

There is, of course, significance in the mere act of making eye contact regardless of the expressions that the two interactants have put on the remainder of their faces. These expressions may be very neutral yet the experience of eye contact is usually a deeply meaningful one in most interaction contexts and the use of eye contact is rather carefully regulated in most interactions. Researchers are now beginning to find out some of the implicit rules governing eye contact in social interaction. Kendon (1967) for example has demonstrated that eye contact is a signal for an exchange of speaker-hearer roles during social interaction. As one person comes to the end of what he wishes to say he looks at the person who is listening to him, makes eye contact, and the former listener then begins his response and looks away from the former speaker. Another finding is that most people look at another person more frequently when listening than when speaking. This confirms the importance of nonverbal behavior in communication since if one is attempting to understand the message being sent by another he must listen *and* watch in order to monitor both the verbal and the nonverbal channels. However, when one is speaking rather than listening it would be distracting from one's own speech generating process to be concerned about the nonverbal behavior of the other person, and so when we speak we do not look so directly nor so often at those who are listening.

There is one interesting exception to the general lack of expressiveness of the eyeball itself and that is the ability of the pupil to dilate and contract. Eckhard Hess (1965) rediscovered and empirically verified some ancient wisdom concerning pupil dilation. His observation, at first informal, and later more formally verified, was that the pupils dilated as a person looked at an object that evoked favorable or positive response from him. The first informal verification of this phenomenon was accomplished by including a *Playboy* centerfold picture among a set of more neutral stimuli and simply observing the dilation of a person's pupils as he shuffled through the set of cards. I mention that this phenomenon was rediscovered by Hess. It is rumored that jade merchants for centuries used the pupil dilation cue as an index of interest in a particular piece and a shrewd merchant could thereby adjust the price of the piece by knowing the degree of interest a customer had in it. But if a dilated pupil indicates approval or some positive response to what is being looked at, then it should follow that if a person's pupils are dilated as he looks at us we should find that event itself reinforcing and be more attracted to a person with dilated pupils than to a person with contracted pupils. This hypothesis is supported by some other folk wisdom in that the use of belladonna to dilate pupils of women to make themselves more attractive was widespread at certain times and in certain cultures. Again, it has been empirically demonstrated that a pictured person is judged to be warmer, friendlier, and more attractive if in the picture the pupils are dilated rather than contracted. But notice how neatly reciprocal this relationship then becomes, if I am looking at someone that I find attractive there is some pupil dilation which, when the other person returns my gaze, enhances the warmth, friendliness, and attractiveness of my countenance. But this is simply a speculation at this point, there is no hard empirical evidence that in natural settings pupil dilation plays an important role in mutual attraction.

The complex task of analyzing the meaning of facial expressions, including the meaning of eye contact has really just begun. My speculation is that eye contact indicates engagement with the other person in an interaction, but the entire context of the interaction and the expressions of the entire face and body determine the meaning of the glance to be flirtation, aggression, disbelief, or any of the wide range of emotions that are supposed to be expressed by the eyes.

The selection from Robert Sommer's book, *Personal Space*, focused on the effects of spatial invasion, that is, moving one's own body to a point closer to another person than he would like to have it. While Sommer has focused on the use of space, Robert Kleck has described the effects on a variety of nonverbal behaviors of interacting with a stigmatized person. Rather than elaborate on either of those reports, I want to discuss briefly the hypothesized interrelationships of the wide variety of nonverbal behaviors that we all emit. Argyle and Dean (1965) have suggested a sort of equilibrium model for nonverbal behaviors in interaction. Their idea is that each of these behaviors expresses a certain level of intimacy or intensity of the interaction. Thus, as Hall (1966) has pointed out, the distance at which we place ourselves from another person expresses the kind of interaction we expect to have. Similarly, the amount of eye contact that we attempt to make with the partner in an interaction expresses the level of intensity or intimacy of engagement. Argyle and Dean then propose that all of these parameters of nonverbal behavior are adjusted until an equilibrium is reached so that both parties to interaction are expressing by their nonverbal behavior a mutually acceptable level of intensity or intimacy for that particular interaction. What it seems that we are saying, then, in the nonverbal behaviors we emit is how we feel about the interaction, the kind of interaction we want it to be, and the level of intimacy that we wish to exchange with the partner in that particular interaction. In this light it is not surprising that moving too close to a person in an impersonal public setting, as in Robert Sommer's studies and those conducted by his student Nancy Russo, caused the target person to adjust his own nonverbal behavior, the distance he wanted to maintain, to something more satisfactory for him. Since these persons in fact desired no interaction with the invader, we can understand their flight as merely attempting to achieve the acceptable level of interaction for them, namely a zero level. Furthermore, in Kleck's work we can understand the adjustments in behavior when one interacts with a physically stigmatized person as a response to the emotion that stigmatization arouses in us. We then adjust our manner of behavior in accord with our response to the stigmatized person and to express the kind of interaction we wish to have. Of course, these speculations, even if true, are only descriptions of behavior and do not constitute a satisfying explanation. The pursuit of a full understanding of the determinants and functions of nonverbal behavior will, I think, happily occupy researchers for some time to come.

One facet of the study of nonverbal behavior that has not yet received much empirical attention is the question of whether a person's personality traits or characteristics determine in some ways the nonverbal behaviors that he emits. Our language implies that personality does express itself through nonverbal behaviors. We say of certain people that they look kind, or trustworthy, or sneaky, or sinister, or criminal, implying that personality traits are expressed in the appearance and movements of a person. Less than a century ago it was asserted that a person's criminal tendencies could be discerned by examining his physiognomy. I think that both our own nonverbal behavior and our responses to the nonverbal behaviors of others are determined, in part, by our personal traits or personality characteristics. While we generally obey the societal norms for interaction distance, and the frequency of eye contact, there is no doubt that we also express ourselves uniquely in the combinations of movements, gestures and expressions that we emit, and that we uniquely interpret the nonverbal behaviors of other persons. But the study of individual differences in nonverbal behavior has barely begun, and I cannot even guess what relationships will be found between personality traits and nonverbal patterns of behavior.

How much can we communicate nonverbally? I think that it is impossible to place limits on the applicability of nonverbal behavior and foolish to try to make statements that indicate the percentage of human communication that is carried by the nonverbal channel. Both verbal and nonverbal behavior are important modes of human communication. In attempting to understand the kinds of interactions that people are having or the determinants of the persuasive impact that one person has upon another, it is essential to look at both verbal and nonverbal behavior. Some recent experiments by Albert Mehrabian (Mehrabian and Williams, 1969) have indicated that we do adopt different kinds of behavior when we attempt to persuade others. I don't doubt that much of what we mean when we say that a man is an eloquent speaker refers to his ability to use gestures and expressions to emphasize and punctuate his message. But perhaps we can best learn how much we can say without speaking by observing the French mime, Marcel Marceau, who uses no words at all to express eloquently feelings and conditions that are very real to all of us.

REFERENCES

Argyle, M., and Dean, J., Eye contact, distance, and affiliation. *Sociometry*, 1965, *28*, 289–304.

Birdwhistell, R. L., *Kinesics and Context: Essays on Body Motion Communication*. Philadelphia: University of Pennsylvania Press, 1970.

Hall, E. T., *The Hidden Dimension*. Garden City, N.Y.: Doubleday, 1966.

Hess, E. H., Attitude and pupil size. *Scientific American*, 1965, *212*, 46–54.

Kendon, A., Some functions of gaze direction in social interaction. *Acta Psychologica*, 1967, *26*, 22–63.

Mehrabian, A., and Williams, M., Nonverbal concomitants of perceived and intended persuasiveness. *J. Personality soc. Psychol.*, 1969, *13*, 37–58.

11
Interaction in Some Particular Dyads

Darwyn E. Linder

Dyadic interaction occurs for all sorts of reasons. People come together for courtship, for cooperation, for simple human companionship, and to pass the time. There seems to be no simple set of dimensions along which one can categorize all of the kinds of dyadic interactions that do occur. Some theorists have proposed that interactions can be divided into those that are cooperative versus those that are competitive. Another dimension that might be suggested is the extent to which the interacting pair is task oriented, or group oriented. That is, the extent to which they are seeking to accomplish some concrete goal, or are motivated to obtain interpersonal rewards from the process of interacting. As dichotomies these assertions fail to satisfy us because we can always find examples in which there is both competition and cooperation, in which there is at the same time a task orientation and an interpersonal orientation.

Rather than attempt to map out the dyadic landscape, trying to assign each possible dyad some coordinates by which we could identify its location in this theoretical scheme, I have chosen to present some examples of interaction in particular dyads.

Stanley Milgram examines some of the dimensions of power between an authority and a subordinate, and the factors that may allow subordinates to perform actions that are distasteful or immoral at the mere request of the authority. Anatol Rapoport has used an exceedingly simple game to study conflict and cooperation in dyads. Robert Carson, a colleague and friend at Duke University, is a clinical psychologist who has a great deal of experience as a therapist and as a researcher in clinical psychology. In his paper he presents an essentially social psychological analysis of the relationship and power dynamics between client and therapist.

These papers are tied together by two theoretical threads. First, and obviously, they all deal with interaction in dyads. Second, they all deal with the distribution and use of power in social interaction. In an earlier section of this book, I said that attraction was perhaps the most important dimension in the analysis of dyadic interaction. But as I pointed out, attractiveness confers the ability to mediate rewards, and that ability is a source of power that may be used to shape the behavior of one's partner in a dyadic interaction. While attractiveness may be converted to power in relatively informal dyads, power can be determined by one's role in more structured interactions. In the three selections that follow, the dyads studied are structured in particular ways and the use of power by each member to achieve his own goals will be the focus of our interest.

12
Some Conditions of Obedience and Disobedience to Authority

Stanley Milgram

In this experimental design, the function studied is obedience: if X tells Y to hurt Z, under what conditions will Y obey and under what conditions will he refuse? The laboratory procedure consists of ordering a naive S to administer increasingly more severe punishment (electric shock) to a victim in the context of a learning experiment. The victim is a confederate of the E. The primary dependent variable is the maximum shock the S is willing to administer before he refuses to continue. The results showed, first, that it was more difficult for many people to defy the experimenter's authority than expected. A broad range of situational variables was then examined. Several of these were found to have an important effect upon the subject's level of obedience.

The situation in which one agent commands another to hurt a third turns up time and again as a significant theme in human relations. It is powerfully expressed in the story of Abraham, who is commanded by God to kill his son. It is no accident that Kierkegaard, seeking to orient his thought to the central themes of human experience, chose Abraham's conflict as the springboard to his philosophy.

War too moves forward on the triad of an authority which commands a person to destroy the enemy, and perhaps all organized hostility

From *Human Relations*, 1968, Vol. 18, pages 57–76. Reprinted by permission of Plenum Publishing Co. Ltd.

may be viewed as a theme and variation on the three elements of authority, executant, and victim.[1] We describe an experimental program, recently concluded at Yale University, in which a particular expression of this conflict is studied by experimental means.

In its most general form the problem may be defined thus: if X tells Y to hurt Z, under what conditions will Y carry out the command of X and under what conditions will he refuse. In the more limited form possible in laboratory research, the question becomes: if an experimenter tells a subject to hurt another person, under what conditions will the subject go along with this instruction, and under what conditions will he refuse to obey. The laboratory problem is not so much a dilution of the general statement as one concrete expression of the many particular forms this question may assume.

One aim of the research was to study behavior in a strong situation of deep consequence to the participants, for the psychological forces operative in powerful and lifelike forms of the conflict may not be brought into play under diluted conditions.

This approach meant, first, that we had a special obligation to protect the welfare and dignity of the persons who took part in the study; subjects were, of necessity, placed in a difficult predicament, and steps had to be taken to ensure their wellbeing before they were discharged from the laboratory. Toward this end, a careful, post-experimental treatment was devised and has been carried through for subjects in all conditions.[2]

TERMINOLOGY

If Y follows the command of X we shall say that he has obeyed X; if he fails to carry out the command of X, we shall say that he has disobeyed X. The terms *to obey* and *to disobey*, as used here, refer to the subject's overt action only, and carry no implication for the motive or experiential states accompanying the action.[3]

To be sure, the everyday use of the word *obedience* is not entirely free from complexities. It refers to action within widely varying situations, and connotes diverse motives within those situations: a child's obedience differs from a soldier's obedience, or the love, honor, and *obey* of the marriage vow. However, a consistent behavioral relationship is indicated in most uses of the term: in the act of obeying, a person does what another person tell him to do. Y obeys X if he carries out the prescription for action which X has addressed to him; the term suggests, moreover, that some form of dominance, or hierarchical element, is part of the situation in which the transaction between X and Y occurs.

A subject who complies with the entire series of experimental commands will be termed an *obedient* subject; one who at any point in the command series defies the experimenter will be called a *disobedient* or *defiant* subject. As used in this report, the terms refer only to the subject's performance in the experiment, and do not necessarily imply a general personality disposition to submit to or reject authority.

SUBJECT POPULATION

The subjects used in all experimental conditions were male adults, residing in the greater New Haven and Bridgeport areas, aged 20 to 50 years, and engaged in a wide variety of occupations. Each experimental condition described in this report employed 40 fresh subjects and was carefully balanced for age and occupational types. The occupational composition for each experiment was: workers, skilled and unskilled: 40 percent; white collar, sales, business: 40 percent; professionals: 20 percent. The occupations were intersected with three age categories (subjects in 20s, 30s, and 40s, assigned to each condition in the proportions of 20, 40, and 40 percent respectively).

THE GENERAL LABORATORY PROCEDURE

The focus of the study concerns the amount of electric shock a subject is willing to administer to another person when ordered by an experimenter to give the "victim" increasingly more severe punishment. The act of administering shock is set in the context of a learning experiment, ostensibly designed to study the effect of punishment on memory. Aside from the experimenter, one naive subject and one accomplice perform in each session. On arrival each subject is paid $4.50. After a general talk by the experimenter, telling how little scientists know about the effect of punishment on memory, subjects are informed that one member of the pair will serve as teacher and one as learner. A rigged drawing is held so that the naive subject is always the teacher, and the accomplice becomes the learner. The learner is taken to an adjacent room and strapped into an "electric chair."[4]

The naive subject is told that it is his task to teach the learner a list of paired associates, to test him on the list, and to administer punishment whenever the learner errs in the test. Punishment takes the form of electric shock, delivered to the learner by means of a shock generator controlled by the naive subject. The teacher is instructed to increase the intensity of electric shock one step on the generator on each error. The learner, according to plan, provides many wrong answers, so that before long the naive subject must give him the strongest shock on the generator. Increases in shock level are met by increasingly insistent demands from the learner that the experiment be stopped because of the growing discomfort to him. However, in clear terms the experimenter orders the teacher to continue with the procedure in disregard of the learner's protests. *Thus, the naive subject must resolve a conflict between two mutually incompatible demands from the social field. He may continue to follow the orders of the experimenter and shock the learner with increasing severity, or he may refuse to follow the orders of the experimenter and heed the learner's pleas. The experimenter's authority operates not in a free field, but against ever-mounting countervailing pressures from the person being punished.*

A few technical points need to be considered before the findings of the study are described. For the purpose of delivering shock, a simulated shock generator is used, with 30 clearly marked voltage levels that range from 15 to 450 volts (and each activated by one of 30 individual lever switches set in a horizontal line). The naive subject is given a sample shock of 45 volts to convince him of the authenticity of the instrument. The generator bears verbal designations that range from "Slight Shock" to "Danger: Severe Shock."

The responses of the victim are standardized on tape, and each protest is coordinated to a particular voltage level on the shock generator. Starting with 75 volts the learner begins to grunt and moan. At 150 volts he demands to be let out of the experiment. At 180 volts he cries out that he can no longer stand the pain. At 300 volts he refuses to provide any more answers to the memory test, insisting that he is no longer a participant in the experiment and must be freed. In response to this last tactic, the experimenter instructs the naive subject to treat the absence of an answer as equivalent to a wrong answer, and to follow the usual shock procedure. The experimenter reinforces his demand with the statement: "You have no other choice, you must go on!" (This imperative is used whenever the naive subject tries to break off the experiment.) If the subject refuses to give the next higher level of shock, the experiment is considered at an end. A quantitative value is assigned to the subject's performance based on the maximum intensity shock he administered before breaking off. Thus any subject's score may range from zero (for a subject unwilling to administer the first shock level) to 30 (for a subject who proceeds to the highest voltage level on the board). For any particular subject and for any particular experimental condition the degree to which participants have followed the experimenter's orders may be specified with a numerical value, corresponding to the metric on the shock generator.

This laboratory situation gives us a framework in which to study the subject's reactions to the principal conflict of the experiment. Again, this conflict is between the experimenter's demands that he continue to administer the electric shock, and the learner's demands, which become increasingly more insistent, that the experiment be stopped. The crux of the study is to vary systematically the factors believed to alter the degree of obedience to the experimental commands, to learn under what conditions submission to authority is most probable, and under what conditions defiance is brought to the fore.

PILOT STUDIES

Pilot studies for the present research were completed in the winter of 1960; they differed from the regular experiments in a few details; for one, the victim was placed behind a silvered glass, with the light balance on the glass such that the victim could be dimly perceived by the subject (Milgram, 1961).

Though essentially qualitative in treatment, these studies pointed to several significant features of the experimental situation. At first no vocal feedback was used from the victim. It was thought that the verbal and voltage designations on the control panel would create sufficient pressure to curtail the subject's obedience. However, this was not the case. In the absence of protests from the learner, virtually all subjects, once commanded, went blithely to the end of the board, seemingly indifferent to the verbal designations ("Extreme Shock" and "Danger: Severe Shock"). This deprived us of an adequate basis for scaling obedient tendencies. A force had to be introduced that would strengthen the subject's resistance to the experimenter's commands, and reveal individual differences in terms of a distribution of break-off points.

This force took the form of protests from the victim. Initially, mild protests were used, but proved inadequate. Subsequently, more vehement protests were inserted into the experimental procedure. To our consternation, even the strongest protests from the victim did not prevent all subjects from administering the harshest punishment ordered by the experimenter; but the protests did lower the mean maximum shock somewhat and created some spread in the subject's performance; therefore, the victim's cries were standardized on tape and incorporated into the regular experimental procedure.

The situation did more than highlight the technical difficulties of finding a workable experimental procedure: it indicated that subjects would obey authority to a greater extent than we had supposed. It also pointed to the importance of feedback from the victim in controlling the subject's behavior.

One further aspect of the pilot study was that subjects frequently averted their eyes from the person they were shocking, often turning their heads in an awkward and conspicuous manner. One subject explained: "I didn't want to see the consequences of what I had done." Observers wrote:

> ... subjects showed a reluctance to look at the victim, whom they could see through the glass in front of them. When this fact was brought to their attention they indicated that it caused them discomfort to see the victim in agony. We note, however, that although the subject refuses to look at the victim, he continues to administer shocks.

This suggested that the salience of the victim may have, in some degree, regulated the subject's performance. If, in obeying the experimenter, the subject found it necessary to avoid scrutiny of the victim, would the converse be true? If the victim were rendered increasingly more salient to the subject, would obedience diminish? The first set of regular experiments was designed to answer this question.

Immediacy of the Victim

This series consisted of four experimental conditions. In each condition the victim was brought "psychologically" closer to the subject giving him shocks.

In the first condition (Remote Feedback) the victim was placed in another room and could not be heard or seen by the subject, except that, at 300 volts, he pounded on the wall in protest. After 315 volts he no longer answered or was heard from.

The second condition (Voice Feedback) was identical to the first except that voice protests were introduced. As in the first condition the victim was placed in an adjacent room, but his complaints could be heard clearly through a door left slightly ajar, and through the walls of the laboratory.[5]

The third experimental condition (Proximity) was similar to the second, except that the victim was now placed in the same room as the subject, and one and a half feet from him. Thus he was visible as well as audible, and voice cues were provided.

The fourth, and final, condition of this series (Touch-Proximity) was identical to the third, with this exception: the victim received a shock only when his hand rested on a shockplate. At the 150-volt level the victim again demanded to be let free and, in this condition, refused to place his hand on the shockplate. The experimenter ordered the naive subject to force the victim's hand onto the plate. Thus obedience in this condition required that the subject have physical contact with the victim in order to give him punishment beyond the 150-volt level.

Forty adult subjects were studied in each condition. The data revealed that obedience was significantly reduced as the victim was rendered more immediate to the subject. The mean maximum shock for the conditions is shown in Figure 1.

Expressed in terms of the proportion of obedient to defiant subjects, the findings are that 34 percent of the subjects defied the experimenter in the Remote condition, 37.5 percent in Voice Feedback, 60 percent in Proximity, and 70 percent in Touch-Proximity.

How are we to account for this effect? A first conjecture might be that as the victim was brought closer the subject became more aware of the intensity of his suffering and regulated his behavior accordingly. This makes sense, but our evidence does not support the interpretation. There are no consistent differences in the attributed level of pain across the four conditions (i.e. the amount of pain experienced by the victim as estimated by the subject and expressed on a 14-point scale). But it is easy to speculate about alternative mechanisms:

Empathic cues. In the Remote and to a lesser extent the Voice Feedback condition, the victim's suffering possesses an abstract, remote quality for the subject. He is aware, but only in a conceptual sense, that his actions cause pain to another person; the fact is apprehended, but not felt. The phenomenon is common enough. The bombardier can

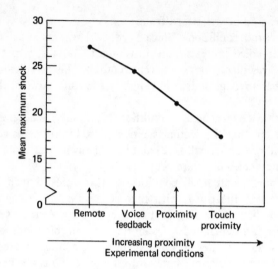

Figure 1

reasonably suppose that his weapons will inflict suffering and death, yet this knowledge is divested of affect, and does not move him to a felt, emotional response to the suffering resulting from his actions. Similar observations have been made in wartime. It is possible that the visual cues associated with the victim's suffering trigger empathic responses in the subject and provide him with a more complete grasp of the victim's experience. Or it is possible that the empathic responses are themselves unpleasant, possessing drive properties which cause the subject to terminate the arousal situation. Diminishing obedience, then, would be explained by the enrichment of empathic cues in the successive experimental conditions.

Denial and narrowing of the cognitive field.   The Remote condition allows a narrowing of the cognitive field so that the victim is put out of mind. The subject no longer considers the act of depressing a lever relevant to moral judgment, for it is no longer associated with the victim's suffering. When the victim is close it is more difficult to exclude him phenomenologically. He necessarily intrudes on the subject's awareness since he is continuously visible. In the Remote conditions his existence and reactions are made known only after the shock has been administered.

The auditory feedback is sporadic and discontinuous. In the Proximity conditions his inclusion in the immediate visual field renders him a continuously salient element for the subject. The mechanism of denial can no longer be brought into play. One subject in the Remote condition said: "It's funny how you really begin to forget that there's a guy out there, even though you can hear him. For a long time I just concentrated on pressing the switches and reading the words.'

Reciprocal fields.   If in the Proximity condition the subject is in an improved position to observe the victim, the reverse is also true. The actions of the subject now come under proximal scrutiny by the victim. Possibly, it is easier to harm a person when he is unable to observe our actions than when he can see what we are doing. His surveillance of the action directed against him may give rise to shame, or guilt, which may then serve to curtail the action. Many expressions of language refer to the discomfort or inhibitions that arise in face-to-face confrontation. It is often said that it is easier to criticize a man "behind his back" than to "attack him to his face". If we are in the process of lying to a person it is reputedly difficult to "stare him in the eye". We "turn away from others in shame" or in "embarrassment" and this action serves to reduce our discomfort. The manifest function of allowing the victim of a firing squad to be blindfolded is to make the occasion less stressful for him, but it may also serve a latent function of reducing the stress of the executioner. In short, in the Proximity conditions, the subject may sense that he has become more salient in the victim's field of awareness. Possibly he becomes more self-conscious, embarrassed, and inhibited in his punishment of the victim.

Phenomenal unity of act.   In the Remote conditions it is more difficult for the subject to gain a sense of *relatedness* between his own actions and the consequences of these actions for the victim. There is a physical and spatial separation of the act and its consequences. The subject depresses a lever in one room, and protests and cries are heard from another. The two events are in correlation, yet they lack a compelling phenomenological unity. The structure of a meaningful act—*I am hurting a man*—breaks down because of the spatial arrangements, in a manner somewhat analogous to the disappearance of phi phenomena when the blinking lights are spaced too far apart. The unity is more fully achieved in the Proximity conditions as the victim is brought closer to the action that causes him pain. It is rendered complete in Touch-Proximity.

Incipient group formation.   Placing the victim in another room not only takes him further from the subject, but the subject and the experimenter are drawn relatively closer. There is incipient group formation between the experimenter and the subject, from which the victim is excluded. The wall between the victim and the others deprives him of an intimacy which the experimenter and subject feel. In the Remote condition, the victim is truly an outsider, who stands alone, physically and psychologically.

When the victim is placed close to the subject, it becomes easier to form an alliance with him against the experimenter. Subjects no longer have to face the experimenter alone. They have an ally who is close at hand and eager to collaborate in a revolt against the experimenter. Thus, the changing set of spatial relations leads to a potentially shifting set of alliance over the several experimental conditions.

Acquired behavior dispositions.   It is commonly observed that laboratory mice will rarely fight with their litter mates. Scott (1958) explains this in terms of passive inhibition. He writes: "By doing nothing under ... circumstances [the animal] learns to do nothing, and this may be spoken of as passive inhibition ... this principle has great importance in teaching an individual to be peaceful, for it means that he can learn not to fight simply by not fighting." Similarly, we may learn not to harm others simply by not harming them in everyday life. Yet this learning occurs in a context of proximal relations with others, and may not be generalized to that situation in which the person is physically removed from us. Or possibly, in the past, aggressive actions against others who were physically close resulted in retaliatory punishment which extinguished the original form of response. In contrast, aggression against others at a distance may have only sporadically led to retaliation. Thus the organism learns that it is safer to be aggressive toward others at a distance, and precarious to be so when the parties are within arm's reach. Through a pattern of rewards and punishments, he acquires a disposition to avoid aggression at close quarters, a disposition which does not extend to harming others at a distance. And this may account for experimental findings in the remote and proximal experiments.

Proximity as a variable in psychological research has received far less attention than it deserves. If men were sessile it would be easy to understand this neglect. But we move about; our spatial relations shift from one situation to the next, and the fact that we are near or remote may have a powerful effect on the psychological processes that mediate our behavior toward others. In the present situation, as the victim is brought closer to the man ordered to give him shocks, increasing numbers of subjects break off the experiment, refusing to obey. The concrete, visible, and proximal presence of the victim acts in an important way to counteract the experimenter's power and to generate disobedience.[6]

Closeness of Authority

If the spatial relationship of the subject and victim is relevant to the degree of obedience, would not the relationship of subject to experimenter also play a part?

There are reasons to feel that, on arrival, the subject is oriented primarily to the experimenter rather than to the victim. He has come to the laboratory to fit into the structure that the experimenter—not the victim—would provide. He has come less to understand his behavior than to *reveal* that behavior to a competent scientist, and he is willing to display himself as the scientist's purposes require. Most subjects seem quite concerned about the appearance they are making before the experimenter, and one could argue that this preoccupation in a relatively new and strange setting makes the subject somewhat insensitive to the triadic nature of the social situation. In other words, the subject is so concerned about the show he is putting on for the experimenter that influences from other parts of the social field do not receive as much weight as they ordinarily would. This overdetermined orientation to the experimenter would account for the relative insensitivity of the subject to the victim, and would also lead us to believe that alterations in the relationship between subject and experimenter would have important consequences for obedience.

In a series of experiments we varied the physical closeness and degree of surveillance of the experimenter. In one condition the experimenter sat just a few feet away from the subject. In a second condition, after giving initial instructions, the experimenter left the laboratory and gave his orders by telephone; in still a third condition the experimenter was never seen, providing instructions by means of a tape recording activated when the subjects entered the laboratory.

Obedience dropped sharply as the experimenter was physically removed from the laboratory. The number of obedient subjects in the first condition (Experimenter Present) was almost three times as great as in the second, where the experimenter gave his orders by telephone. Twenty-six subjects were fully obedient in the first condition, and only 9 in the second (Chi square obedient vs. defiant in the two conditions, 1 d.f. = 14.7; $p < .001$). Subjects seemed able to take a far stronger stand against the experimenter when they did not have to encounter him face to face, and the experimenter's power over the subject was severely curtailed.[7]

Moreover, when the experimenter was absent, subjects displayed an interesting form of behavior that had not occurred under his surveillance. Though continuing with the experiment, several subjects administered lower shocks than were required and never informed the experimenter of their deviation from the correct procedure. (Unknown to the subjects, shock levels were automatically recorded by an Esterline-Angus event recorder wired directly into the shock generator; the instrument provided us with an objective record of the subjects' performance.) Indeed, in telephone conversations some subjects specifically assured the experimenter that they were raising the shock level according to instruction, whereas in fact they were repeatedly using the lowest shock on the board. This form of behavior is particularly interesting: although these subjects acted in a way that clearly undermined the avowed purposes of the experiment, they found it easier to handle the conflict in this manner than to precipitate an open break with authority.

Other conditions were completed in which the experimenter was absent during the first segment of the experiment, but reappeared at the point that the subject definitely refused to give higher shocks when commanded by telephone. Although he had exhausted his power via telephone, the experimenter could frequently force further obedience when he reappeared in the laboratory.

Experiments in this series show that the physical *presence* of an authority is an important force contributing to the subject's obedience or defiance. Taken together with the first experimental series on the proximity of the victim, it would appear that something akin to fields of force, diminishing in effectiveness with increasing psychological distance from their source, have a controlling effect on the subject's performance. As the victim is brought closer, the subject finds it harder to administer shocks to him. When the victim's position is held constant relative to the subject, and the authority is made more remote, the subject finds it easier to break off the experiment. This effect is substantial in both cases, but manipulation of the experimenter's position yielded the more powerful results. Obedience to destructive commands is highly dependent on the proximal relations between authority and subject.

Tensions

The description of final scores does not fully convey the character of the subjects' performance, and it would be useful to interrupt our reporting of quantitative relationships to remark on the subjects' general reaction to the situation.

One might suppose that a subject would simply break off or continue as his conscience and temperament dictated. Yet this is very far from what happened. There were powerful reactions of tension and emotional strain in a substantial proportion of the participants. Persons were observed to sweat, tremble, stutter, bite their lips, and groan as they found themselves increasingly implicated in the experimental conflict. Some sense of the subjects' mood can be gotten from a transcript of their remarks at break-off point. Here are the remarks of two defiant subjects:

> Is he banging? ... Is he hurt out there? Well, I don't want to be responsible for anything that happens to him. No, I can't go on with it. I don't know whether he's all right or not. I mean he may have a heart condition or something; I wouldn't feel right doing it. He's banging for help. He's evidently in trouble or he wouldn't bang ... I don't see any sense to this—to knocking him out or something. I just can't see it.
>
> (*Subject refuses to administer shocks*)
>
> [*Subject 0108*]
>
> The man is banging. He wants to get out ... I'm sorry. If the man wants to get out I'd just as soon stop ... I don't want to administer any more [extremely excited] ... I will gladly refund the check, but I will not harm this man ... I'm sorry, I will not give him any more if he obviously wants to get out. There is no money in the world that will make me hurt another individual.
>
> [*Subject 010X*]

And here is a transcript from an obedient subject. He began the experiment calmly, but became increasingly tense as the experiment proceeded. After administering the 150-volt shock, he began to address the experimenter in agitated tones:

> *150 volts delivered.* You want me to keep going?
> *165 volts delivered.* That guy is hollering in there. There's a lot of them here. He's liable to have heart condition. You want me to go?
> *180 volts delivered.* He can't stand it! I'm not going to kill that man in

there! You hear him hollering? He's hollering. He can't stand it. What if something happens to him? . . . I'm not going to get that man sick in there. He's hollering in there. You know what I mean? I mean I refuse to take responsibility. He's getting hurt in there. He's in there hollering. Too many left here. Geez, if he gets them wrong. There's too many of them left. I mean who is going to take responsibility if anything happens to that gentleman?
[*The experimenter accepts responsibility.*]
All right.
195 volts delivered. You see he's hollering. Hear that. Gee, I don't know. [*The experimenter says: 'The experiment requires that you go on.'*] —I know it does, sir, but I mean—hugh—he don't know what he's in for. He's up to 195 volts.
210 volts delivered
225 volts delivered
240 volts delivered. Aw, no. You mean I've got to keep going up with the scale? No sir. I'm not going to kill that man! I'm not going to give him 450 volts! [*The experimenter says: "The experiment requires that you go on."*] —I know it does, but that man is hollering in there, sir . . .

Despite his numerous, agitated objections, which were constant accompaniments to his actions, the subject unfailingly obeyed the experimenter, proceeding to the highest shock level on the generator. He displayed a curious dissociation between word and action. Although at the verbal level he had resolved not to go on, his actions were fully in accord with the experimenter's commands. This subject did not want to shock the victim, and he found it an extremely disagreeable task, but he was unable to invent a response that would free him from E's authority. Many subjects cannot find the specific verbal formula that would enable them to reject the role assigned to them by the experimenter. Perhaps our culture does not provide adequate models for disobedience.

One puzzling sign of tension was the regular occurrence of nervous laughing fits. In the first four conditions 71 of the 160 subjects showed definite signs of nervous laughter and smiling. The laughter seemed entirely out of place, even bizarre. Full-blown, uncontrollable seizures were observed for 15 of these subjects. On one occasion we observed a seizure so violently convulsive that it was necessary to call a halt to the experiment. In the post-experimental interviews subjects took pains to point out that they were not sadistic types and that the laughter did not mean they enjoyed shocking the victim.

In the interview following the experiment subjects were asked to indicate on a 14-point scale just how nervous or tense they felt at the point of maximum tension (Figure 2). The scale ranged from "Not at all tense and nervous" to "Extremely tense and nervous". Self-reports of this sort are of limited precision, and at best provide only a rough indication of the subject's emotional response. Still, taking the reports for what they are worth, it can be seen that the distribution of responses spans the entire range of the scale, with the majority of subjects concentrated at the center and upper extreme. A further breakdown showed that obedient subjects reported themselves as having been slightly more tense and nervous than the defiant subjects at the point of maximum tension.

How is the occurrence of tension to be interpreted? First, it points to the presence of conflict. If a tendency to comply with authority were the

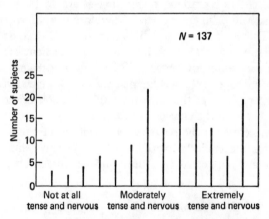

Fig. 2 This shows the self-reports on "tension and nervousness" for 137 subjects in the Proximity experiments. Subjects were given a scale with 14 values ranging from "Not at all tense and nervous" to "Extremely tense and nervous". They were instructed: "Thinking back to that point in the experiment when you felt the most tense and nervous, indicate just how you felt by placing an X at the appropriate point on the scale." The results are shown in terms of midpoint values.

only psychological force operating in the situation, all subjects would have continued to the end and there would have been no tension. Tension, it is assumed, results from the simultaneous presence of two or more incompatible response tendencies (Miller, 1944). If sympathetic concern for the victim were the exclusive force, all subjects would have calmly defied the experimenter. Instead, there were both obedient and defiant outcomes, frequently accompanied by extreme tension. A conflict develops between the deeply ingrained disposition not to harm others and the equally compelling tendency to obey others who are in authority. The subject is quickly drawn into a dilemma of a deeply dynamic character, and the presence of high tension points to the considerable strength of each of the antogonistic vectors.

Moreover, tension defines the strength of the aversive state from which the subject is unable to escape through disobedience. When a person is uncomfortable, tense, or stressed, he tries to take some action that will allow him to terminate this unpleasant state. Thus tension may serve as a drive that leads to escape behavior. But in the present situation, even where tension is extreme, many subjects are unable to perform the response that will bring about relief. Therefore there must be a competing relief. Therefore there must be a competing drive, tendency, or inhibition that precludes activation of the disobedient response. The strength of this inhibiting factor must be of greater magnitude than the stress experienced, else the terminating act would occur. Every evidence of extreme tension is at the same time an indication of the strength of the forces that keep the subject in the situation.

Finally, tension may be taken as evidence of the reality of the situations for the subjects. Normal subjects do not tremble and sweat unless they are implicated in a deep and genuinely felt predicament.

Background Authority

In psychophysics, animal learning, and other branches of psychology, the fact that measures are obtained at one institution rather than another is irrelevant to the interpretation of the findings, so long as the technical facilities for measurement are adequate and the operations are carried out with competence.

But it cannot be assumed that this holds true for the present study. The effectiveness of the experimenter's commands may depend in an important way on the larger institutional context in which they are issued. The experiments described thus far were conducted at Yale University, an organization which most subjects regarded with respect and sometimes awe. In post-experimental interviews several participants remarked that the locale and sponsorship of the study gave them confidence in the integrity, competence, and benign purposes of the personnel; many indicated that they would not have shocked the learner if the experiments had been done elsewhere.

This issue of background authority seemed to us important for an interpretation of the results that had been obtained thus far; moreover it is highly relevant to any comprehensive theory of human obedience. Consider, for example, how closely our compliance with the imperatives of others is tied to particular institutions and locales in our day-to-day activities. On request, we expose our throats to a man with a razor blade in the barber shop, but would not do so in a shoe store; in the latter setting we willingly follow the clerk's request to stand in our stockinged feet, but resist the command in a bank. In the laboratory of a great university, subjects may comply with a set of commands that would be resisted if given elsewhere. *One must always question the relationship of obedience to a person's sense of the context in which he is operating.*

To explore the problem we moved our apparatus to an office building in industrial Bridgeport and replicated experimental conditions, without any visible tie to the university.

Bridgeport subjects were invited to the experiment through a mail circular similar to the one used in the Yale study, with appropriate changes in letterhead, etc. As in the earlier study, subjects were paid $4.50 for coming to the laboratory. The same age and occupational distributions used at Yale, and the identical personnel, were employed.

The purpose in relocating in Bridgeport was to assure a complete dissociation from Yale, and in this regard we were fully successful. On the surface, the study appeared to be conducted by RESEARCH ASSOCIATES OF BRIDGEPORT, an organization of unknown character (the title had been concocted exclusively for use in this study).

The experiments were conducted in a three-room office suite in a somewhat rundown commercial building located in the downtown shopping area. The laboratory was sparsely furnished, though clean, and marginally respectable in appearance. When subjects inquired about professional affiliations, they were informed only that we were a private firm conducting research for industry.

Some subjects displayed skepticism concerning the motives of the

Bridgeport experimenter. One gentleman gave us a written account of the thoughts he experienced at the control board:

> ... Should I quit this damn test? Maybe he passed out? What dopes we were not to check up on this deal. How do we know that these guys are legit? No furniture, bare walls, no telephone. We could of called the Police up or the Better Business Bureau. I learned a lesson tonight. How do I know that Mr. Williams [the experimenter] is telling the truth ... I wish I knew how many volts a person could take before lapsing into unconsciousness ...

> [Subject 2414]

Another subject stated:

> I questioned on my arrival my own judgment [about coming]. I had doubts as to the legitimacy of the operation and the consequences of participation. I felt it was a heartless way to conduct memory or learning processes on human beings and certainly dangerous without the presence of a medical doctor.

> [Subject 2440 V]

There was no noticeable reduction in tension for the Bridgeport subjects. And the subjects' estimation of the amount of pain felt by the victim was slightly, though not significantly, higher than in the Yale study.

A failure to obtain complete obedience in Bridgeport would indicate that the extreme compliance found in New Haven subjects was tied closely to the background authority of Yale University; if a large proportion of the subjects remained fully obedient, very different conclusions would be called for.

As it turned out, the level of obedience in Bridgeport, although somewhat reduced, was not significantly lower than that obtained at Yale. A large proportion of the Bridgeport subjects were fully obedient to the experimenter's commands (48 percent of the Bridgeport subjects delivered the maximum shock vs 65 percent in the corresponding condition at Yale).

How are these findings to be interpreted? It is possible that if commands of a potentially harmful or destructive sort are to be perceived as legitimate they must occur within some sort of institutional structure. But it is clear from the study that it need not be a particularly reputable or distinguished institution. The Bridgeport experiments were conducted by an unimpressive firm lacking any credentials; the laboratory was set up in a respectable office building with title listed in the building directory. Beyond that, there was no evidence of benevolence or competence. It is possible that the *category* of institution, judged according to its professed function, rather than its qualitative position within that category, wins our compliance. Persons deposit money in elegant, but also in seedy-looking banks, without giving much thought to the differences in security they offer. Similarly, our subjects may consider one laboratory to be as competent as another, so long as it *is* a scientific laboratory.

It would be valuable to study the subjects' performance in other contexts which go even further than the Bridgeport study in denying institutional support to the experimenter. It is possible that, beyond a certain point, obedience disappears completely. But that point had not been reached in the Bridgeport office: almost half the subjects obeyed the experimenter fully.

Further Experiments

We may mention briefly some additional experiments undertaken in the Yale series. A considerable amount of obedience and defiance in everyday life occurs in connection with groups. And we had reason to feel in the light of many group studies already done in psychology that group forces would have a profound effect on reactions to authority. A series of experiments was run to examine these effects. In all cases only one naive subject was studied per hour, but he performed in the midst of actors who, unknown to him, were employed by the experimenter. In one experiment (Groups for Disobedience) two actors broke off in the middle of the experiment. When this happened 90 percent of the subjects followed suit and defied the experimenter. In another condition the actors followed the orders obediently; this strengthened the experimenter's power only slightly. In still a third experiment the job of pushing the switch to shock the learner was given to one of the actors, while the naive subject performed a subsidiary act. We wanted to see how the teacher would respond if he were involved in the situation but did not actually give the shocks. In this situation only three subjects out of forty broke off. In a final group experiment the subjects themselves determined the shock level they were going to use. Two actors suggested higher and higher shock levels; some subjects insisted, despite group pressure, that the shock level be kept low; others followed along with the group.

Further experiments were completed using women as subjects, as well as a set dealing with the effects of dual, unsanctioned, and conflicting authority. A final experiment concerned the personal relationship between victim and subject. These will have to be described elsewhere, lest the present report be extended to monographic length.

It goes without saying that future research can proceed in many different directions. What kinds of response from the victim are most effective in causing disobedience in the subject? Perhaps passive resistance is more effective than vehement protest. What conditions of entry into an authority system lead to greater or lesser obedience? What is the effect of anonymity and masking on the subject's behavior? What conditions lead to the subject's perception of responsibility for his own actions? Each of these could be a major research topic in itself, and can readily be incorporated into the general experimental procedure described here.

Levels of Obedience and Defiance

One general finding that merits attention is the high level of obedience manifested in the experimental situation. Subjects often expressed deep disapproval of shocking a man in the face of his objections, and others denounced it as senseless and stupid. Yet many subjects complied even while they protested. The proportion of obedient subjects greatly exceeded the expectations of the experimenter and his colleagues. At the outset, we had conjectured that subjects would not, in general, go above the level of "Strong Shock." In practice, many subjects were willing to administer the most extreme shocks available when commanded by the experimenter. For some subjects the experiment provides an occasion for aggressive release. And for others it demonstrates the intent to which obedient dispositions are deeply ingrained, and are engaged irrespective of their consequences for others. Yet this is not the whole story. Somehow, the subject becomes implicated in a situation from which he cannot disengage himself.

The departure of the experimental results from intelligent expectation, to some extent, has been formalized. The procedure was to describe the experimental situation in concrete detail to a group of competent persons, and to ask them to predict the performance of 100 hypothetical subjects. For purposes of indicating the distribution of break-off points judges were provided with a diagram of the shock generator, and recorded their predictions before being informed of the actual results.

Judges typically underestimated the amount of obedience demonstrated by subjects.

In Figure 3, we compare the predictions of forty psychiatrists at a leading medical school with the actual performance of subjects in the experiment. The psychiatrists predicted that most subjects would not go beyond the tenth shock level (150 volts; at this point the victim makes his first explicit demand to be freed). They further predicted that by the twentieth shock level (300 volts; the victim refuses to answer) 3.73 percent of the subjects would still be obedient; and that only a little over one-tenth of one percent of the subjects would administer the highest shock on the board. But, as the graph indicates, the obtained behavior was very different. Sixty-two percent of the subjects obeyed the experimenter's commands fully. Between expectation and occurrence there is a whopping discrepancy.

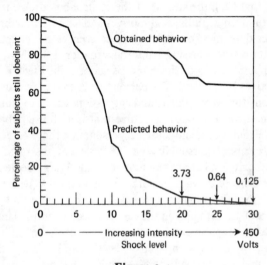

Figure 3

Why did the psychiatrists underestimate the level of obedience? Possibly, because their predictions were based on an inadequate conception that focuses on motives *in vacuo*. This orientation may be entirely adequate for the repair of bruised impulses as revealed on the psychiatrist's couch, but as soon as our interest turns to action in larger settings, attention must be paid to the situations in which motives are expressed. A situation exerts an important press on the individual. It exercises constraints and may provide push. In certain circumstances it is not so much the kind of person a man is, as the kind of situation in which he is placed, that determines his actions.

Many people, not knowing much about the experiment, claim that subjects who go to the end of the board are sadistic. Nothing could be more foolish as an overall characterization of these persons. It is like saying that a person thrown into a swift-flowing stream is necessarily a fast swimmer, or that he has great stamina because he moves so rapidly relative to the bank. The context of action must always be considered. The individual, upon entering the laboratory, becomes integrated into a situation that carries its own momentum. The subject's problem then is how to become disengaged from a situation which is moving in an altogether ugly direction.

The fact that disengagement is so difficult testifies to the potency of the forces that keep the subject at the control board. Are these forces to be conceptualized as individual motives and expressed in the language of personality dynamics, or are they to be seen as the effects of social structure and pressures arising from the situational field?

A full understanding of the subject's action will, I feel, require that both perspectives be adopted. The person brings to the laboratory enduring dispositions toward authority and aggression, and at the same time he becomes enmeshed in a social structure that is no less an objective fact of the case. From the standpoint of personality theory one may ask: What mechanisms of personality enable a person to transfer responsibility to authority? What are the motives underlying obedient and disobedient performance? Does orientation to authority lead to a short-circuiting of the shame-guilt system? What cognitive and emotional defenses are brought into play in the case of obedient and defiant subjects?

The present experiments are not, however, directed toward an exploration of the motives engaged when the subject obeys the experimenter's commands. Instead, they examine the situational variables responsible for the elicitation of obedience. Elsewhere, we have attempted to spell out some of the structural properties of the experimental situation that account for high obedience, and this analysis need not be repeated here (Milgram, 1963). The experimental variations themselves represent our attempt to probe that structure, by systematically changing it and noting the consequences for behavior. It is clear that some situations produce greater compliance with the experimenter's commands than others. However, this does not necessarily imply an increase or decrease in the strength of any single definable motive. Situations producing the greatest obedience could do so by triggering the most powerful, yet perhaps the most idiosyncratic, of motives in each subject confronted by the setting. Or they may simply recruit a greater number and variety of motives in their service. But whatever the motives involved—and it is far from certain that they can ever be known—action may be studied as a direct function of the situation in which it occurs. This has been the approach of the present study, where we sought to plot behavioral irregularities against manipulated properties of the social field. Ultimately, social psychology would like to have a compelling *theory of situations* which will, first, present a language in terms of which situations can be defined; proceed to a typology of situations; and then point to the manner in which definable properties of situations are transformed into psychological forces in the individual.[8]

Postscript

Almost a thousand adults were individually studied in the obedience research, and there were many specific conclusions regarding the variables that control obedience and disobedience to authority. Some of these have been discussed briefly in the preceding sections, and more detailed reports will be released subsequently.

There are now some other generalizations I should like to make, which do not derive in any strictly logical fashion from the experiments as carried out, but which, I feel, ought to be made. They are formulations of an intuitive sort that have been forced on me by observation of many subjects responding to the pressures of authority. The assertions represent a painful alteration in my own thinking; and since they were acquired only under the repeated impact of direct observation, I have no illusion that they will be generally accepted by persons who have not had the same experience.

With numbing regularity good people were seen to knuckle under the demands of authority and to perform actions that were callous and severe. Men who are in everyday life responsible and decent were seduced by the trappings of authority, by the control of their perceptions, and by the uncritical acceptance of the experimenter's definition of the situation, into performing harsh acts.

What is the limit of such obedience? At many points we attempted to establish a boundary. Cries from the victim were inserted; not good enough. The victim claimed heart trouble; subjects still shocked him on command. The victim pleaded that he be let free, and his answers no longer registered on the signal box; subjects continued to shock him. At the outset we had not conceived that such drastic procedures would be needed to generate disobedience, and each step was added only as the ineffectiveness of the earlier techniques became clear. The final effort to establish a limit was the Touch-Proximity condition. But the very first subject in this condition subdued the victim on command, and proceeded to the highest shock level. A quarter of the subjects in this condition performed similarly.

The results, as seen and felt in the laboratory, are to this author disturbing. They raise the possibility that human nature, or—more specifically—the kind of character produced in American democratic society, cannot be counted on to insulate its citizens from brutality and inhumane treatment at the direction of malevolent authority. A substantial proportion of people do what they are told to do, irrespective of the content of the act and without limitations of conscience, so long as they perceive that the command comes from a legitimate authority. If in this study an anonymous experimenter could successfully command adults to subdue a fifty-year-old man, and force on him painful electric shocks against his protests, one can only wonder what government, with its vastly greater authority and prestige, can command of its subjects. There is, of course, the extremely important question of whether malevolent political institutions could or would arise in American society. The present research contributes nothing to this issue.

In an article entitled "The Dangers of Obedience," Harold J. Laski wrote:

> ... civilization means, above all, an unwillingness to inflict unnecessary pain. Within the ambit of that definition, those of us who heedlessly accept the commands of authority cannot yet claim to be civilized men.
>
> ... Our business, if we desire to live a life not utterly devoid of meaning and significance, is to accept nothing which contradicts our basic experience merely because it comes to us from tradition or convention or authority. It may well be that we shall be wrong; but our self-expression is thwarted at the root unless the certainties we are asked to accept coincide with the certainties we experience.

That is why the condition of freedom in any state is always a widespread and consistent skepticism of the canons upon which power insists.

NOTES

This research was supported by two grants from the National Science Foundation: NSF G-17916 and NSF G-24152. Exploratory studies carried out in 1960 were financed by a grant from the Higgins Funds of Yale University. The author is grateful to John T. Williams, James J. McDonough, and Emil Elges for the important part they played in the project. Thanks are due also to Alan Elms, James Miller, Taketo Murata, and Stephen Stier for their aid as graduate assistants. The author's wife, Sasha, performed many valuable services. Finally, a profound debt is owed to the many persons in New Haven and Bridgeport who served as subjects.

1. Consider, for example, J. P. Scott's analysis of war in his monograph on aggression:
   '. . . while the actions of key individuals in a war may be explained in terms of direct stimulation to aggression, vast numbers of other people are involved simply by being part of an organized society.
   '. . . For example, at the beginning of World War I an Austrian archduke was assassinated in Sarajevo. A few days later soldiers from all over Europe were marching toward each other, not because they were stimulated by the archduke's misfortune, but because they had been trained to obey orders.' (Slightly rearranged from Scott (1958), *Aggression*, p. 103.)

2. It consisted of an extended discussion with the experimenter and, of equal importance, a friendly reconciliation with the victim. It is made clear that the victim did not receive painful electric shocks. After the completion of the experimental series, subjects were sent a detailed report of the results and full purposes of the experimental program. A formal assessment of this procedure points to its overall effectiveness. Of the subjects, 83.7 percent indicated that they were glad to have taken part in the study; 15.1 percent reported neutral feelings; and 1.3 percent stated that they were sorry to have participated. A large number of subjects spontaneously requested that they be used in further experimentation. Four-fifths of the subjects felt that more experiments of this sort should be carried out, and 74 percent indicated that they had learned something of personal importance as a result of being in the study. Furthermore, a university psychiatrist, experienced in outpatient treatment, interviewed a sample of experimental subjects with

the aim of uncovering possible injurious effects resulting from participation. No such effects were in evidence. Indeed, subjects typically felt that their participation was instructive and enriching. A more detailed discussion of this question can be found in Milgram (1964).

3. *To obey* and *to disobey* are not the only terms one could use in describing the critical action of Y. One could say that Y is cooperating with X, or displays conformity with regard to X's commands. However, *co-operation* suggests that X agrees with Y's ends, and understands the relationship between his own behavior and the attainment of those ends. (But the experimental procedure, and, in particular, the experimenter's command that the subject shock the victim even in the absence of a response from the victim, preclude such understanding.) Moreover, co-operation implies status parity for the coacting agents, and neglects the asymmetrical, dominance-subordination element prominent in the laboratory relationship between experimenter and subject. *Conformity* has been used in other important contexts in social psychology, and most frequently refers to imitating the judgments or actions of others when no explicit requirement for imitation has been made. Furthermore, in the present study there are two sources of social pressure: pressure from the experimenter issuing the commands, and pressure from the victim to stop the punishment. It is the pitting of a common man (the victim) against an authority (the experimenter) that is the distinctive feature of the conflict. At a point in the experiment the victim demands that he be let free. The experimenter insists that the subject continue to administer shocks. Which act of the subject can be interpreted as conformity? The subject may conform to the wishes of his peer or to the wishes of the experimenter, and conformity in one direction means the absence of conformity in the other. Thus the word has no useful reference in this setting, for the dual and conflicting social pressures cancel out its meaning.

In the final analysis, the linguistic symbol representing the subject's action must take its meaning from the concrete context in which that action occurs; and there is probably no word in everyday language that covers the experimental situation exactly, without omissions or irrelevant connotations. It is partly for convenience, therefore, that the terms *obey* and *disobey* are used to describe the subject's actions. At the same time, our use of the words is highly congruent with dictionary meaning.

4. A more detailed account of the laboratory procedure can be found in Milgram (1963). A similar and independently evolved experimental procedure, employing a shock generator, victim, and learning task, was reported by Buss (1961). Buss used the technique for studying aggression, not obedience, and did not make use of the fundamental measure employed

in the present study: break-off points. His investigation promises to be a useful compliment to the present research.

5. It is difficult to convey on the printed page the full tenor of the victim's responses, for we have no adequate notation for vocal intensity, timing, and general qualities of delivery. Yet these features are crucial to producing the effect of an increasingly severe reaction to mounting voltage levels. (They can be communicated fully only by sending interested parties the recorded tapes.) In general terms, however, the victim indicates no discomfort until the 75-volt shock is administered, at which time there is a light grunt in response to the punishment. Similar reactions follow the 90- and 105-volt shocks, and at 120 volts the victim shouts to the experimenter that the shocks are becoming painful. Painful groans are heard on administration of the 135-volt shock, and at 150 volts the victim cries out, "Experimenter, get me out of here! I won't be in the experiment any more! I refuse to go on!" Cries of this type continue with generally rising intensity, so that at 180 volts the victim cries out, "I can't stand the pain", and by 270 volts his response to the shock is definitely an agonized scream. Throughout, he insists that he be let out of the experiment. At 300 volts the victim shouts in desperation that he will no longer provide answers to the memory tests; and at 315 volts, after a violent scream, he reaffirms with vehemence that he is no longer a participant. From this point on, he provides no answers, but shrieks in agony whenever a shock is administered; this continues through 450 volts. Of course, many subjects will have broken off before this point.

A revised and stronger set of protests was used in all experiments outside the Proximity series. Naturally, new baseline measures were established for all comparisons using the new set of protests.

There is overwhelming evidence that the great majority of subjects, both obedient and defiant, accepted the victims' reactions as genuine. The evidence takes the form of: (a) tension created in the subjects (see discussion of tension); (b) scores on "estimated pain" scales filled out by subjects immediately after the experiment; (c) subjects' accounts of their feelings in post-experimental interviews; and (d) quantifiable responses to questionnaires distributed to subjects several months after their participation in the experiments. This matter will be treated fully in a forthcoming monograph.

(The procedure in all experimental conditions was to have the naive subject announce the voltage level before administering each shock, so that —independently of the victim's responses—he was continually reminded of delivering punishment of ever-increasing severity.)

6. Admittedly, the terms *proximity, immediacy, closeness,* and *salience-of-the-victim* are used in a loose sense, and the experiments themeselves represent a

very coarse treatment of the variable. Further experiments are needed to refine the notion and tease out such diverse factors as spatial distance, visibility, audibility, barrier interposition, etc.

The Proximity and Touch-Proximity experiments were the only conditions where we were unable to use taped feedback from the victim. Instead, the victim was trained to respond in these conditions as he had in Experiment 2 (which employed taped feedback). Some improvement is possible here, for it should be technically feasible to do a proximity series using taped feedback.

7. The third condition also led to significantly lower obedience than this first situation, in which the experimenter was present, but it contains technical difficulties that require extensive discussion.

8. My thanks to Professor Howard Leventhal of Yale for strengthening the writing in this paragraph.

REFERENCES

Buss, Arnold H., *The Psychology of Aggression*. New York and London: John Wiley, 1961.

Kierkegaard, S. (1843). *Fear and Trembling*. English edition, Princeton: Princeton University Press, 1941.

Laski, Harold J., The dangers of obedience. *Harper's Monthly Magazine 159*, June, 1–10, 1929.

Milgram, S., Dynamics of Obedience: Experiments in Social Psychology. Mimeographed report, *National Science Foundation*, January 25, 1961.

Milgrim, S., Behavioral study of obedience. *J. abnorm. soc. Psychol.*, 1963, 67; 371–8.

Milgrim, S., Issues in the study of obedience: A reply to Baumrind. *Amer. Psychol.*, 1964, 19; 848–52.

Miller, N. E., Experimental studies of conflict. In J. McV. Hunt (ed.), *Personality and the Behavior Disorders*. New York: Ronald Press, 1944.

Scott, J. P., *Aggression*. Chicago: University of Chicago Press, 1958.

13
Experiments in Dyadic Conflict and Cooperation

Anatol Rapoport, Ph.D.

It is impossible to reproduce in the laboratory a real life situation in all its richness. Since the purpose of laboratory work is avowedly the study of events under controlled conditions with a view of discovering precisely describable regularities, the events selected for study are for the most part those which can be precisely, preferably quantitatively described.

For the most part, aspects of behavior which lend themselves easily to precise, quantitative description are the more superficial ones, e.g., reactions to stimuli, rote learning, etc. The question before us is whether the scope of the laboratory method can be enlarged so as to include the study of events closely connected to what is of central interest in psychology.

It must be admitted that attempts to extend the laboratory method to include the study of "deeper" events have been extensive and persistent. The link with "hard science" is maintained in these attempts by the development of so-called scaling techniques, that is, schemes of converting observed behavioral events into quantifiable variables. In personality studies, for example verbal responses constitute a great bulk of the data. These responses can be scaled either by restricting the repertoire of the responses at the outset (as in multiple choice questions) or by statistical techniques of content analysis.

In general, there is a trade-off between the objectivity so achieved and the depth of the phenomena under scrutiny. The deeper the probe, the less reliable become the schemes aimed at converting the data into tractable variables.

Can conflict be studied in the laboratory under controlled conditions? In view of what has been said, it would seem that the deeper the aspects of conflict proposed to be studied, the less tractable the observations would become in the context of data. Moreover, we are faced with

Reprinted with permission from the *Bulletin of the Menninger Clinic*, Vol. 30, pp. 284–91, copyright 1966 by the Menninger Foundation. Work on which this paper is based was supported by the National Institutes of Health Grants M-423801, -02, -03, -04.

still another difficulty. It is practically impossible to reproduce a really serious conflict in the laboratory. To a large extent this is due to the constraints imposed by experimental ethics. But even aside from that, the very atmosphere of the laboratory—sterile, congenial, and urbane—inhibits the development of genuine emotional involvement.

SIMULATED CONFLICT

There remains one promising area, namely *simulated* conflict. A parlor game is a classical example of such conflict. Indeed, one might guess that parlor games were invented as outlets for aggression in which the participants are not exposed to physical harm and, given sufficient sophistication known as "sportsmanship," remain fairly safe from psychological harm.

Even a parlor game, however, is too complex to allow a complete analysis of behavior in it. Moreover, since the objective of such a game is usually clearly defined, variations of behavior can be ascribed to the players' failure to find the most efficient winning strategies. It is possible, however, to design games, which are strategically trivial but which present the subject with a dilemma, namely a choice between cooperative or non-cooperative behavior. These we designate choice C and choice D respectively. Such games combine the utmost simplicity of data with a richness of psychological implications.

This is the approach we have taken at the University of Michigan. In our experiments each dyadic "conflict" takes on the average six seconds and involves two subjects. We are thus able to get vast numbers of replications under controlled and varied conditions, and our results, being statistically stable, lend themselves to the formulation and the testing of specific hypotheses.

The essential feature of our simulated dyadic conflict is that the motivations of the participants are "mixed." Specifically, a motive to cooperate with the other clashes with a motive to compete with him or to exploit him. Situations of this sort are readily discernible in real life. Imagine two firms competing for the same market. Suppose each has a choice of selling its product at a high price or at a low price. In the absence of other competitors (which we assume), if both firms sell at a high price, they divide the market among them (say in equal proportions) and reap a large profit. If they both sell at a low price, they still divide the market (say in the same proportion) but make a low profit (or possibly even sustain a loss, as in a price war). If, however, firm A sells at a low price, while firm B stays with the high price, then we suppose that firm A captures the entire market and reaps the largest profit, while firm B goes out of business.

Obviously it is in the conventional interest of both firms to collude, i.e., to fix the price high and share the benefits. But if price fixing is prohibited by law or is otherwise inhibited, how should a firm decide? Strategic calculation indicates low price. For if firm B should sell at a high price, it is clearly advantageous for firm A to sell at a low price and so to capture the market. If, on the other hand, firm B should sell at a low price, then firm A should do likewise "in self defense." It follows that firm A should sell at a low price no matter what firm B decides to do. Similar considerations apply to firm B. Consequently "rational calculation of self interest" leads both firms to sell at a low price, whereas they could cut the public's throat instead of their own if they somehow could agree to sell at a high price.

The *logical structure* of this species of conflict is completely known. Also the method of resolution is clear. Both parties gain if they cooperate. But in the absence of communication, cooperation can be achieved only on the basis of a *tacit* agreement, i.e., on the basis of mutual trust. To put it another way, the two start to cooperate to their common benefit as soon as each identifies his personal interest with the common interest (of the two firms, that is), and *rejects* the decision dictated by "strategic analysis."

The systematic study of such situations demands the singling out of certain independent and certain dependent variables. The independent variables are those which are either given or can be manipulated by the experimenter, for example, the sex, age, personality profile, etc., of the subjects; the numerical values of the game payoffs, and the controlled conditions under which the game is played.

Experiments of the sort just described have been conducted by several investigators in the United States in the past several years. The range of the chosen independent variables has been quite large, including instructions given to the subjects, independently assessed personality measures, information given to each about the other, etc. The range of dependent variables, on the other hand, has been quite narrow. For the most part the relative frequency of the cooperative choice, i.e., the index C, was the single behavioral index examined. (As expected practically all subjects oscillate between the C and the D choice in the course of iterated plays of the game.)

In the University of Michigan experiments, the range of independent variables was not wide, mostly confined to (1) the payoffs, (2) selected easily identifiable categories of subjects, specifically sex, and (3) controlled play strategies of one of the subjects. The range of dependent variables, on the other hand, was much broader than heretofore studied. The dependent variables included a large variety of statistics obtained from the protocols, both static (averaged over the entire sessions of 300 plays) and dynamic (obtained as time courses averaged over the subjects).

RESULTS

The simplest and the most straightforward results are with respect to the payoffs. If we take the grand average of a large population of players with respect to the relative frequency of C (cooperative responses), we see that:

1. as the payoff for the double cooperative response increases, so does C;

2. as the payoff for being the single defector increases, C decreases;

3. as the loss for being the single cooperator increases, C decreases;

4. as the loss for double defection increases, C increases.

All these results are expected on common sense grounds and are therefore of little interest except as indications that our subjects are indeed motivated by the monetary payoffs. However, questions are immediately. raised which cannot be answered on a priori grounds. For example, which is more important in reinforcing the cooperative response, the reward associated with the double cooperative response or the punishment associated with the double defective response?

It turns out that a gross index such as relative frequency of C responses is much too crude to describe the process. Therefore it is premature simply to relate the observed C to variables extrinsic to the process, such as personality traits of the participants, etc. I shall illustrate by citing a simple finding. If we calculate the correlation coefficient across the population of pairs between the relative frequency of C responses of one pair member vs. that of the other, we find this coefficient to be in the middle nineties. The indication, therefore, is that what a subject does in a long run of such choices is determined to a very large degree by what the other does. This is by no means to say that different populations will exhibit the same patterns. Comparison of *noninteracting* populations may be extremely instructive.

We carried out such comparisons on three populations, namely (1) all-male pairs, (2) all-female pairs, and (3) mixed pairs in which men played against women. The gross results indicate that cooperation among men is about twice as frequent as that among women. On the other hand, when men play against women, the ones are hardly distinguishable from the others. It is as if the men were "pulled down" by the women, while the women were "pulled up" by the men.

These results tempt one to conclude that "women are less cooperative than men." Aside from the fact that our results stem only from a sample (admittedly a fairly large one) of college students and may not be replicated in population at large, the simple conclusion is not warranted even with regard to our samples. A finer analysis, involving the time courses of the variable C, reveals that the all-male pairs and all-female pairs start on the average with exactly the same frequency of cooperation. The initial trend is initially downward, i.e., toward less cooperation in both populations. However, after about 30 plays the men begin to "recover," eventually reaching a considerably larger level of cooperation than initially. It is as if men at first learn to distrust each other and so resort predominantly to defecting responses. Eventually, however, an opposite trend toward tacit collusion sets in. The women, on the other hand, do not start to "recover" until after about 150 plays, and their recovery is much slower. The mixed pairs start at a level of cooperation higher than that of either the all-male or the all-female pairs, indicating, perhaps, that initially the reservoir of good will vis-a-vis the opposite sex is considerably larger than vis-a-vis one's own. But the initial decline in cooperation sets in also in the mixed pairs, and eventually the time course settles to a position between the other two courses. Evidently not an initial propensity to cooperate but subsequent interactions determine to a large degree what will happen in the course of such a game iterated many times.

Further light on this problem is thrown by the preliminary results we have obtained in experiments where the plays of one of the subjects are controlled. That is to say, one of the subjects is a "stooge" who plays as he has been directed. Five different strategies were used as the independent vabiable. At one extreme was the 100 percent C strategy by the stooge; at the other the 100 percent defecting strategy. Between the two was the so-called tit-for-tat strategy, in which the stooge did exactly what the subject did on the preceding play. Certain mixed strategies filled in the other two points of the scale. The completely non-cooperative strategy on the part of the stooge elicited almost no cooperation in the subject, as we expected. The tit-for-tat strategy elicited the largest amount of cooperation in both men and women, specifically 70–80 percent in a game which yields 27–46 percent cooperation (from women and men respectively) when both players are bona fide subjects. The results of the 100 percent cooperative strategy are most interesting. This strategy seemed to elicit either almost complete cooperation or complete defection in the real subject, perhaps separating most effectively the would-be cooperators from the would-be exploiters.

Coming back to the comparison between the men and the women, the high yield of the tit-for-tat strategy may be the explanation of the results, for statistical analysis shows that men are more prone to play tit-for-tat than women, and it may be this proneness, rather than a greater propensity for cooperation, which is responsible for the men's higher cooperative scores.

DISCUSSION AND PROJECTION

These, then, are samples of the sort of results we have obtained so far. In the light of such results, what can we say about the relevance of the experiments to real conflict situations? Do the experiments help us understand conflict better? Do they suggest ways of controlling conflict? In the laboratory, yes; in real life, we do not know. But we hope we are on the right track because of the questions which are suggested by the data, which questions can be unambiguously answered in the experimental context. As an example, now that we know that the totally defecting strategy elicits practically no cooperation, while the tit-for-tat strategy elicits much cooperation, we can ask and answer the following question: How many initial defecting responses does it take to impair significantly the "therapeutic" power of the tit-for-tat strategy subsequently undertaken? The answers should not be regarded as conclusions about real life conflicts but as sources of hypotheses about them. Once one is enabled to make explicit hypotheses and has acquired a certain experience with indices of conflict behavior, perhaps ways will be suggested of how to put these hypotheses to tests in real life.

We said a while ago that the single index C is too crude as a behavioral measure in the situation depicted. Because of its crudeness, this index does not lend itself to extrapolation to real life. People may well cooperate under given conditions in the trivial game and fail to do so in real life, or vice versa. However, it is possible to refine the index C so as to get four different indices which probe deeper, as it were. Namely, one can consider the *conditional* frequencies of cooperation following each of the four possible outcomes of the previous play. These conditional frequencies are richly suggestive. For example, the propensity to cooperate when everything is going well (*i.e.*, following a double C) is indicative of one psychological state (perhaps "trustworthiness"), while the propensity to cooperate after one has been betrayed by the other indicates quite another psychological state (perhaps "forgiveness"). Next, the propensity to defect following a successful defection suggests still another state (perhaps "greed"), while the propensity to continue to defect after the pair has locked in on the double D, suggests a different state (perhaps "mistrust"). The value of our experiments is in the opportunity they provide to get statistically stable numerical values of these derived variables under a variety of conditions and from a variety of populations. For example, our results suggest that in the all-male population, "trustworthiness" (as we have operationalized it) has the greatest numerical value, followed by "mistrust," "greed," and "forgiveness." In the all-female population, "mistrust" has the largest numerical value, followed by "trustworthiness," "greed," and "forgiveness." That both "trustworthiness" and "mistrust" are high (if these indices are to be taken seriously) is not surprising since both may well be self-perpetuating tendencies. Each reflects the characteristic "lock-in" effect observed throughout.

In this way, our experiments, although they suggest considerable richness of psychological content, nevertheless permit us to build a theory strictly from the data appeal to a priori explanatory notions.

Another way in which the method can be brought closer to reality is by a gradual build-up toward greater realism. It is in principle possible to go from the simple game depicted here to a full-dress simulation of international relations, by gradually adding quasi-realistic features. One such program is currently in progress at the University of Michigan. We began with a simple armament-disarmament game, modeled exactly after the games just described, except that the either-or choices were replaced by a graded range of cooperation. Having investigated the simplest situation, we began adding features, for example, "inspections" which place a limit on the secrecy of the individual decisions concerning the "level of armaments," i.e., the degree of non-cooperation contemplated. In this connection we plan to introduce other features like "surprise attack," "ultimatums," etc., in short, all the gimmicks of interest to the diplo-military gamesters.

Sometimes we feel uneasy about this program. It sometimes seems to us that we are being sucked into the psychopathic world of would-be deterrers, preemptors, and calculators of scores in the "game" of nuclear exchange. However, one cannot deny the heuristic value of these games, not, of course, in the sense of suggesting "effective strategies" of conducting the cold war blackmail, which is frequently the tacit or even the avowed goal of the strategies, but in the sense of supplementing Lewis F. Richardson's pithy explanation of his armament race equations. These equations, Richardson wrote, "only indicate what would happen if people did not stop to think." Similarly the adults of diplo-military games, which frequently end in debilitating stalemates or in nuclear war, may serve to indicate what is likely to happen if people persist in thinking exclusively in strategic terms. On the other hand, "happy" solutions can be included in the reportoires of outcomes of these games as easily as disastrous ones. We can then see under which conditions people, subjected to conflicting motivations to cooperate, to compete, and to exploit, to trust and to mistrust, are most likely to end the game cooperatively. This knowledge may not be relevant to international affairs in their present state, but it may, if wide-spread, help change men's ideas about the nature of the game which the strategists are playing with our lives and the lives of our children as stakes. Therein lies the main hope.

14
A Conceptual Approach to the Problem of Therapist-Client Matching

Robert C. Carson, Ph.D.

A substantial amount of research in the past few years on the A–B variable, as well as other individual difference measures of therapists and their clients, has made it abundantly clear that psychotherapy is not a unitary technical procedure having inherently predictable results. The consequences of psychotherapeutic relationships are powerfully determined by the manner in which the personal characteristics of the two parties happen to mesh, and these effects appear to be, to a large extent, independent of the degree of disorder of the client, the experience level of the therapist, or other factors attributable wholly to one or the other member of the therapeutic dyad. In other words, the consequences of a therapy relationship, in terms of benefit to the client, are in a very basic sense truly the product of interpersonal interaction.

At one time not so very long ago it would have been possible, and even likely, that an observation of this sort would be consigned to the realm of established thereapeutic clichés, there to reside forever without in any way affecting the behavior of researchers, therapists, clinic administrators, or other mental health personnel. Increasingly sophisticated and critical investigations of the outcome of psychotherapy now make such a comfortable nonsolution to the problem indefensible. Consider, for example, recent reviews of psychotherapy outcome research by Bergin, at Columbia.[1] Bergin has reanalyzed the data of the seven best-controlled outcome studies to be found in the literature, emerging with the startling and sobering conclusion that, *in every study*, some of the treated clients improved with therapy and some *deteriorated*. That is, the principal effect of psychotherapy was to increase the *variance* in functionability among the treated group, relative to control cases. A substantial proportion of the clients in these studies would apparently have been better off never to have met their therapists, even though in many instances the therapists were extremely well qualified formally, and had

---

Reprinted by permission from the author and *The Journal of the American College Health Association*, Feb. 1970, Vol. 18, No. 3.

had *successful* experiences with *other* clients. Findings of this sort make the problem of therapist—client matching a suitable object for more than idle interest and speculation. It is a vital issue that cries for serious investigation and rational solution. I am strongly encouraged to see it so prominently and competently displayed here, although it is disappointing to note that, so far as I know, the current session is in this respect a first.

What I want to do in the brief time available is to try to sketch in general and programmatic terms a conception of the therapeutic process that has grown out of serious concern over a period of years, as both researcher and practitioner, with the kinds of issues we have been addressing. I shall not have time to engage in detailed empirical documentation and assessment of the ideas I want to present, although it would otherwise be entirely possible to do so. I shall also avoid any attempt at precise articulation of the theory with A—B research findings, because the implications of these findings are as yet not as clear as one would hope them to be for detailed theoretical treatment. The title of my talk, as originally announced, was in this respect excessively optimistic.

I would assert as something of a first principle that the trade of the psychotherapist, qua therapist, is basically that of social influence. The therapist engages the client in an interpersonal relationship for the intended purpose of changing the client in certain ways. With the possible exception of the more radically behavioristic therapists, who sometimes incorporate various *im*personal props in their work, the principal change-producing instrument is the person of the therapist himself. This formulation of therapist-as-social-influence-agent has been given very explicit and detailed attention recently by Goldstein, Heller, and Sechrest in their influential book, *Psychotherapy and the Psychology of Behavior Change.*[2]

If the role of the psychotherapist is basically one of *social influence agent*, we may ask what it is that he is supposed to influence. The simple answer to this—one that has become practically an article of faith in certain circles—is that he should influence the client's behavior. From a certain point of view, there is not much to argue here. Most therapists would see positive behavior change in a client as a reasonable indication of the success of their efforts. But persons, after all, are not mere physico-chemical machines having the capacity to convert *stimuli* into *responses*, behavioristic propaganda notwithstanding. Recognition of this fact, which is in part responsible for the re-emergence of cognitive alter-

natives to the mechanistic behavior theories of the recent past, forces our
attention to another and more bssic target of the influence efforts of the
therapist, that is, the client's personal cosmology, the templates by
means of which he orders and construes his experiences; his cognitive
map or image of the universe, including of course his *self* and his notions
of his proper relation to the rest of it. Changes in behavior are dependent
on and follow from changes in the basic congitive or belief system of the
behaving person.

This view of the therapist's task is of course not an altogether new
one. It involves certain aspects of what is sometimes called "insight."
Carl Rogers, Albert Ellis, and George Kelly, among others, have developed entire systems of therapy around central notions that are very
similar to this one.[3] One of the special virtues of referring to it in the
terms I have is that it encourages an opening to the entire field of attitude and belief change—a vigorous and active area of research in contemporary social psychology. In general, we can say that anything which
enhances the therapist's capacity to influence *in a corrective way* the
cognitive system of his client will benefit therapy, while anything which
interferes with or reduces this capacity will have negative therapeutic
results. We are touching here on the issue of the therapist's *power* in the
interpersonal situation. I want to return to this issue later.

The typical psychotherapy candidate is a person whose construct
system, including his self-system, is poorly adapted to the characteristics
of the real situation in which he in fact lives. The input and feedback
information that he receives makes a poor match with his existing construct system—especially perhaps with its self-system components—
as a result of which he is insecure and anxious a good part of the time.
Out of desperation, he enacts behaviors that are designed to increase
the match between his self-system and the social feedback he receives,
but these self-defensive behaviors, being inflexible or unduly intense,
are apt to be maladaptive in the long run. In the short run, they often
succeed in inducing others to provide in their own interactive behaviors
social feedback that is complementary to the disturbed person's constricted self. The disturbed person has his own power resources which,
if limited in subtlety, are often impressive in effect.

Seen from this perspective, then, what the typical psychotherapy
candidate needs is a new cognitive map, an altered conception of himself
and his relationship to the world which would more closely approximate
the realities of his current life situation. One way this might be accom-

plished is by persuasive instruction. I suspect that most therapists do at least some of this, and it is used as the prime technique in Ellis's Rational–Emotive therapy.[4] Social psychological research findings suggest that the effectiveness of the persuasive appeal would be a function, among other things, of the credibility and attractiveness of the therapist, which would in turn presumably vary to some extent depending on predilections and tastes of the client. Most therapists, however, are not particularly impressed with persuasive instruction as a technique of therapy and, in fact, most contemporary social psychologists are unimpressed with it as a technique of attitude change. In the latter field, the big thing now is called counter-attitudinal advocacy. In short, it has been found in repeated investigations that one of the best and most efficient ways of changing peoples' attitudes and beliefs is to induce them by some means or other to *behave* in a way that is discrepant from their current beliefs but concordant with the beliefs it is desired that they have. There is already an analogue in the therapy field, namely, in George Kelly's fixed-role therapy and in Moreno's psychodrama, but techniques of this sort have not been systematically exploited to the extent they deserve.[5] I suspect on the other hand that many experienced therapists have learned implicitly and unsystematically to apply comparable techniques in their relationships with their clients.

Now, let us try to become more specific about the matter of the therapeutic induction of construct-system change in the client and its relationship to the problem of client-therapist matching. This will also lead us back to a consideration of interpersonal power, and its converse, dependence, as factors in psychotherapy. Stated simply, the therapist's task is to conduct himself in his interactions with his client in such a way as to fail to provide confirmatory and complementary feedback in response to the disorder-maintaining behaviors of the client, while at the same time providing the client with an experience that is sufficiently positive to maintain him in treatment. Additionally, the therapist should encourage further positive modifications in the client's construct system, largely through inducing him to sample forms of social behavior not originally in his repertoire. It is a difficult task, and to accomplish it the therapist will have to be *powerful* in the relationship. The conception of interpersonal power I am using here derives from social exchange theory, as developed chiefly by Thibaut and Kelley.[6] According to this conception, a person is powerful in a relationship to the degree that he can, at little cost to himself, cause the other person to experience a wide range of hedonic effects (pleasure–displeasure) above that other person's *comparison level for alternatives*, abbreviated CL_{alt}. A person's CL_{alt} is a subjective standard representing the level of hedonic experience he believes to be available currently in his next best alternative relationship; if hedonic experience in a relationship drops below CL_{alt} for any appreciable period, the individual will normally leave the relationship. A person is *dependent* in a relationship to the degree that his hedonic experience in it exceeds his CL_{alt}. The commodities involved in such satisfaction or in security, using those terms in approximately the Sullivanian sense. In the therapy relationship, we are dealing mainly with behaviors relating to the *security* of the participants.

Now, in order to bring this discussion down to a somewhat more concrete level, let me introduce a brief case example at this point. It is taken from a paper by Halpern and will, I think, have a familiar ring to therapists in the audience.[7]

A male anxiety neurotic, in his early thirties, defines himself as a passive, bewildered, helpless little boy—precisely in the way his parents defined him. In one session the patient announced that he was going to put into action a scheme on his job that was consciously designed to win him plaudits and a promotion but which the therapist could easily see would get him into deep trouble and, at the very least, result in his being fired. The therapist felt tremendous pressure [that is, he was responding to the power resources of the patient] to point out to the patient the self-defeating nature of what he was doing and to explore, probably with profit, the patient's need to harm himself. But the therapist was also aware that bringing this to the patient's attention would be a way of reassuring this particular patient that he really is a helpless, bewildered little boy who needs someone to tell him what is and what is not appropriate behavior. So the therapist said nothing and waited as the patient, in session after session, increased his pressure to win the therapist's intervention. Finally, the day before the patient was to spring his scheme, the patient said, "You know, the more I think about my plan, the more I feel it will probably lead to nothing but trouble." This moment represented the essence of change.

Halpern's example nicely illustrates what I call the therapeutic paradox. The therapist must consistently avoid the interpersonal position that is complementary to the client's own favored one, while at the same time providing sufficient rewards to keep the client above CL_{alt} and *in* the relationship.

Inevitably, the therapist, if he is to be successful, will have to provide the client with a series of experiences of rather low hedonic outcome for the client—first to block his disorder-maintaining behavior, and then to induce him into new interpersonal positions with which he needs to have some construct-revising experience. In maintaining the client's dependence upon him, the therapist cannot afford to deliver the type of reward that would be confirmatory of the client's constricted self-system. Therefore, the therapist strives to deliver his generalized rewards, such as warmth and acceptance, in a noncontingent manner— unconditionally, if you will—in order to maintain his attractiveness to the client, as recently emphasized by Goldstein, Heller, and Sechrest.[8] Attractiveness, of course, is convertible to power. All schools of psychotherapy, in addition, teach their practitioners various techniques whose largely inadvertent effect is to repudiate impunitively the client's claim to his favored interpersonal position. Generically, Beier calls these therapist tactics "asocial responses."[9] Asocial responses have the interesting property of maintaining contact without confirming *anything* the client has just said or done. Silence, I suppose, is the prototypic asocial response, but an incredible array of other kinds exist, such as restatement of the client's last remark, or "interpreting" it to the client in a way that renders it totally without meaning in the present context. Haley has amusingly catalogued the ploys of this type that are taught to budding psychoanalysts, and I have the impression that much of the ritualistic paraphernalia of behavior therapy serves the same function.[10]

In any case, the client, repeatedly frustrated in his efforts to make his relationship with the therapist a security-enhancing replica of all of his other relationships, is soon departing from his more suave and well-practiced methods of confirmatory response-evocation, and begins to produce rather more gross and forceful, if transparent, power tactics in order to get the therapist into a more satisfactory vis-a-vis position. In some circles this is known as a transference reaction, or even transference neurosis. If all goes well, the therapist neither falls into the trap nor loses his client; and he can go on from there to plan and execute new inputs to the client's congitive structures concerning the world and his relationship to it—utilizing, among other things, his own power over the client to induce him into positions vis-a-vis another human being—the therapist—that he has heretofore rarely or never sampled.

But sometimes, as we have seen, therapeutic relationships do not go well. A particular client and therapist *may* mesh in such a way that long-lasting positive results accrue to the client; it seems also to be the case, however, that a particular client-therapist combination may not only fail to result in benefit for the client, but may actually damage him further. How can such differential effects be accounted for? A partial answer is provided by the implications of the analysis that I have tried to develop here.

As I have implied above, one important power source in inter-personal relationships is the capacity of one person to affect the security of another by producing behavior that enhances or diminishes that security. An important limitation on the use of this power source by any person, however, is imposed by his own security requirements. It will not be possible for A to exercise this kind of power over B, whose security requires, let us say, a lovingly dominant stance from the other, if A's own security needs do not permit him to engage in that type of behavior. Less obviously, A's power over B will be limited if A's maintenance of security requires that he *always* enact loving dominance, for in this case he will be unable to *vary* B's security income, except perhaps by leaving, or threatening to leave, the relationship. Generally speaking, the person who is able with comfort to occupy virtually any interpersonal position when it is appropriate for him to do so will be powerful, in the sense that he can provide or refuse to provide responses of which other persons are in need for the maintenance of their security. Contrariwise, if a person's security needs impose greater or lesser constraints on the interpersonal positions he can occupy—as is typical, for example, of maladjusted persons—such a person will be to that degree dependent on certain others—that is, they can control his hedonic experience to some extent. How would this work in the case of the personality of the psychothera-pist? I hope you can now see what I am driving at.

If these ideas have any validity, it may be suggested that the most *generally* effective therapist—across all manner of clients—should be one who can move comfortably to any required interpersonal position, a characteristic that may be tantamount to maximum personal adjust-ment. There is considerable empirical evidence, by the way, that the latter is associated with general effectiveness as a therapist. I suppose one implication here is that, if the A–B variable relates to preferred inter-personal style, as I suspect it does, the best *all-round* therapist should be neither an A nor a B, but something in between. Therapists having

security-imposed constraints of one kind or another on their free interpersonal movement should suffer a corresponding reduction in the types
of clients they are likely to be successful in treating. The therapist who
is unable to move to positions which block the disturbance-perpetuating
behaviors of his client will almost certainly be unsuccessful.

But even beyond that, what of the therapist who has strong security
needs of his own for occupying a particular interpersonal position and for
receiving a complementary variety of social feedback. And what if his
client happens to be "hooked" on exactly that complementary stance.
In such a situation it would be difficult to say who is more dependent,
in the technical sense, on whom. I would propose for this situation a new
type of interpersonal game, suitable as an addition to Eric Berne's
museum.[11] It is called IT, I–T, for Interminable Therapy. One of its
principal variants is "Chronic Mental Hospital Patient;" the latter is
a game wherein the participants—patients and predisposed hospital
personnel—do little else but support each others' assumptions about how
grim and hateful life really is. Only a minority of persons in any population are attracted to this type of security-enhancing interchange, so the
players on both sides tend to have low CL_{alts} and therefore a high degree
of interdependence on each other.

One would hope that the therapist in any therapeutic relationship
will be capable of sticking to the task of inducing modification in his
client's maladaptive image of himself and his universe, rather than in
the maintenance and enhancement of that of his own. Seen in this light,
it is hardly surprising that therapeutic outcome is, to a large extent,
determined by the particular combination of personal characteristics
that the client and therapist bring to their relationship.

NOTES

1. A. E. Bergin, Some implications of Psychotherapy Research for Therapeutic Practice, *J. abnorm. Psychol.*, 71: 235–246, 1966.

2. A. P. Goldstein, K. Heller, and L. B. Sechrest, *Psychotherapy and the Psychology of Behavior Change* (New York: Wiley, 1966).

3. C. R. Rogers, "A Theory of Therapy, Personality, and Interpersonal Rela-
   tionships, as Developed in the Client-Centered Framework," in *Psychology:
   A Study of a Science*, ed. by S. Koch (New York: McGraw-Hill, 1959), pp.
   184–256; A. Ellis, *Reason and Emotion in Psychotherapy* (New York: Lyle
   Stuart, 1962); and, G. A. Kelly, *The Psychology of Personal Constructs* (New
   York: W. W. Norton, 1955).

4. Ellis, *op. cit.*

5. Kelly, *op cit.*; and J. L. Moreno, *Psychodrama* (Beacon, N.Y.: Beacon House, (1946).

6. J. W. Thibaut and H. H. Kelley, The Social Psychology of Groups (New York: Wiley, 1959).

7. H. M. Halpern, An Essential Ingredient in Successful Psychotherapy, *Psychother.*, 2: 177–180, 1965.

8. Goldstein, Heller, and Sechrest, *op cit.*

9. E. G. Beier, *The Silent Language of Psychotherapy* (Chicago: Aldine, 1966).

10. J. Haley, The Art of Psychoanalysis, *Etc.*, *15*: 190–200, 1958.

11. E. Berne, *Games People Play* (New York: Grove Press, 1964).

15
Conflict and Accommodation in Dyads

Darwyn E. Linder

In the summer of 1971 Philip Zimbardo of the Stanford University Department of Psychology conducted a study in which he created a simulated prison. The people who participated in the study were students from a variety of colleges and universities who were spending the summer in the San Francisco Bay Area. They were offered $15 a day to participate in a two-week study of a simulated prison. They were randomly assigned to roles as either guards or prisoners. The simulation was carefully planned and realistically conducted. Prisoners were picked up by police, booked, brought blindfolded to the location of the simulated prison, stripped, deloused, given prison uniforms, assigned numbers and put in cells. The most remarkable thing about the simulation was the extent to which prisoners began to obey the autocratic and capricious orders of the guards. There were rebellions and resistance, but all of these were broken by the simple application of authority on the part of the guards. Without using physical force or any form of tangible threat, the guards were able finally to elicit complete obedience from the prisoners. Zimbardo terminated the study after the 5th day when he realized that his simulated prison had become a real prison.

Why were these student prisoners so docilely obedient? There seems to be no simple explanation. Certainly they were playing the role of prisoners and perhaps their conception of a prisoner's role included obedience. Yet they performed acts that went beyond the role requirements that they might reasonably have set for themselves. They vilified other prisoners, they allowed themselves to be debased, and yet did not defy the guards and terminate their participation. Zimbardo did not set out to study obedience as did Stanley Milgram, and yet the results of both studies surprise us, I think for the same reason. We are surprised at the kinds of acts individuals will perform at the simple request of an arbitrary authority. The kind of coercive power that this ability usually depends upon seems absent in Milgram's experimental situation and in Zimbardo's simulation. The experimenter in Milgram's case and the guards in Zimbardo's case had no real or tangible source of power, the subjects were not bound in either case by any real force to continue to perform the actions requested of them. Perhaps the power to elicit these kinds of actions derives from the role relationship established between the experimenter and the subject and the guards and the prisoners. But then it must be that most people are taught the subordinate role very well, and fall into it very easily. Milgram points out that perhaps we do not have adequate models for disobedience, perhaps we have overlearned the role of subordinate.

We may be puzzled by the absence of a tangible power source in Milgram's experiments, but in Rapoport's games the source of power is obvious, the two players are competing for tangible monetary rewards. In the usual instance of these kinds of games both players have equivalent power over one another. The power in these games and in most dyadic interactions derives from the difference that changes in your behavior make to the other person in the interaction. That is, if by changing your behavior you alter greatly the level of positive outcome that the other person receives, you have great power over him, your behavior is important and he will conform to your wishes in order to receive the more favorable, for him, of your behaviors. The payoff matrices in these games can be altered to manipulate the power that one player has over another and a great deal of very interesting behavior can be observed when there is differential power between the two participants. Quite naturally the low power participant in such an interaction will attempt to increase his power so that he may interact in a more equitable fashion. In many naturally occurring dyads the main basis of power is the attraction that the two participants have for one another and their consequent ability to administer or withhold approval from one another. An effective strategy, then, for the low-power person is to attempt to increase his attractiveness to the high-power person, to ingratiate himself with the high-power person so that his own approval or disapproval will have greater impact on the high-power person. Experiments by Jones, Gergen, Gumpert, and Thibaut (1965) and Davis and Florquist (1965) and other studies reported by Jones (1964) indicate some of the subtle ways in which individuals will attempt to use ingratiation strategies to equalize the power distribution in a dyad.

This kind of an analysis may seem coldly analytic and overly concerned with the economics of social interaction and yet it is very useful for understanding even complex and authentic interaction. Robert Carson's discussion of the dynamics of the therapeutic situation in terms of the Thibaut and Kelley (1959) model makes certain assumptions about the relationship between therapist and patient, but given those assumptions the analysis is appealing and has implications for the behavior of the therapist. The assumptions are that the therapist's role is to direct behavior change in the patient so that his actions and interactions are healthier and more rewarding for him. Not all therapists agree that the clinician should take such an active role in reshaping the behavior of the patient, but it seems to me that the therapeutic enterprise is just that. If the therapist is to elicit behavior change from the patient he must be in a position of power that allows him to do so, and the basis of this power is the attraction that the patient has for the relationship. This attraction may be determined by how unrewarding his interactions outside the therapeutic hour have become, and in part by his attraction to the therapist. Since power depends upon the amount of difference that one's behavior makes to the other person involved in the interaction, the therapist must maintain his power by being able to move the patient through a relatively wide range of outcomes and he himself must not be susceptible to manipulation by the patient. That is, he must keep the patient in a position of relatively low power in the interaction. At the same time, as Carson points out, the therapist must be careful to maintain the level of outcomes for the patient at a level sufficiently high so that the patient wishes to maintain the therapeutic relationship. Treading this line, then, the therapist attempts to change the patient's behavior by withholding the approval and reinforcement that is usually elicited by those behaviors the patient has devised to deal with his life outside the therapeutic setting.

Two people interacting, the simplest possible social system, and yet there are an immense variety of settings in which dyads may occur and of power structures that may underly each dyadic interaction. A few simple concepts have helped us to understand some of the dynamics of dyadic interaction, but just as each person is unique he brings to each interaction his uniqueness and each interaction therefore is different from every other interaction that has occurred. This implies that we may never have a complete understanding of even this simplest form of social interaction, and perhaps we shall never be able to predict accurately the course and outcome of these encounters. But I do not regret this either as a scientist who observes social interactions nor as a person who participates in them. For the scientist this complexity means that I will continue to confront intriguing questions about interaction in dyads, and for the participant it means that I will continue to enjoy the surprises that unfold as I meet and interact with new people.

REFERENCES

Davis, K. E., and Florquist, Carolie C., Perceived threat and dependence as determinants of the tactical usage of opinion conformity. *J. exp. soc. Psychol.*, 1965, *1*, 219–236.

Jones, E. E., *Ingratiation: A Social Psychological Analysis*. New York: Appleton-Century Crofts, 1964.

Jones, E. E., Gergen, K. J., Gumpert, P., and Thibaut, J. W., Some conditions affecting the use of ingratiation to influence performance evaluation. *J. of Personality and soc. Psychol.*, 1965, *1*, 613–626.

Thibaut, J. W., and Kelley, H. H., *The Social Psychology of Groups*. New York: Wiley, 1959.

Part 3
Interaction in Small Groups

I
An Introduction to Social Interactions in Groups

Darwyn E. Linder

The study of small groups is one of the oldest concerns of social psychologists. In the nineteenth century thinkers such as Le Bon (1896), were concerned with the effects of groups on individual behavior. It was during this period that the "group mind" hypothesis, now discredited, was used to explain the development of supposedly abnormal behaviors within groups. It was thought that a group consciousness developed that allowed men to behave in a manner that would be morally repugnant to each person, were he acting as an individual. The vicious and cruel behavior of some mobs was explained in this way. It seems quite appropriate then to begin this section with a selection by Charles Horton Cooley, who theorized that primary groups shaped human nature, that we in fact become human through primary group contact. Cooley's argument reminds me of the report by Harlow and Harlow (1962) that infant monkeys were effectively socialized by exposure only to other infant monkeys. Even when isolated from adults they developed monkeylike social behavior if allowed to interact with other infant monkeys. There can be no doubt that membership in primary groups, the family, the neighborhood play group, and others, have a great impact on the socialization of human beings. However, this is not the time to reopen a discussion of the nature-nurture question or to reconsider the problem of the relative contributions of inheritance and environment to human behavior. Instead we shall consider the more straightforward question of the effects of group membership on individual behavior.

The empirical study of the effects on individual behavior of being in a group begins with Triplett (1898), who studied the differences caused by performing a simple task while alone or while in the presence of other individuals. He found that performance was enhanced by the presence of others engaged in the task. It might be argued that the mere presence of other individuals is not really a form of social interaction and yet in some ways we are in interaction whenever another person is present to our senses. If this primitive form of social interaction can affect individual behavior, we must start by analyzing those effects and then proceed to the effects of more complicated interactions. In this section we will be concerned with the behavior of the individual as a function of the social setting in which he acts. In the next section the behavior of the group will become our focus and we will consider the group as the unit of analysis.

Being a group member can have a wide variety of effects on attitudes and behavior. The empirical question in one form is quite simple. Does a person's behavior or performance when he is alone differ from his behavior or performance when he is in the presence of others or in some kind of social interaction with them? The experimental design suggested by this question is relatively straightforward and has been used by Triplett (1898), Sherif (1935), Asch (1956), and other investigators concerned with the effects of group membership on behavior. Some subjects are observed acting singly while others are asked to respond to the experimental task while in groups of varying size or character. The differences in behavior in these two settings become the focus of analysis. Much of the experimental work on conformity, risk taking in groups and bystander intervention has used this classic experimental design. For some aspects of social behavior, however, the behavior of the individual while alone is not the appropriate comparison. In some instances the relevant behavior cannot be emitted by a single person but requires a group setting in order to occur. For example, one cannot study the distance between members in a small discussion group by considering the distance between people when they are alone and when they are in a group. Obviously, it makes no sense to attempt to consider the distance between persons when only one person is present.

Another kind of concern is with the effects of a different kind of group atmosphere on the behavior of individual group members. Kurt Lewin was the first investigator to have the audacity to attempt to manipulate so complex a variable as group atmosphere, but by doing so he opened for empirical study an entire field of group dynamics. His very well known study (Lewin, Lippit, and White, 1939) succeeded in showing that group atmosphere could be manipulated and controlled by the experimenter and that such manipulations did affect the behavior of individual group members. In this study groups of boys of elementary school age met to form clubs. The adult leader of each club manipulated the group atmosphere to be either "democratic," "authoritarian," or "laissez faire." The behavior of the boys with the leader present and the leader absent was carefully recorded and group productivity was measured. The interested reader can find a complete report in the original paper or in secondary sources such as Cartwright and Zander (1968) and I shall not describe the results here. Lewin's work became the prototype of a number of studies in which the atmosphere or some aspect of the group setting was either measured or manipulated and some aspects of individual behavior became the dependent variable.

In addition to paving the way for the experimental study of group dynamics, Kurt Lewin helped to found the National Training Laboratories as a method of providing individuals with practical training in group dynamics and group behavior. Founded in 1947 the National Training Laboratories developed the idea of a basic training or T-group in which an individual participated in order to learn more about his own functioning in groups and to be better able to use groups and group dynamics in business and education. This basic T-group is a direct ancestor of the basic encounter group discussed by Carl Rogers. It becomes a very difficult task to write nonoverlapping definitions of T-groups, encounter groups, and group therapy. One way to define the differences between these sorts of groups is to emphasize the goal of each group experience. I am sure that there are a great number of practitioners who would not agree with the definitions I am about to propose but I think they may be useful in understanding the range of activities that are available in these kinds of group settings. I define a T-group or training group as one in which the goal is to become better able to lead and function in a group setting. Group therapy has as its goal the cure or improvement of some psychopathic condition. Members of therapy groups are in those groups seeking to improve their psychological adjustment, just as persons in individual therapy wish to do. Encounter groups occupy a sort of large mid range between T-groups and group therapy. I think that the goal of most encounter groups is to provide a kind of growth experience for the participants, an experience that allows them to expand the ways in which they can interact with others and to deepen the meaning of their interactions. It is primarily this kind of group experience, oriented toward personal growth, that Carl Rogers considers in the selection that concludes the next section of this book.

These then are some aspects of interaction in small groups—some of the things people do when in small groups that differ from what they would do or could do when alone, some of the ways in which individuals are affected by group membership. There is much more to be considered in a complete discussion of group dynamics or small group interaction. I can recommend two excellent sources, Cartwright and Zander (1968) and Shaw (1971), for a deeper and broader study of group dynamics.

REFERENCES

Asch, S., Studies of independence and conformity: A minority of one against a unanimous majority. *Psychological Monographs*, 1956, 70, No. 9 (Whole No. 416)

Cartwright, D. C., and Zander, A. (eds.), *Group Dynamics: Research and Theory*. (3rd. ed.) New York: Harper and Row, 1968.

Harlow, H. F., and Harlow, Margaret K., The effect of rearing conditions on behavior, *Bulletin of the Menninger Clinic*, 1962, 26, 213–224.

Le Bon, G., *The Crowd*. Unwin, 1896. (Translated from *Psychologies des foules*. Paris: Oleon, 1895.)

Lewin, K., Lippitt, R., and White, R. K., Patterns of aggressive behavior in experimentally created "social climates." *J. Soc. Psychol.*, 1939, 10, 271–299.

Shaw, M. E., *Group Dynamics: The Psychology of Small Group Behavior*. New York: McGraw-Hill, 1971.

Sherif, M., A study of some social factors in perception. *Archives of Psychology*, 1935, No. 187.

Triplett, N., The dynamogenic factors in pacemaking and competition. *Amer. J. Psychol.*, 1898, 2, 507–533.

2
Primary Groups

Charles H. Cooley

By primary groups I mean those characterized by intimate face-to-face
association and coöperation. They are primary in several senses, but
chiefly in that they are fundamental in forming the social nature and
ideals of the individual. The results of intimate association, psychologically, is a certain fusion of individualities in a common whole, so that
one's very self, for many purposes at least, is the common life and purpose of the group. Perhaps the simplest way of describing this whole-
ness is by saying that it is a "we"; it involves the sort of sympathy and
mutual identification for which "we" is the natural expression. One
lives in the feeling of the whole and finds the chief aims of his will in that
feeling.

It is not to be supposed that the unity of the primary group is one
of mere harmony and love. It is always a differentiated and usually a
competitive unity, admitting of self-assertion and various appropriative
passions; but these passions are socialized by sympathy, and come, or
tend to come, under the discipline of a common spirit. The individual
will be ambitious, but the chief object of his ambition will be some
desired place in the thought of the others, and he will feel allegiance to
common standards of service and fair play. So the boy will dispute with
his fellows a place on the team, but above such disputes will place the
common glory of his class and school.

The most important spheres of this intimate association and cooperation—though by no means the only ones—are the family, the
play-group of children, and the neighborhood or community group of
elders. These are practically universal, belonging to all times and all
stages of development; and are accordingly a chief basis of what is
universal in human nature and human ideals. The best comparative
studies of the family, such as those of Westermarck[1] or Howard,[2] show
it to us as not only a universal institution, but as more alike the world
over than the exaggeration of exceptional customs by an earlier school

had led us to suppose. Nor can any one doubt the general prevalence of play-groups among children or of informal assemblies of various kinds among their elders. Such association is clearly the nursery of human nature in the world about us, and there is no apparent reason to suppose that the case has anywhere or at any time been essentially different.

As regards play, I might, were it not a matter of common observation, multiply illustrations of the universality and spontaneity of the group discussion and coöperation to which it gives rise. The general fact is that children, especially boys after about their twelfth year, live in fellowships in which their sympathy, ambition and honor are engaged even more, often, than they are in the family. Most of us can recall examples of the endurance by boys of injustice and even cruelty, rather than appeal from their fellows to parents or teachers—as, for instance, in the hazing so prevalent at schools, and so difficult, for this very reason, to repress. And how elaborate the discussion, how cogent the public opinion, how hot the ambitions in these fellowships.

Nor is this facility of juvenile association, as is sometimes supposed, a trait peculiar to English and American boys; since experience among our immigrant population seems to show that the offspring of the more restrictive civilizations of the continent of Europe form self-governing play-groups with almost equal readiness. Thus Miss Jane Addams, after pointing out that the "gang" is almost universal, speaks of the interminable discussion which every detail of the gang's activity receives, remarking that "in these social folk-motes, so to speak, the young citizen learns to act upon his own determination."[3]

Of the neighborhood group it may be said, in general, that from the time men formed permanent settlements upon the land, down, at least, to the rise of modern industrial cities, it has played a main part in the primary, heart-to-heart life of the people. Among our Teutonic forefathers the village community was apparently the chief sphere of sympathy and mutual aid for the commons all through the "dark" and middle ages, and for many purposes it remains so in rural districts at the present day. In some countries we still find it with all its ancient vitality, notably in Russia, where the mir, or self-governing village group, is the main theatre of life, along with the family, for perhaps fifty millions of peasants.

In our own life the intimacy of the neighborhood has been broken up by the growth of an intricate mesh of wider contacts which leaves us strangers to people who live in the same house. And even in the country the same principle is at work, though less obviously, diminishing our economic and spiritual community with our neighbors. How far this change is a healthy development, and how far a disease, is perhaps still uncertain.

Besides these almost universal kinds of primary association, there are many others whose form depends upon the particular state of civilization; the only essential thing, as I have said, being a certain intimacy and fusion of personalities. In our own society, being little bound by place, people easily form clubs, fraternal societies and the like, based on congeniality, which may give rise to real intimacy. Many such relations are formed at school and college, and among men and women brought together in the first instance by their occupations—as workmen in the same trade, or the like. Where there is a little common interest and activity, kindness grows like weeds by the roadside.

But the fact that the family and neighborhood groups are ascendant in the open and plastic time of childhood makes them even now incomparably more influential than all the rest.

Primary groups are primary in the sense that they give the individual his earliest and completest experience of social unity, and also in the sense that they do not change in the same degree as more elaborate relations, but form a comparatively permanent source out of which the latter are ever springing. Of course they are not independent of the larger society, but to some extent reflect its spirit; as the German family and the German school bear somewhat distinctly the print of German militarism. But this, after all, is like the tide setting back into creeks, and does not commonly go very far. Among the German, and still more among the Russian, peasantry are found habits of free coöperation and discussion almost uninfluenced by the character of the state; and it is a familiar and well-supported view that the village commune, self-governing as regards local affairs and habituated to discussion, is a very widespread institution in settled communities, and the continuator of a similar autonomy previously existing in the clan. "It is man who makes monarchies and establishes republics, but the commune seems to come directly from the hand of God."[4]

In our own cities the crowded tenements and the general economic and social confusion have sorely wounded the family and the neighborhood, but it is remarkable, in view of these conditions, what vitality they show; and there is nothing upon which the conscience of the time is more determined than upon restoring them to health.

These groups, then, are springs of life, not only for the individual but for social institutions. They are only in part moulded by special traditions, and, in larger degree, express a universal nature. The religion or government of other civilizations may seem alien to us, but the children or the family group wear the common life, and with them we can always make ourselves at home.

By human nature, I suppose, we may understand those sentiments and impulses that are human in being superior to those of lower animals, and also in the sense that they belong to mankind at large, and not to any particular race or time. It means, particularly, sympathy and the innumerable sentiments into which sympathy enters, such as love, resentment, ambition, vanity, hero-worship, and the feeling of social right and wrong.

Human nature in this sense is justly regarded as a comparatively permanent element in society. Always and everywhere men seek honor and dread ridicule, defer to public opinion, cherish their goods and their children, and admire courage, generosity, and success. It is always safe to assume that people are and have been human.

To return to primary groups: the view here maintained is that human nature is not something existing separately in the individual, but a *group-nature or primary phase of society*, a relatively simple and general condition of the social mind. It is something more, on the one hand, than the mere instinct that is born in us—though that enters into it—and something less, on the other, than the more elaborate development of ideas and sentiments that makes up institutions. It is the nature which is developed and expressed in those simple, face-to-face groups that are somewhat alike in all societies; groups of the family, the playground, and the neighborhood. In the essential similarity of these is to be found the basis, in experience, for similar ideas and sentiments in the human mind. In these, everywhere, human nature comes into existence. Man does not have it at birth; he cannot acquire it except through fellowship, and it decays in isolation.

If this view does not recommend itself to commonsense I do not know that elaboration will be of much avail. It simply means that application at this point of the idea that society and individuals are inseparable phases of a common whole, so that wherever we find an individual fact we may look for a social fact to go with it. If there is a universal nature in persons there must be something universal in association to correspond to it.

What else can human nature be than a trait of primary groups? Surely not an attribute of the separate individual—supposing there were any such thing—since its typical characteristics, such as affection, ambition, vanity, and resentment, are inconceivable apart from society. If it belongs, then, to man in association, what kind or degree of association is required to develop it? Evidently nothing elaborate, because elaborate phases of society are transient and diverse, while human nature is comparatively stable and universal. In short the family and neighborhood life is essential to its genesis and nothing more is.

Here as everywhere in the study of society we must learn to see mankind in psychical wholes, rather than in artificial separation. We must see and feel the communal life of family and local groups as immediate facts, not as combinations of something else. And perhaps we shall do this best by recalling our own experience and extending it through sympathetic observation. What, in our life, is the family and the fellowship; what do we know of the we-feeling? Thought of this kind may help us to get a concrete perception of that primary group-nature of which everything social is the outgrowth.

NOTES

1. *The History of Human Marriage.*
2. *A History of Matrimonial Institutions.*
3. *Newer Ideals of Peace,* 177.
4. De Tocqueville, *Democracy in America,* vol. i, chap. 5.

3
The Nature of Conformity and its Investigation

Charles A. Kiesler and Sara B. Kiesler

If you had been reading a newspaper in a particular city in the Northern United States in late September of 1954, you might have seen a back-page headline reading: "PROPHECY FROM PLANET. CLARION CALL TO CITY: FLEE THAT FLOOD. IT'LL SWAMP US ON DEC. 21, OUTER SPACE TELLS SUBURBANITE." The item had been supplied by a "Mrs. Keech," who maintained that the prophecy was not her own. She said that she had received many messages by automatic writing, sent to her by superior beings from a planet called "Clarion." The beings, who had visited the earth in flying saucers, had noticed fault lines in the earth's crust that foretold the deluge. Mrs. Keech reported that the flood would spread from the Arctic Circle to the Gulf of Mexico. At the same time, she said, a cataclysm would engulf the West Coast from Seattle to Chile.

Mrs. Keech had gathered about her a number of followers who also believed in the prophecy and were preparing for the great event. When no flood appeared on December 21, many of the group left. However, the people most committed to the prophecy not only persisted in their beliefs after disconfirmation, but started to recruit new believers and group members.

Several psychologists and their students seized this opportunity to study what happens to people when their beliefs are disconfirmed, and they observed Mrs. Keech and her unusual group of followers over a period of months. Some, pretending to be believers, even joined the group. Their research was reported in a book called *When Prophecy Fails* (Festinger, Riecken, and Schachter, 1956).[1] This detailed report describes a number of activities and attitudes which can be subsumed under the heading of *conformity*. Examples from the prophecy group will be used throughout this chapter to illustrate various aspects of conformity.

Reprinted by permission from Charles A. Kiesler and Sarah B. Kiesler, *Conformity*, © 1969, Addison-Wesley, Reading, Mass.

DEFINING CONFORMITY

Conformity as Change toward A Group

Whether we are discussing the "true believer," ourselves, or the man in the street, conformity is defined in the same way: *a change in behavior or belief toward a group as a result of real or imagined group pressure.* We will first discuss what we mean by "change toward a group."

Everyone belongs to groups of people. Moreover, these groups influence us. Our behavior and attitudes change as we interact with others. A group will want an individual member to act and believe as the others do. Consequently, the end result of group influence is that our beliefs and actions will be more similar to those of others in the group. For example, the leader of a group, or a united clique within the group, may be more influential than other members. Of course, any member of a group may be influenced by any of the others. If each member influences others and is influenced himself, the members will become more and more like each other in attitude and action. In many groups, then, each member of a group changes his attitudes and actions to be more like those of the others, and, overall, the group becomes more uniform in belief and behavior.

It won't happen quite like this for all people, of course. If you belong to a group in name only, the members may not influence you at all. Or if you belong to a group only because you have to (say, your parents insist that you join a club for which you have no affection), then you may resist all influence attempts. We have simply described what *can* happen as a result of membership in a group.

Mrs. Keech's group illustrates our conformity paradigm quite well. Here was a conglomeration of friends, married couples, and strangers who just seemed to happen along, all brought together because of some attraction or another to Mrs. Keech and the activities she was engaged in. There was a core membership of fifteen persons and a few others who drifted in and out. Some of the members of the group, especially the two leaders, Mrs. Keech and a Dr. Armstrong, entered the group with a common set of beliefs: belief in extrasensory perception, in the spirit world, in reincarnation, and in the possibility of communication with outer space beings. Mrs. Keech convinced the other members of the imminence of the great flood. But the process of change did not stop there.

The members who met with Mrs. Keech and Dr. Armstrong were constantly cajoled or more subtly pressured into believing and acting more as their leaders expected. At group meetings, the members were asked to discuss their mystical experiences and dreams so that their "correct" meanings could be found. (This proved to be a little embarrassing for the researching infiltrators.) The group prayed together for common guidance and in doing so they tried to adjust their "vibrations" so that they would be in tune with each other. Newcomers to the group were given lessons by the more committed (one of the less subtle persuasive techniques); individuals who outwardly refused to accept the major beliefs (e.g., belief in ESP) were rejected or suspected of spying.

These techniques were rather successful in influencing the membership, at least before the disconfirmation of the prophecy. The beliefs of group members became more like those of the leaders, and the activities and attitudes of all the members became more and more uniform. Even after disconfirmation, the members most committed to the group conform to the group's standards of belief and behavior.

These events illustrate what the study of conformity is directed at: changes in belief and behavior that a member of a group may undergo as a result of pressure from one or more other members of the group. We may also want to study how the combined changes of members result in group uniformity, how persistent the changes are, and what further changes take place when the circumstances are different. Of course, we are not interested in just any change. When we study conformity, we study change *toward the group*, i.e., movement in beliefs and behavior that make them more like those of other group members.

The Compliant Skeptic versus the True Believer

Not all of Mrs. Keech's circle really believed in her prophecy. There were some (including the spying researchers) who were skeptical, but who nevertheless had other reasons for acting as the group expected and demanded. Both kinds of people—the compliant skeptics and the true believers—were conformers, since they both displayed some sort of change in the direction of group expectations. However, it should be obvious that we must make some distinction between these two kinds of conformity.

Social psychologists have labeled these two types of conformity *compliance* and *private acceptance*. Compliance refers to overt behavior which becomes more like the behavior that the group wishes its members to show. The term refers to outward actions without consideration of the private convictions of the actor. When we speak of "compliance only," we mean that the person is behaving as the group wants him to but does not really believe in what he is doing. That is, he is going along with the group without privately agreeing with the group. Private acceptance means a change in attitude or belief in the direction of group attitudes and beliefs. In this case, the person may not only act as the group wishes, but changes his opinions so that he believes as the group believes. This term has its parallel in the term "attitude change" used in studies of persuasive communications.

Two members of Mrs. Keech's group can be used to illustrate the difference between compliance and private acceptance. Cleo Armstrong was the "compliant skeptic." She was the college-age daughter of two of the most committed members of the group. Her father was Dr. Armstrong, whom we have described as one of the leaders of the group. Because of her parents, Cleo was "stuck" with the group. At times she remarked that she had a great deal to lose if the flood prediction were not confirmed because of the community's certain resultant disrespect for her father. Thus she participated in the meetings and discussions, and never openly denied a belief in the prophecy. In all outward respects she conformed with the group. Yet her private convictions wavered a great deal. She did not proselytize on her own, she devoted little effort to studying Mrs. Keech's mimeographed lessons, and she argued extensively with her father. Cleo Armstrong, then, showed outward compliance without much private acceptance of the group's belief system.

Bob Eastman was a "true believer." He had once been a cynical, hard-living individual, who, after a stint in the Army, had entered college. He had come under the tutorship of Dr. Armstrong and became his faithful disciple. Eastman attended every meeting of the group; gave up smoking, drinking, and swearing; studied the lessons on his own; and worked hard in a secretarial capacity for the group. He sold property to pay off his debts before the flood, said goodbye to his parents after failing to convince them of the imminent catastrophe, and actively proselytized other students. He seemed to believe completely in the prophecy. By our definition, he displayed compliance with the group's norms and private acceptance of them.

Although both compliance and private acceptance are subsumed under the general notion of conformity, the conditions under which each occurs may be quite different. This is one reason why we have partitioned our later discussion into separate chapters on compliance and private acceptance. Also, most studies in the psychological literature have employed either measures of compliance or measures of private acceptance, but rarely both together. This historical fact is perhaps unfortunate because it would be of interest to examine how the two types of conformity interact. For example, we might want to examine the conditions under which private acceptance occurs but not overt compliance. Perhaps this occurs when it is easy for a person to change his beliefs but difficult to behave as the group does. For example, a smoker thinking of quitting may join a "smoking clinic" and be persuaded that to stop smoking is extremely important but still find it very hard to act on this belief.

Compliance and private acceptance may also have different psychological implications. Take, for example, the complier. The person who outwardly complies with the group but does not privately accept the group's beliefs is doing this for one or more of a number of reasons. Perhaps he thinks others will look up to him if he acts as the group does, as when a draftee walks down the street in that certain manner we call "military bearing." Perhaps the complier thinks the group will get him where he wants to go, as with the debutante who hates coming-out parties, but thinks if she attends them she may find a rich husband. Maybe he complies because he is forced to, as with the prisoner who labors diligently all day. Compliant behavior, itself, has implications for subsequent events. The person may feel a need to justify to himself what he is doing, so he may exaggerate the importance of his "motive" for complying, or he may eventually decide that he really does believe in what he is doing; or, upon examining his behavior, he may decide (if he can) to quit the group altogether. What happens will depend upon the situation: the extent to which the person is stuck with the group, the pressures on him to comply, and so forth.

Sometimes a complier never comes to the point where he feels the need to examine his behavior. Perhaps he well knows that he was forced to act as he is acting, or maybe the behavior is too insignificant in his life to bother with. In the case where the person feels he has no choice in behaving as he does, he will probably stop complying the minute the group turns its back or releases its hold on him.

The psychological implications of private acceptance may be very different. The person who believes in what he does will probably persist in his behavior long after the group has stopped monitoring his behavior—as long, in fact, as he continues to believe. When the person considers what he is doing, he thinks, "I'm doing these things because I believe in them." Further actions on the issue will be dictated by his belief. The person may also change other attitudes to bring them in line with his new belief.

In addition, private acceptance is likely to intensify the person's relationship to the other group members, since he feels similar to them in belief as well as action. If the group is ideologically attacked, he may defend it. (After all, when the group's beliefs are attacked, so are his.) In a sense, a person who privately accepts the group's beliefs has a greater investment in the group. Not only is he likely to devote more time and effort to its activities, but these efforts are whole-hearted. The group has far more potential influence in other areas of his life than if he were only complying.

On the other hand, we cannot conclude that the person who changes his beliefs will always increase his affection for the group more than the person who just complies. We mentioned above that the complier may need to justify his behavior because it is discrepant with his beliefs. When he asks himself, "Why am I doing these things?", he cannot say, "... because I believe in them." Consequently, he may attempt to justify his behavior by increasing his liking for the group. He says, "I do these things, even though I don't believe, because the group members are marvelous people." The person who acts out of private conviction does not have to justify his behavior, so he may be less likely to increase his attention to the group. We shall later discuss in some detail when the complier will be a more enthusiastic group member. To sort out the differential predictions, we have to know more about the conditions under which compliance and private acceptance occur. Let it suffice to know that the person may be in an entirely different psychological situation, depending on whether he has complied overtly or has privately changed his beliefs.

Measuring Compliance and Private Acceptance

We mentioned before that, historically, few studies have employed measures of both compliance and private acceptance. The techniques for studying compliance and private acceptance usually require very different strategies, and to combine the two in the same experiment would be quite difficult. By understanding how the two kinds of conformity are investigated, the implications of the distinction between them will become clearer.

We can more or less readily observe whether or not a person overtly complies with a particular group demand. It is a little more difficult to find out if the same person privately accepts group influence, since we cannot directly observe his private, personal opinions. Psychologists who studied compliance in the past ordinarily exposed people to group influence attempts and then, with the group still around, simply waited to see if the individuals copied the group's example. When interest in private acceptance grew, psychologists learned that this method was inadequate, so they devised more subtle methods for investigating private acceptance. Sometimes they exposed people to group influence and then withdrew the group so that they could observe their subjects when the group was no longer present. Sometimes they kept the group intact, but let members express their opinions on anonymous questionnaires.

A classic study of compliance. The method in this study was first employed by Solomon Asch. A number of confederates, after being told what to do beforehand, participate with a naive subject who thinks they are also subjects. Suppose we have four confederates. They enter the experiment room with the subject and sit in a semicircle with the subject forced to take an end seat. The experimenter tells the group that they will make judgments of a series of lines. They are to compare one line with three others and choose the one of the same length (see Fig. 1). The confederates, instead of choosing the line which obviously matches the comparison line, choose one of a different length. The subject is then in a dilemma: should he identify the correct line, or should he yield to social pressure and pick the line the others chose? Two measures of compliance in this situation could be the number of subjects who pick the incorrect line and the number of trials on which subjects yield.

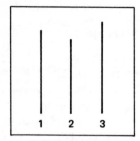 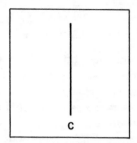

Fig. 1. A sample judgmental stimulus used in Asch-type studies of compliance.

A number of independent variables can be studied in this type of experimental setting. For example, if we are interested in the effect of group size on conformity, we can vary the number of confederates. If we are interested in the effect of status, we can vary the status of the confederates by introducing them differently or by having them wear different clothes.

The Asch technique allows us to study compliance under a number of different conditions. But we have no way of knowing what the subjects are privately thinking. Do they actually come to believe that the line the confederates chose is the correct line? Not often. One line and only one line is correct, even though the others say it isn't. No matter how the subject squirms and squints, he cannot make their choice look correct. Thus, there is no room for private acceptance in this situation.

Now let's shorten the longest line and lengthen the shortest one until it really isn't too clear which is correct. The situation then becomes ambiguous enough so that the subject's private opinion might indeed be swayed by the confederates. Could we measure private acceptance by perhaps having him whisper his answer to the experiment? Probably not. The subject might guess that conformity was the experimenter's real interest. If a subject guesses the real purpose of an experiment, we cannot depend on his response. If he were to tell the experimenter that he privately agreed with the confederates, we wouldn't know if he actually did or if he just wished to please the experimenter. If he told the experimenter that he disagreed with the confederates, he might only be trying to convince the experimenter that he was an independent sort of person. For the same reasons, an anonymous questionnaire would be inadequate. Without any rationale for the questionnaire, the subject would still wonder what the purpose of the experiment was. Originally, the subject was involved in what he thought was a judgmental task. But when we ask him to repeat his judgment, either on a questionnaire or by whispering to the experimenter, he becomes suspicious. The situation is both artificial and unbelievable. In short, it is difficult to measure private acceptance with the Asch technique. It is not even clear that the Asch technique provides an adequate measure of compliance.

In recent years, psychologists have discovered that if they really want to study conformity—both private acceptance *and* compliance—they must be far more subtle. This subtlety requires that: (1) the experimenter not reveal his hypothesis to the subject (called "experimenter demand," because a revealed hypothesis puts pressure on the subject to satisfy it); (2) the experimental situation not be so contrived that the results cannot be generalized to other situations; and (3) the situation not be so artificial that the subject reacts suspiciously or defensively rather than as he would if the same variables were operating naturally. These considerations are taken into account in the following example of a study of private acceptance.

A hypothetical study of private acceptance.   Suppose a person has never thought one way or the other about why he brushes his teeth. He just does it. He participates in our experiment with some confederates who discuss toothbrushing under the guise of a seminar on "cultural truisms." The confederates take the position that toothbrushing is actually harmful to the teeth (it wears down the enamel) and should be substituted by rinsing with a mouthwash. To measure compliance, we can observe whether the subject overtly agrees with the confederates.

Overt agreement, however, would not indicate private acceptance. A more complicated technique is required. One reasonable method would be to use another subject who also is exposed to the group but is never asked to express his opinion. We will measure his opinion later. (There are two reasons why we do not ask the subject to express his opinion in the group. First, this might make him suspicious when we later measure his opinion, and second, the act of complying, itself, might affect his private acceptance of the group's opinion.) Later, he is asked to participate in another experiment. In the second experiment, a new experimenter tells him that the study is concerned with "reading skills" and that his reading speed and comprehension will be tested. Among the materials he reads is a persuasive communication (say, from the "Dental Institute") which advocates brushing the teeth three times a day. An anonymous questionnaire (the "comprehension test") is then given to the subject. Imbedded among several questions is one which asks, "How often should a person brush his teeth?" If the subject had been convinced by the discussion group that toothbrushing is harmful, he should be more resistant to the communication than would a control subject who had not participated in the discussion group. That is, the experimental subject should be more likely to answer that one should rarely brush one's teeth. But if the subject had not been convinced by the group, then both he and the control subject should be influenced by the communication. They might answer that one must brush his teeth two or three times a day. Thus, one way to measure private acceptance is to see whether the subject still endorses the group's opinion after attack.

The experiment outlined above illustrates some important problems in defining conformity. First, the behavior of interest must be precisely described so that it can be measured. In particular, it is essential to distinguish between behavior that merely goes along with the group's and behavior reflecting true agreement with the group. Second, measures of conformity must be taken within a context that is believable to the subject.

Does One Have to Change in Order to Conform?

The answer to our subtitle is that it depends partly on how one defines conformity. However, conformity could not be defined to include behavior that just happened to coincide with that of a group because behavior that is truly coincidental has nothing to do with the psychological effect of a group. Conformity, as we have defined it, involves an alteration of behavior and belief toward a group. It is not just any alteration—it is alteration that occurs as a result of some group pressure. If a person agrees with a group just by coincidence, we would not call this conformity. Let us examine this notion more thoroughly.

Conformity was clearly demonstrated in the behavior of Kitty O'Donnell, one of Mrs. Keech's prophecy group. She first came to a meeting at Bob Eastman's urging. At first, she considered the group a "bunch of crackpots." But she consented to listen to what the group had to say. Later, she had a dream which convinced her she had been "chosen" to be one of the group. Eventually, she accepted the group's beliefs and plunged herself into group activities, quit her job, and left her parents' home. She obviously changed toward the group's beliefs. It was not a coincidental agreement with the group, nor even a chance movement toward the group. The group had an effect on her. Kitty O'Donnell illustrates our definition of conformity: a change toward the group as a result of real (or imagined) group pressure.

To illustrate coincidental agreement let us suppose that a person in India had consulted the stars and decided that on December 21 a great flood would appear on the American continent. However, he had never heard of Mrs. Keech and knew nothing of her group. We would not call him a conformer, even though he came to believe as Mrs Keech and her group did. She and her group did not influence him (unless one believes in ESP). Regardless of the fascinating coincidence, his behavior is psychologically irrelevant when we are studying the effect of Mrs. Keech and her co-believers.

We have limited our definition of conformity to changes in belief and behavior as a result of group pressure. But a bright student may still make the point that one can be interested in the effect of group pressure without necessarily confining oneself to change. What if a person were in a group, happened to agree with its standards before he joined, but *maintained* his beliefs as a result of group pressure? What follows is an example from the Keech group.

Dr. Armstrong was a physician working on the staff of a college health service. He and his wife were active in religious organizations and Dr. Armstrong organized "The Seekers," a group of young people who met weekly to discuss various topics, including one of Dr. Armstrong's favorites, flying saucers. He joined with Mrs. Keech because they were of like mind. The group did not change him—he already had a set of beliefs consistent with Mrs. Keech's prophecy. However, it is possible that without the constant presence of Mrs. Keech and the group Dr. Armstrong may have reverted to a more conventional belief system. Can we not, then, speak of his conformity?[2]

Why don't we say that maintenance of a belief in a group is also conformity? Because without other information, we cannot demonstrate that the group had any effect on the person. We would know that the individual, like Dr. Armstrong, did not abandon his beliefs while in the group, but we would not know that the group caused the belief maintenance. Perhaps the belief would have remained intact without the group. However, there is one instance when belief maintenance can be called conformity. That is when comparable people outside the group abandon their opinions. In this case, by proper comparison with these control subjects, one could conclude that the group made the individual resistant to change—he would have held a different opinion had he not been in the group. Since the control subjects alter their opinions and those in the group do not, the difference between them represents a change, albeit an indirect one. In a sense, the difference between the two conditions reflects the change in the group member that would have occurred without group support. This argument is analogous to the one presented in our previous discussion of how to measure private acceptance.

Let us summarize our point. In research on conformity, we are forced to examine change, directly or by inference, to be assured that the group has had some effect on the individual. This is why we limit our definition of conformity to changes in belief and behavior toward a group. There are two main ways to examine this change. Sometimes we compare subjects' behavior after group interaction with the behavior of other subjects who were not in the group. A difference between them allows us to infer change. A second method is to expose both of these groups of subjects to an attack on their beliefs. Again, we can infer change by comparing relative resistance to attack in the two subject groups. Both methods allow us to conclude whether the group has had an effect on the person, in short, whether conformity had occurred.

Conformity to What?

As we mentioned previously, a person belongs to many groups. In an uncontrolled setting, it can be very misleading to restrict oneself to an examination of a person's behavior with respect to only one group or to one situation. If we fail to analyze the whole psychological environment, we may eventually draw the wrong conclusions. That is, we may infer that a particular variable was influencing the person when actually something quite different may have caused him to change his behavior.

Say we are interested in the effect of parental attitudes on the behavior of children. As a small study, we might correlate the dating behavior of teenagers with the "permissiveness" of their parents. Permissiveness is defined as few restrictions on behavior. Suppose we find that teenagers with permissive parents are more frequent daters than teenagers with nonpermissive parents. Can we conclude that the permissive parents want their children to date more and have influenced them to do so? We cannot. Perhaps the children of permissive parents, because the parents dictate less of their behavior, become more dependent on their peers. If frequent dating is positively valued in the teenage culture, the children might as easily be conforming to teenage norms as to parental norms, if they are conforming at all. In short, only with more information about the whole context of the behavior could we draw any conclusion about conformity.

Conformity as a Personality Trait

The layman often thinks of conformity as a personality trait: there are the conformers and then there are the nonconformers. Whether the layman thinks of himself as a conformer or not may depend upon whom he is comparing himself to. If he is considering himself relative to those he considers beatniks, hippies, or bums, he is a staunch conformer—he is not, in his own eyes, one of those awful nonconformers who are likely to reject Mother, God, and Country all at once. However, if he is asked if he believes in "changes for the better" (whatever they are), he will suddenly assume that he is a brave nonconformer, unshackled by the inhibitions and fears of the old fogies. While we often are attracted by the idea of conformity as an enduring personality trait, we may be unwilling to accept it in ourselves.

A number of psychologists are interested in conformity as a personality trait, but complete discussion of this topic is beyond the scope of this book. We will limit ourselves to presenting two major pitfalls that one may encounter if he assumes that conformity is a personality trait.

The first pitfall has already been hinted at in our discussion of the layman's psychology of conformity. That is, by labeling people as "conformers" and "nonconformers" we may be encouraged to let value judgments intrude into our thinking. Take Mrs. Keech's group again. We have seen how Mrs. Keech convinced her followers of the outlandish flood prophecy—or if not convinced, got them to cooperate in her spiritual ventures. Why were these people willing to go along with such notions? One argument might be that these were "weak" persons who were influenced because of their acquiescent personalities. This hypothesis is not objective since it ignores the parallels between the behavior of Mrs. Keech's disciples and our own behavior (as when we copy the dress styles of our peers or the political opinions of our parents).

A second problem with the idea that conformity reflects an acquiescent or "conformer" personality is that this explanation is no explanation at all. All it really says is that conformers conform. But why do they conform? Do they conform in every situation? Obviously not, for some of Mrs. Keech's group left in disillusionment when the prophecy failed. The argument that these people were *more* prone to conformity than the rest of us, had more acquiescent or conforming personalities, is not very helpful either. For one thing, one could argue that the members of the prophecy group were *less* conformist than most of us, because they did not accept many of the beliefs that the rest of our society holds. That is, they did not conform to the majority idea of the pragmatic, realistic, "objective" American, who goes to a conventional church and would never accept such a fatalistic prophecy. Again we must ask, conformity to what? They were conforming to their group, but we conform to ours. For the long-range goal of finding out why people conform, labels are not profitable.

A Note on Group Pressure

We repeat our definition of conformity: conformity is a change in behavior or belief toward a group as a result of real or imagined group pressure. We have not yet discussed the phrase, "as a result of real or imagined group pressure." We have, however, emphasized that we are interested in changes that occur due to the group. Group pressure refers to the process by which the group seeks to impose its influence on the person. Group pressure is sometimes an explicit attempt by group members to impose standards on the person, but not always. All that is required is that the group expect the person to act or believe in a certain way, or that that person think such things are expected of him. The whole process by which group pressure is exerted is reserved for the next chapter, where we discuss the concept of group in more detail.

NOTES

1. Festinger, L., Riecken, H. W., and Schachter, S., *When Prophecy Fails*. Minneapolis: University of Minnesota Press, 1956.

2. Some psychologists (e.g. Hollander, E. P., and Willis, R. H., some current issues in the psychology of conformity and nonconformity, *Psychological Bulletin*, 1967, *68*, 62–76) call this "congruence conformity," as opposed to "movement conformity," which we have been discussing.

4
Social Determinants of Bystander
Intervention in Emergencies[1]

Bibb Latané and John M. Darley

Almost 100 years ago, Charles Darwin wrote: "As man is a social animal, it is almost certain that he would ... from an inherited tendency be willing to defend, in concert with others, his fellow-men; and be ready to aid them in any way, which did not too greatly interfere with his own welfare or his own strong desires" (*The Descent of Man*). Today, although

Reprinted by permission from *Altruism and Helping Behavior*, J. Macaulay and L. Berkowitz (eds.), New York: Academic Press, 1970.

many psychologists would quarrel with Darwin's assertion that altruism is inherited, most would agree that men will go to the aid of others even when there is no visible gain for themselves. At least, most would have agreed until a March night in 1964. That night, Kitty Genovese was set upon by a maniac as she returned home from work at 3:00 A.M. Thirty-eight of her neighbors in Kew Gardens came to their windows when she cried out in terror; but none came to her assistance, even though her stalker took over half an hour to murder her. No one even so much as called the police.

Since we started our research on bystander response to emergencies, we have heard about dozens of such incidents. We have also heard many explanations: "I would assign this to the effect of the megalopolis in which we live, which makes closeness very difficult and leads to the alienation of the individual from the group," contributed a psychoanalyst. "A disaster syndrome," explained a sociologist, "that shook the sense of safety and sureness of the individuals involved and caused psychological withdrawal from the event by ignoring it." "Apathy," others claim. "Indifference." "The gratification of unconscious sadistic impulses." "Lack of concern for our fellow men." "The Cold Society." These explanations and many more have been applied to the surprising failure of bystanders to intervene in emergencies—failures which suggest that we no longer care about the fate of our neighbors.

But can this be so? We think not. Although it is unquestionably true that the witnesses in the incidents above did nothing to save the victim, "apathy," "indifference," and "unconcern" are not entirely accurate descriptions of their reactions. The 38 witnesses of Kitty Genovese's murder did not merely look at the scene once and then ignore it. Instead they continued to stare out of their windows at what was going on. Caught, fascinated, distressed, unwilling to act but unable to turn away, their behavior was neither helpful nor heroic; but it was not indifferent or apathetic either.

Paradoxically, the key to understanding these failures of intervention may be found exactly in the fact that so surprises us about them: so many bystanders fail to intervene. If we think of 38, or 11, or 100 individuals, each looking at an emergency and callously deciding to pass by, we are horrified. But if we realize that each bystander is picking up cues about what is happening and how to react to it from the other bystanders, understanding begins to emerge. There are several ways in which a crowd of onlookers can make each individual member of that crowd less likely to act.

DEFINING THE SITUATION

Most emergencies are, or at least begin as, ambiguous events. A quarrel in the street may erupt into violence or it may be simply a family argument. A man staggering about may be suffering a coronary, or an onset of diabetes, or he simply may be drunk. Smoke pouring from a building may signal a fire, but on the other hand, it may be simply steam or air-conditioner vapor. Before a bystander is likely to take action in such ambiguous situations, he must first define the events as an emergency and decide that intervention is the proper course of action.

In the course of making these decisions, it is likely that an individual bystander will be considerably influenced by the decisions he perceives other bystanders to be taking. If everyone else in a group of onlookers seems to regard an event as nonserious and the proper course of action as nonintervention, this consensus may strongly affect the perceptions of any single individual and inhibit his potential intervention.

The definitions that other people held may be discovered by discussing the situation with them, but they may also be inferred from their facial expressions or behavior. A whistling man with his hands in his pockets obviously does not believe he is in the midst of a crisis. A bystander who does not respond to smoke obviously does not attribute it to fire. An individual, seeing the inaction of others, will judge the situation as less serious than he would if alone.

But why should the others be inactive? Probably because they are aware that other people are also watching them. The others are an audience to their own reactions. Among American males, it is considered desirable to appear poised and collected in times of stress. Being exposed to the public view may constrain the actions and expressions of emotion of any individual as he tries to avoid possible ridicule and embarrassment. Even though he may be truly concerned and upset about the plight of a victim, until he decides what to do, he may, maintain a calm demeanor.

If each member of a group is, at the same time, trying to appear calm and also looking around at the other members to gauge their reactions, all members may be led (or misled) by each other to define the situations as less critical than they would if alone. Until someone acts, each person sees only other nonresponding bystanders and is likely to be influenced not to act himself. A state of "pluralistic ignorance" may develop.

It has often been recognized that a crowd can cause contagion of panic, leading each person in the crowd to overreact to an emergency to the detriment of everyone's welfare. What we suggest here is that a crowd can also force inaction on its members. It can suggest by its passive behavior that an event is not to be reacted to as an emergency, and it can make any individual uncomfortably aware of what a fool he will look for behaving as if it is.

Where There's Smoke, There's (Sometimes) Fire[2]

In this experiment we presented an emergency to individuals either alone or in groups of three. It was our expectation that the constraints on behavior in public combined with social influence processes would lessen the likelihood that members of three-person groups would act to cope with the emergency.

College students were invited to an interview to discuss "some of the problems involved in life at an urban university." As they sat in a small room waiting to be called for the interview and filling out a preliminary questionnaire, they faced an ambiguous but potentially dangerous situation. A stream of smoke began to puff into the room through a wall vent.

Some subjects were exposed to this potentially critical situation while alone. In a second condition, three naive subjects were tested together. Since subjects arrived at slightly different times, and since they each had individual questionnaires to work on, they did not introduce themselves to each other or attempt anything but the most rudimentary conversation.

As soon as the subjects had completed two pages of their questionnaires, the experimenter began to introduce the smoke through a small vent in the wall. The "smoke," copied from the famous Camel cigarette sign in Times Square, formed a moderately fine-textured but clearly visible stream of whitish smoke. It continued to jet into the room in irregular puffs, and by the end of the experimental period, it obscured vision.

All behavior and conversation were observed and coded from behind a one-way window (largely disguised on the subject's side by a large sign giving preliminary instructions). When and if the subject left the experimental room and reported the smoke, he was told that the situation "would be taken care of." If the subject had not reported the smoke within 6 minutes from the time he first noticed it, the experiment was terminated.

The typical subject, when tested alone, behaved very reasonably. Usually, shortly after the smoke appeared, he would glance up from his questionnaire, notice the smoke, show a slight but distinct startle reaction, and then undergo a brief period of indecision, perhaps returning briefly to his questionnaire before again staring at the smoke. Soon, most subjects would get up from their chairs, walk over to the vent and investigate it closely, sniffing the smoke, waving their hands in it, feeling its temperature, etc. The usual Alone subject would hesitate again, but finally would walk out of the room, look around outside, and, finding somebody there, calmly report the presence of the smoke. No subject showed any sign of panic, most simply said: "There's something strange going on in there, there seems to be some sort of smoke coming through the wall. . . ." The median subject in the Alone condition had reported the smoke within 2 minutes of first noticing it. Three-quarters of the 24 people run in this condition reported the smoke before the experimental period was terminated.

Because there are three subjects present and available to report the smoke in the Three Naive Bystanders condition as compared to only one subject at a time in the Alone condition, a simple comparison between the two conditions is not appropriate. We cannot compare speeds in the Alone condition with the average speed of the three subjects in a group because, once one subject in a group had reported the smoke, the pressures on the other two disappeared. They could feel legitimately that the emergency had been handled and that any action on their part would be redundant and potentially confusing. Therefore, we used the speed of the first subject in a group to report the smoke as our dependent variable. However, since there were three times as many people available to respond in this condition as in the Alone condition, we would expect an increased likelihood that at least one person would report the smoke by chance alone. Therefore, we mathematically created "groups" of three scores from the Alone condition to serve as a baseline.[3]

In constrast to the complexity of this procedure, the results were quite simple. Subjects in the three-person-group condition were markedly inhibited from reporting the smoke. Since 75 percent of the Alone subjects reported the smoke, we would expect over 98 percent of the three-person groups to include at least one reporter. In fact, in only 38 percent of the eight groups in this condition did even one person report ($p < .01$). Of the 24 people run in these eight groups, only one person reported the smoke within the first 4 minutes before the room got noticeably unpleasant. Only three people reported the smoke within the entire experimental period. Social inhibition of reporting was so strong that the smoke was reported faster when only one person saw it than when groups of three were present ($p < .01$).

Subjects who had reported the smoke were relatively consistent in later describing their reactions to it. They thought the smoke looked somewhat "strange." They were not sure exactly what it was or whether it was dangerous, but they felt it was unusual enough to justify some examination. "I wasn't sure whether it was a fire, but it looked like something was wrong." "I thought it might be steam, but it seemed like a good idea to check it out."

Subjects who had not reported the smoke were also unsure about exactly what it was, but they uniformly said that they had rejected the idea that it was a fire. Instead, they hit upon an astonishing variety of alternative explanations, all sharing the common characteristic of interpreting the smoke as nondangerous event. Many thought the smoke was either steam or airconditioning vapors, several thought it was smog, purposely introduced to simulate an urban environment, and two actually suggested that the smoke was a "truth gas" filtered into the room to induce them to answer the questionnaire accurately! Predictably, some decided that "it must be some sort of experiment" and stoically endured the discomfort of the room rather than overreact.

The results of this study clearly support the prediction. Groups of three naive subjects were less likely to report the smoke than solitary bystanders. Our predictions were confirmed—but this does not necessarily mean that our explanation of these results is the correct one. As a matter of fact, several alternative explanations center around the fact that the smoke represented a possible danger to the subject himself as well as to others in the building. For instance, it is possible that the subjects in groups saw themselves as engaged in a game of "chicken" in which the first person to report would admit his cowardliness. Or it may have been that the presence of others made subjects feel safer, and thus reduced their need to report.

To rule out such explanations, a second experiment was designed to see whether similar group inhibition effects could be observed in situations where there is no danger to the individual himself for not acting. In this study, male Columbia University undergraduates waited either alone or with a stranger to participate in a market research study. As they waited they heard a woman fall and apparently injure herself in the room next door. Whether they tried to help and how long they took to do so were the main dependent variables of the study.

The Fallen Woman[4]

Subjects were telephoned and offered $2 to participate in a survey of game and puzzle preferences conducted at Columbia by the Consumer Testing Bureau (CTB), a market research organization. When they arrived, they were met at the door by an attractive young woman and taken to the testing room. On the way, they passed the CTB office, and through its open door they were able to see a desk and bookcase piled high with papers and filing cabinets. They entered the adjacent testing room which contained a table and chairs and a variety of games, and they were given questionnaires to fill out. The representative told subjects that she would be working next door in her office for about 10 minutes while they were completing the questionnaire and left by opening the collapsible curtain which divided the two rooms. She made sure that subjects were aware that the curtain was unlocked and easily opened and that it provided a means of entry to her office. The representative stayed in her office, shuffling papers, opening drawers, and making enough noise to remind the subjects of her presence. Four minutes after leaving the testing area, she turned on a high fidelity stereophonic tape recorder.

The Emergency

If the subject listened carefully, he heard the representative climb up on a chair to reach for a stack of papers on the bookcase. Even if he were not listening carefully, he heard a loud crash and a scream as the chair collapsed and she fell to the floor. "Oh, my God, my foot ... I ... I ... can't move ... it. Oh ... my ankle," the representative moaned. "I ... can't get this ... thing ... off me." She cried and moaned for about a minute longer, but the cries gradually got more subdued and controlled. Finally she muttered something about getting outside, knocked over the chair as she pulled herself up and thumped to the door, closing it behind her as she left. The entire incident took 130 seconds.

The main dependent variable of the study, of course, was whether the subjects took action to help the victim and how long it took them to do so. There were actually several modes of intervention possible: a subject could open the screen dividing the two rooms, leave the testing room and enter the CTB office by the door, find someone else, or most simply, call out to see if the representative needed help. In one condition, each subject was in the testing room alone while he filled out the questionnaire and heard the fall. In the second condition, strangers were placed in the testing room in pairs. Each subject in the pair was unacquainted with the other before entering the room and they were not introduced.

Across all experimental groups, the majority of subjects who intervened did so by pulling back the room divider and coming into the CTB office (61 percent). Few subjects came the round-about way through the door to offer their assistance (14 percent), and a surprisingly small number (24 percent) chose the easy solution of calling out to offer help. No one tried to find someone else to whom to report the accident.

Since 70 percent of Alone subjects intervened, we should expect that at least one person in 91 percent of all two-person groups would offer help if members of a pair had no influence upon each other. In fact, members did influence each other. In only 40 percent of the groups did even one person offer help to the injured woman. Only eight subjects of the 40 who were run in this condition intervened. This response rate is significantly below the hypothetical baseline ($p < .001$). Social inhibition of helping was so strong that the victim was actually helped more quickly when one person heard her distress than when two did ($p < .01$).

When we talked to subjects after the experiment, those who intervened usually claimed that they did so either because the fall sounded very serious or because they were uncertain what had occurred and felt they should investigate. Many talked about intervention as the "right thing to do" and asserted they would help again in any situation.

Many of the noninterveners also claimed that they were unsure what had happened (59 percent), but had decided that it was not too serious (46 percent). A number of subjects reported that they thought other people would or could help (25 percent), and three said they refrained out of concern for the victim—they did not want to embarrass her. Whether to accept these explanations as reasons or rationalizations is moot—they certainly do not explain the differences among conditions. The important thing to note is that noninterveners did not seem to feel that they had behaved callously or immorally. Their behavior was generally consistent with their interpretation of the situation. Subjects almost uniformly claimed that in a "real" emergency they would be among the first the help the victim.

These results strongly replicate the findings of the Smoke study. In both experiments, subjects were less likely to take action if they were in the presence of others than if they were alone. This congruence of findings from different experimental settings supports the validity and generality of the phenomenon; it also helps rule out a variety of alternative explanations suitable to either situation alone. For example, the possibility that smoke may have represented a threat to the subject's personal safety and that subjects in groups may have had a greater concern to appear "brave" than single subjects does not apply to the present experiment. In the present experiment, nonintervention cannot signify bravery. Comparison of the two experiments also suggests that the absolute number of nonresponsive bystanders may not be a critical factor in producing social inhibition of intervention; pairs of strangers in the present study inhibited each other as much as did trios in the former study.

Other studies we have done show that group inhibition effects hold in real life as well as in the laboratory, and for members of the general population as well as college students. The results of these experiments clearly support the line of theoretical argument advanced earlier. When bystanders to an emergency can see the reactions of other people, and when other people can see their own reactions, each individual may, through a process of social influence, be led to interpret the situation as less serious than he would if he were alone, and consequently be less likely to take action.

These studies, however, tell us little about the case that stimulated our interest in bystander intervention: the Kitty Genovese murder. Although the 38 witnesses to that event were aware, through seeing lights and silhouettes in other windows, that others watched, they could not see what others were doing and thus be influenced by their reactions. In the privacy of their own apartments, they could not be clearly seen by others, and thus inhibited by their presence. The social influence process we have described above could not operate. Nevertheless, we think that the presence of other bystanders may still have affected each individual's response.

DIFFUSION OF RESPONSIBILITY

In addition to affecting the interpretations that he places on a situation, the presence of other people can also alter the rewards and costs facing an individual bystander. Perhaps most importantly, the presence of other people can reduce the cost of not acting. If only one bystander is present at an emergency, he carries all of the responsibility for dealing with it, he will feel all of the guilt for not acting; he will bear all of any blame others may level for nonintervention. If others are present, the onus of responsibility is diffused, and the individual may be more likely to resolve his conflict between intervening and not intervening in favor of the latter alternative.

When only one bystander is present at an emergency, if help is to come it must be from him. Although he may choose to ignore them out of concern for his personal safety, or desire "not to get involved," any pressures to intervene focus uniquely on him. When there are several observers present, however, the pressures to intervene do not focus on any one of the observers; instead, the responsibility for intervention is shared among all the onlookers and is not unique to any one. As a result, each may be less likely to help.

Potential blame may also be diffused. However much we wish to think that an individual's moral behavior is divorced from considerations of personal punishment or reward, there is both theory and evidence to the contrary. It is perfectly reasonable to assume that under circumstances of group responsibility for a punishable act, the punishment or blame that accrues to any one individual is often slight or nonexistent.

Finally, if others are known to be present, but their behavior cannot be closely observed, any one bystander may assume that one of the other observers is already taking action to end the emergency. If so, his own intervention would only be redundant—perhaps harmfully or confusingly so. Thus, given the presence of other onlookers whose behavior cannot be observed, any given bystander can rationalize his own inaction by convincing himself that "somebody else must be doing something."

The considerations suggest that even when bystanders to an emergency cannot see or be influenced by each other, the more bystanders who are present, the less likely any one bystander would be to intervene and provide aid. To test this suggestion, it would be necessary to create an emergency situation in which each subject is blocked from communicating with others to prevent his getting information about their behavior during the emergency.

A Fit to be Tried[5]

A college student arrived in the laboratory, and was ushered into an individual room from which a communication system would enable him to talk to other participants (who were actually figments of the tape recorder). Over the intercom, the subject was told that the experimenter was concerned with the kinds of personal problems faced by normal college students in a high-pressure, urban environment, and that he would be asked to participate in a discussion about these problems. To avoid embarrassment about discussing personal problems with strangers, the experimenter said, several precautions would be taken. First, subjects would remain anonymous, which was why they had been placed in individual rooms rather than face-to-face. Second, the experimenter would not listen to the initial discussion himself, but would only get the subject's reactions later by questionnaire.

The plan for the discussion was that each person would talk in turn for 2 minutes, presenting his problems to the group. Next, each person in turn would comment on what others had said, and finally there would be a free discussion. A mechanical switching device regulated the discussion, switching on only one microphone at a time.

The Emergency

The discussion started with the future victim speaking first. He said he found it difficult to get adjusted to New York and to his studies. Very hesitantly and with obvious embarrassment, he mentioned that he was prone to seizures, particularly when studying hard or taking exams. The other people, including the one real subject, took their turns and discussed similar problems (minus the proneness to seizures). The naive subject talked last in the series, after the last prerecorded voice.

When it was again the victim's turn to talk, he made a few relatively calm comments, and then, growing increasingly loud and incoherent, he continued:

> I er I think I I need er if if could er er somebody er er er er er er er
> give me a little or give me a little help here because I er I'm er er h-h-
> having a a a a real problem er right now and I er if somebody could
> help me out it would er er s-s-sure be sure be good ... because er
> there er er a cause I er I uh I've got a a one of the er sie ... er er
> things coming on and and and I could really er use some help so if
> somebody would er give me a little h-help uh er-er-er-er-er c-could
> somebody er er help er uh uh uh (choking sounds. ... I'm gonna
> die er er I'm ... gonna die er help er er seizure (chokes, then quiet).

The major independent variable of the study was the number of people the subject believed also heard the fit. The subject was led to believe that the discussion group was one of three sizes: a two-person group consisting of himself and the victim; a three-person group consisting of himself, the victim and the other person; or a six-person group consisting of himself, the victim, and four other persons.

The major dependent variable of the experiment was the time elapsed from the start of the victim's seizure until the subject left his experimental cubicle. When the subject left his room, he saw the experimental assistant seated at the end of the hall, and invariably went to the assistant to report the seizure. If 5 minutes elapsed without the subject's having emerged from his room, the experiment was terminated.

Ninety-five percent of all the subjects who ever responded did so within the first half of the time available to them. No subject who had not reported within 3 minutes after the fit ever did so. This suggests that even had the experiment been allowed to run for a considerably longer period of time, few additional subjects would have responded.

Eighty-five percent of the subjects who thought they alone knew of the victim's plight reported the seizure before the victim was cut off; only 31 percent of those who thought four other bystanders were present did so. Everyone of the subjects in the two-person condition, but only 62 percent of the subjects in the six-person condition ever reported the emergency. To do a more detailed analysis of the results, each subject's time score was transformed into a "speed" score by taking the reciprocal of the response time in seconds and multiplying by 100. Analysis of variance of these speed scores indicates that the effect of group size was highly significant ($p < .01$), and all three groups differed significantly one from another ($p < .05$).

Subjects, whether or not they intervened, believed the fit to be genuine and serious. "My God, he's having a fit," many subjects said to themselves (and we overheard via their microphones). Others gasped or simply said, "Oh." Several of the male subjects swore. One subject said to herself, "It's just my kind of luck, something has to happen to me!" Several subjects spoke aloud of their confusion about what course of action to take: "Oh, God, what should I do?"

When those subjects who intervened stepped out of their rooms, they found the experimental assistant down the hall. With some uncertainty but without panic, they reported the situation. "Hey, I think Number 1 is very sick. He's having a fit or something." After ostensibly checking on the situation, the experimenter returned to report that "everything is under control." The subjects accepted these assurances with obvious relief.

Subjects who failed to report the emergency showed few signs of the apathy and indifference thought to characterize "unresponsive bystanders." When the experimenter entered her room to terminate the situation, the subject often asked if the victim was all right. "Is he being taken care of?" "He's all right, isn't he?" Many of these subjects showed physical signs of nervousness; they often had trembling hands and sweating palms. If anything, they seemed more emotionally aroused than did the subjects who reported the emergency.

Why, then, didn't they respond? It is not our impression that they had decided not to respond. Rather, they were still in a state of indecision and conflict concerning whether to respond or not. The emotional behavior of these nonresponding subjects was a sign of their continuing conflict, a conflict that other subjects resolved by responding.

The fit created a conflict situation of the avoidance-avoidance type. On the one hand, subjects worried about the guilt and shame they would feel if they did not help the person in distress. On the other hand, they were concerned not to make fools of themselves by overreacting, not to ruin the ongoing experiment by leaving their intercoms, and not to destroy the anonymous nature of the situation, which the experimenter had earlier stressed as important. For subjects in the two-person condition, the obvious distress of the victim and his need for help were so important that their conflict was easily resolved. For the subjects who knew that there were other bystanders present, the cost of not helping was reduced and the conflict they were in was more acute. Caught between the two negative alternatives of letting the victim continue to suffer or rushing, perhaps foolishly, to help, the nonresponding bystanders vacillated between them rather than choosing not to respond. This distinction may be academic for the victim, since he got no help in either case, but it is an extremely important one for understanding the causes of bystanders' failures to help.

Although subjects experienced stress and conflict during the emergency, their general reactions to it were highly positive. On a questionnaire administered after the experimenter had discussed the nature and purpose of the experiment, every single subject found the experiment either "interesting" or "very interesting" and was willing to participate in similar experiments in the future. All subjects felt that they understood what the experiment was all about and indicated that they thought the deceptions were necessary and justified. All but one felt they were better informed about the nature of psychological research in general.

CONCLUSION

We have suggested two distinct processes which might lead people to be less likely to intervene in an emergency if there are other people present than if they are alone. On the one hand, we suggested that the presence of other people may affect the interpretations each bystander puts on an ambiguous emergency situation. If other people are present at an emergency, each bystander will be guided by their apparent reactions in formulating his own impressions. Unfortunately, their apparent reactions may not be a good indication of their true feelings. It is possible for a state of "pluralistic ignorance" to develop, in which each bystander is led by the apparent lack of concern of the others to interpret the situation as being less serious than he would if alone. To the extent that he does not feel the situation is an emergency, he will be unlikely to take any helpful action.

Even if an individual does decide that an emergency is actually in process and that something ought to be done, he still is faced with the choice of whether he himself will intervene. Here again, the presence of other people may influence him—by reducing the costs associated with nonintervention. If a number of people witness the same event, the responsibility for action is diffused, and each may feel less necessity to help.

"There's safety in numbers," according to an old adage, and modern city dwellers seem to believe it. They shun deserted streets, empty subway cars, and lonely dark walks in dark parks, preferring instead to go where others are or to stay at home. When faced with stress, most individuals seem less afraid when they are in the presence of others than when they are alone.

A feeling so widely shared should have some basis in reality. Is there safety in number? If so, why? Two reasons are often suggested: individuals are less likely to find themselves in trouble if there are others about, and even if they do find themselves in trouble, others are likely to help them deal with it. While it is certainly true that a victim is unlikely to receive hlep if nobody knows of his plight, the experiments above cast doubt on the suggestion that he will be more likely to receive help if more people are present. In fact, the opposite seems to be true. A victim may be more likely to get help, or an emergency be reported, the fewer the people who are available to take action.

Although the results of these studies may shake our faith in "safety in numbers," they also may help us begin to understand a number of frightening incidents where crowds have heard but not answered a call for help. Newspapers have tagged these incidents with the label, "apathy." We have become indifferent, they say, callous to the fate of suffering of others. Our society has become "dehumanized" as it has become urbanized. These glib phrases may contain some truth, since startling cases such as the Genovese murder often seem to occur in our large cities, but such terms may also be misleading. Our studies suggest a different conclusion. They suggest that situational factors, specifically factors involving the immediate social environment, may be of greater importance in determining an individual's reaction to an emergency than such vague cultural or personality concepts as "apathy" or "alienation due to urbanization." They suggest that the failure to intervene may be better understood by knowing the relationship among bystanders rather than that between a bystander and the victim.

NOTES

1. The research reported in this paper was supported by National Science Foundation Grants GS1238, GS1239, GS2292, and GS2293, and was conducted at Columbia University and New York University.

2. A more complete account of this experiment is provided in Latané and Darley (1968). Keith Gerritz and Lee Ross provided thoughtful assistance in running the study.

3. The formula for calculating the expected proportion of groups in which at least one person will have acted by a given time is $1 - (1 - p)^n$ where p is the proportion of single individuals who acted by that time and n is the number of persons in the group.

4. This experiment is more fully described in Latané and Rodin (1969).

5. Further details of this experiment can be found in Darley and Latané (1968).

REFERENCES

Darley, J. M., and Latané, B. Bystander intervention in emergencies: Diffusion of responsibility, *J. Personality soc. Psychol*; 1968, *8*, 377–383.

Latané, B., and Darley, J. M. Group inhibition of bystander intervention. *J. Personality soc. Psychol*; 1968, *10*, 215–221.

Latané, B., and Rodin, J., A lady in distress: Inhibition effects of friends and strangers on bystander intervention. *J. exp. soc. Psychol.*, 1969, *5*, 189–202.

5
The Process of the Basic Encounter Group
Carl R. Rogers

I would like to share with you some of my thinking and puzzlement regarding a potent new cultural development—the intensive group experience.[1] It has, in my judgment, significant implications for our society. It has come very suddenly over our cultural horizon, since in anything like its present form it is less than two decades old.

I should like briefly to describe the many different forms and different labels under which the intensive group experience has become a part of our modern life. It has involved different kinds of individuals, and it has spawned various theories to account for its effects.

As to labels, the intensive group experience has at times been called the *T-group* or *lab group*, "T" standing for training laboratory in group dynamics. It has been termed *sensitivity training* in human relationships. The experience has sometimes been called a *basic encounter group* or a *workshop*—a workshop in human relationships, in leadership, in counseling, in education, in research, in psychotherapy. In dealing with one particular type of person— the drug addict—it has been called a *synanon*.

The intensive group experience has functioned in various settings. It has operated in industries, in universities, in church groups, and in resort settings which provide a retreat from everyday life. It has functioned in various educational institutions and in penitentiaries.

An astonishing range of individuals have been involved in these intensive group experiences. There have been groups for presidents of large corporations. There have been groups of delinquent and predelinquent adolescents. There have been groups composed of college students and faculty members, of counselors and psychotherapists, of school dropouts, of married couples, of confirmed drug addicts, of criminals serving sentences, of nurses preparing for hospital service, and of educators, principals, and teachers.

The geographical spread attained by this rapidly expanding movement has reached in this country from Bethel, Maine (starting point of the National Training Laboratory movement), to Idyllwild,

California. To my personal knowledge, such groups also exist in France, England, Holland, Japan, and Australia.

In their outward pattern these group experiences also show a great deal of diversity. There are T-groups and workshops which have extended over three to four weeks, meeting six to eight hours each day. There are some that have lasted only $2\frac{1}{2}$ days, crowding twenty or more hours of group sessions into this time. A recent innovation is the "marathon" weekend, which begins on Friday afternoon and ends on Sunday evening, with only a few hours out for sleep and snacks.

As to the conceptual underpinnings of this whole movement, one may almost select the theoretical flavor he prefers. Lewinian and client-centered theories have been most prominent, but gestalt therapy and various brands of psychoanalysis have all played contributing parts. The experience within the group may focus on specific training in human relations skills. It may be closely similar to group therapy, with much exploration of past experience and the dynamics of personal development. It may focus on creative expression through painting or expressive movement. It may be focused primarily upon a basic encounter and relationship between individuals.

Simply to describe the diversity which exists in this field raises very properly the question of why these various developments should be considered to belong together. Are there any threads of commonality which pervade all these widely divergent activities? To me it seems that they do belong together and can all be classed as focusing on the intensive group experience. They all have certain similar external characteristics. The group in almost every case is small (from eight to eighteen members), is relatively unstructured, and chooses its own goals and personal directions. The group experience usually, though not always, includes some cognitive input, some content material which is presented to the group. In almost all instances the leader's responsibility is primarily the facilitation of the expression of both feelings and thoughts on the part of the group members. Both in the leader and in the group members there is some focus on the process and the dynamics of the immediate personal interaction. These are, I think, some of the identifying characteristics which are rather easily recognized.

There are also certain practical hypotheses which tend to be held in common by all these groups. My own summary of these would be as follows: In an intensive group, with much freedom and little structure, the individual will gradually feel safe enough to drop some of his defenses and facades; he will relate more directly on a feeling basis (come into a basic encounter) with other members of the group; he will come to understand himself and his relationship to others more accurately; he will change in his personal attitudes and behavior; and he will subsequently relate more effectively to others in his everyday life situation. There are other hypotheses related more to the group than to the individual. One is that in this situation of minimal structure, the group will move from confusions, fractionation, and discontinuity to a climate of greater trust and coherence. These are some of the characteristics and hypotheses which, in my judgment, bind together this enormous cluster of activities which I wish to talk about as constituting the intensive group experience.

As for myself, I have been gradually moving into this field for the last twenty years. In experimenting with what I call *student-centered teaching*, involving the free expression of personal feelings, I came to recognize not only the cognitive learnings but also some of the personal changes which occurred. In brief intensive training courses for counselors for the Veterans Administration in 1946, during the postwar period, I and my staff focused more directly on providing an intensive group experience because of its impact in producing significant learning. In 1950, I served as leader of an intensive, full-time, one-week workshop, a postdoctoral training seminar in psychotherapy for the American Psychological Association. The impact of those six days was so great that for more than a dozen years afterward, I kept hearing from members of the group about the meaning it had had for them. Since that time I have been involved in more than forty ventures of what I would like to term—using the label most congenial to me—*basic encounter groups*. Most of these have involved for many of the members experiences of great intensity and considerable personal change. With two individuals, however, in these many groups, the experience contributed, I believe, to a psychotic break. A few other individuals have found the experience more unhelpful than helpful. So I have come to have a profound respect for the constructive potency of such group experiences and also a real concern over the fact that sometimes and in some ways this experience may do damage to individuals.

THE GROUP PROCESS

It is a matter of great interest to me to try to understand what appear to be common elements in the group process as I have come dimly to sense these. I am using this opportunity to think about this problem, not because I feel I have any final theory to give, but because I would like to formulate, as clearly as I am able, the elements which I can perceive at the present time. In doing so I am drawing upon my own experience, upon the experiences of others with whom I have worked, upon the written material in this field, upon the written reactions of many individuals who have participated in such groups, and to some extent upon the recordings of such group sessions, which we are beginning to tap and analyze. I am sure that (though I have tried to draw on the experience of others) any formulation I make at the present time is unduly influenced by my own experience in groups and thus is lacking in the generality I wish it might have.

As I consider the terribly complex interactions which arise during twenty, forty, sixty, or more hours of intensive sessions, I believe that I see some threads which weave in and out of the pattern. Some of these trends or tendencies are likely to appear early and some later in the group sessions, but there is no clear-cut sequence in which one ends and another begins. The interaction is best thought of, I believe, as a varied tapestry, differing from group to group, yet with certain patterns tending to precede and others to follow. Here are some of the process patterns which I see developing, briefly described in simple terms, illustrated from tape recordings and personal reports, and presented in roughly sequential order. I am not aiming at a high-level theory of group process but rather at a naturalistic observation out of which, I hope, true theory can be built.[2]

Milling Around

As the leader or facilitator makes clear at the outset that this is a group with unusual freedom, that it is not one for which he will take directional responsibility, there tends to develop a period of initial confusion, awkward silence, polite surface interaction, "cocktail-party talk," frustration, and great lack of continuity. The individuals come face-to-face with the fact that "there is no structure here except what we provide. We do not know our purposes; we do not even know one another, and we are committed to remain together over a considerable period of time." In this situation, confusion and frustration are natural. Particularly striking to the observer is the lack of continuity between personal expressions. Individual A will present some proposal or concern clearly looking for a response from the group. Individual B has obviously been waiting for his turn and starts off on some completely different tangent as though he had never heard A. One member makes a simple suggestion such as, "I think we should introduce ourselves," and this may lead to several hours of highly involved discussion in which the underlying issues appear to be, "Who is the leader?" "Who is responsible for us?" "Who is a member of the group?" "What is the purpose of the group?"

Resistance to Personal Expression or Exploration

During the milling period, some individuals are likely to reveal some rather personal attitudes. This tends to foster a very ambivalent reaction among other members of the group. One member, writing of his experience, says:

> There is a self which I present to the world and another one which I know more intimately. With others I try to appear able, knowing, unruffled, problem-free. To substantiate this image I will act in a way which at the time or later seems false or artificial or "not the real me." Or I will keep to myself thoughts which if expressed would reveal an imperfect me.
>
> My inner self, by contrast with the image I present to the world, is characterized by many doubts. The worth I attach to this inner self is subject to much fluctuation and is very dependent on how others are reacting to me. At times this private self can feel worthless.

It is the public self which members tend to reveal to one another, and only gradually, fearfully, and ambivalently do they take steps to reveal something of their inner world.

Early in one intensive workshop, the members were asked to write anonymously a statement of some feeling or feelings which they had which they were not willing to tell in the group. One man wrote:

> I don't relate easily to people. I have an almost impenetrable facade. Nothing gets in to hurt me, but nothing gets out. I have repressed so many emotions that I am close to emotional sterility. This situation doesn't make me happy, but I don't know what to do about it.

This individual is clearly living inside a private dungeon, but he does not even dare, except in this disguised fashion, to send out a call for help.

In a recent workshop when one man started to express the concern he felt about an impasse he was experiencing with his wife, another member stopped him, saying essentially:

> Are you sure you want to go on with this, or are you being seduced by the group into going further than you want to go? How do you know the group can be trusted? How will you feel about it when you go home and tell your wife what you have revealed, or when you decide to keep it from her? It just isn't safe to go further.

It seemed quite clear that in his warning, this second member was also expressing his own fear of revealing *him*self and *his* lack of trust in the group.

Description of Past Feelings

In spite of ambivalence about the trustworthiness of the group and the risk of exposing oneself, expression of feelings does begin to assume a larger proportion of the discussion. The executive tells how frustrated he feels by certain situations in his industry, or the housewife relates problems she has experienced with her children. A tape-recorded exchange involving a Roman Catholic nun occurs early in a one-week workshop, when the discussion has turned to a rather intellectualized consideration of anger:

> Bill: What happens when you get mad, Sister, or don't you?
>
> Sister: Yes, I do—yes I do. And I find when I get mad, I, I almost get, well, the kind of person that antagonizes me is the person who seems so unfeeling toward people—now I take our dean as a person in point because she is a very aggressive woman and has certain ideas about what the various rules in a college should be; and this woman can just send me into high "G"; in an angry mood. I *mean this*. But then I find, I. . . .
>
> Facil.:[3] But what, what do you do?
>
> Sister: I find that when I'm in a situation like this, that I strike out in a very sharp, uh, *tone*, or else I just refuse to respond—"All right, this happens to be her way"—I don't think I've ever gone into a tantrum.
>
> Joe: You just withdraw—no use to fight it.
>
> Facil.: You say you use a sharp tone. To *her*, or to other people you're dealing with?
>
> Sister: Oh, no. To *her*.

This is a typical example of a *description* of feelings which are obviously current in her in a sense but which she is placing in the past and which she describes as being outside the group in time and place. It is an example of feelings existing "there and then."

Expression of Negative Feelings

Curiously enough, the first expression of genuinely significant "here-and-now" feeling is apt to come out in negative attitudes toward other group members or toward the group leader. In one group in which members introduced themselves at some length, one woman refused, saying that she preferred to be known for what she was in the group and not in terms of her status outside. Very shortly after this, one of the men in the group attacked her vigorously and angrily for this stand, accusing her of failing to cooperate, of keeping herself aloof from the group, and so forth. It was the first *personal current feeling* which had been brought into the open in the group.

Frequently the leader is attacked for his failure to give proper guidance to the group. One vivid example of this comes from a recorded account of an early session with a group of delinquents, where one member shouts at the leader (Gordon, 1955, p. 214):

> You will be licked if you don't control us right at the start. You have to keep order here because you are older than us. That's what a teacher is supposed to do. If he doesn't do it we will cause a lot of trouble and won't get anything done. [Then, referring to two boys in the group who were scuffling, he continues.] Throw 'em out, throw 'em out! You've just *got* to make us behave!

An adult expresses his disgust at the people who talk too much, but points his irritation at the leader (Gordon, 1955, p. 210):

> It is just that I don't understand why someone doesn't shut them up. I would have taken Gerald and shoved him out the window. I'm an authoritarian. I would have told him he was talking too much and he had to leave the room. I think the group discussion ought to be led by a person who simply will not recognize these people after they have interrupted about eight times.

Why are negatively toned expressions the first current feelings to be expressed? Some speculative answers might be the following: This is one of the best ways to test the freedom and trustworthiness of the group.

"Is it really a place where I can be and express myself positively and negatively? Is this really a safe place, or will I be punished?" Another quite different reason is that deeply positive feelings are much more difficult and dangerous to express than negative ones. "If I say, 'I love you,' I am vulnerable and open to the most awful rejection. If I say, 'I hate you,' I am at best liable to attack, against which I can defend." Whatever the reasons, such negatively toned feelings tend to be the first here-and-now material to appear.

Expression and Exploration of Personally Meaningful Material

It may seem puzzling that following such negative experiences as the initial confusion, the resistance to personal expression, the focus on outside events, and the voicing of critical or angry feelings, the event most likely to occur next is for an individual to reveal himself to the group in a significant way. The reason for this no doubt is that the individual member has come to realize that this is in part *his group*. He can help to make of it what he wishes. He has also experienced the fact that negative feelings have been expressed and have usually been accepted or assimilated without any catastrophic results. He realizes there is freedom here, albeit a risky freedom. A climate of trust (Gibb, 1964, Ch. 10) is beginning to develop. So he begins to take the chance and the gamble of letting the group know some deeper facet of himself. One man tells of the trap in which he finds himself, feeling that communication between himself and his wife is hopeless. A priest tells of the anger which he has bottled up because of unreasonable treatment by one of his superiors. What should he have done? What might he do now? A scientist at the head of a large research department finds the courage to speak of his painful isolation, to tell the group that he has never had a single friend in his life. By the time he finishes telling of his situation, he is letting loose some of the tears of sorrow for himself which I am sure he has held in for many years. A psychiatrist tells of the guilt he feels because of the suicide of one of his patients. A woman of forty tells of her absolute inability to free herself from the grip of her controlling mother. A process which one workshop member has called a "journey to the center of self," often a very painful process, has begun.

Such exploration is not always an easy process, nor is the whole group always receptive to such self-revelation. In a group of institutionalized adolescents, all of whom had been in difficulty of one sort or another, one boy revealed an important fact about himself and immediately received both acceptance and sharp nonacceptance from members of the group:

> George: This is the thing. I've got too many problems at home—uhm, I think some of you know why I'm here, what I was charged with.
>
> Mary: I don't.
>
> Facil.: Do you want to tell us?
>
> George: Well, uh, it's sort of embarrassing.
>
> Carol: Come on, it won't be so bad.
>
> George: Well, I raped my sister. That's the only problem I have at home, and I've overcome that, I think. (*Rather long pause.*)
>
> Freda: Oooh, that *weird*!
>
> Mary: People have problems, Freda, I mean ya know....
>
> Freda: Yeah, I know, but *yeOUW*! ! !
>
> Facil. (*to Freda*): You know about these problems, but they still are weird to you.
>
> George: You see what I mean; it's embarrassing to talk about it.
>
> Mary: Yeah, but it's O.K.
>
> George: It *hurts* to talk about it, but I know I've got to so I won't be guilt-ridden for the rest of my life.

Clearly Freda is completely shutting him out psychologically, while Mary in particular is showing a deep acceptance.

The Expression of Immediate Interpersonal Feelings in the Group

Entering into the process sometimes earlier, sometimes later, is the explicit bringing into the open of the feelings experienced in the immediate moment by one member about another. These are sometimes positive and sometimes negative. Examples would be: "I feel threatened by your silence." "You remind me of my mother, with whom I had a tough time." "I took an instant dislike to you the first moment I saw you." "To me you're like a breath of fresh air in the group." "I like your warmth and your smile." "I dislike you more every time you speak up." Each of these attitudes can be, and usually is, explored in the increasing climate of trust.

The Developing of a Healing Capacity in the Group

One of the most fascinating aspects of any intensive group experience is the manner in which a number of the group members show a natural and spontaneous capacity for dealing in a helpful, facilitative, and therapeutic fashion with the pain and suffering of others. As one rather extreme example of this, I think of a man in charge of maintenance in a large plant who was one of the low-status members of an industrial executive group. As he informed us, he had not been "contaminated by education." In the initial phases the group tended to look down on him. As members delved more deeply into themselves and began to express their own attitudes more fully, this man came forth as, without doubt, the most sensitive member of the group. He knew intuitively how to be understanding and acceptant. He was alert to things which had not yet been expressed but which were just below the surface. When the rest of us were paying attention to a member who was speaking, he would frequently spot another individual who was suffering silently and in need of help. He had a deeply perceptive and facilitating attitude. This kind of ability shows up so commonly in groups that it has led me to feel that the ability to be healing or therapeutic is far more common in human life than we might suppose. Often it needs only the permission granted by a freely flowing group experience to become evident.

In a characteristic instance, the leader and several group members were trying to be of help to Joe, who was telling of the almost complete lack of communication between himself and his wife. In varied ways members endeavored to give help. John kept putting before Joe the feelings Joe's wife was almost certainly experiencing. The facilitator kept challenging Joe's facade of "carefulness." Marie tried to help him discover what he was feeling at the moment. Fred showed him the choice he had of alternative behaviors. All this was clearly done in a spirit of caring, as is even more evident in the recording itself. No miracles were achieved, but toward the end Joe did come to the realization that the only thing that might help would be to express his real feelings to his wife.

Self-acceptance and the Beginning of Change

Many people feel that self-acceptance must stand in the way of change. Actually, in these group experiences, as in psychotherapy, it is the *beginning* of change. Some examples of the kind of attitudes expressed would be these: "I *am* a dominating person who likes to control others. I do want to mold these individuals into the proper shape." Another person says, "I really have a hurt and overburdened little boy inside of me who feels very sorry for himself. I am that little boy, in addition to being a competent and responsible manager."

I think of one governmental executive in a group in which I participated, a man with high responsibility and excellent technical training as an engineer. At the first meeting of the group he impressed me, and I think others, as being cold, aloof, somewhat bitter, resentful, and cynical. When he spoke of how he ran his office it appeared that he administered it "by the book," without any warmth or human feeling entering in. In one of the early sessions when he spoke of his wife, a group member asked him, "Do you love your wife?" He paused for a long time, and the questioner said, "OK, that's answer enough." The executive said, "No. Wait a minute. The reason I didn't respond was that I was wondering if I ever loved anyone. I don't think I *ever* really *loved* anyone." It seemed quite dramatically clear to those of us in the group that he had come to accept himself as an unloving person.

A few days later he listened with great intensity as one member of the group expressed profound personal feelings of isolation, loneliness, and pain, revealing the extent to which he had been living behind a mask, a facade. The next morning the engineer said, "Last night I thought and thought about what Bill told us. I even wept quite a bit by myself. I can't remember how long it has been since I have cried, and I really *felt* something. I think perhaps what I felt was love."

It is not surprising that before the week was over, he had thought through new ways of handling his growing son, on whom he had been placing extremely rigorous demands. He had also begun genuinely to appreciate the love which his wife had extended to him and which he now felt he could in some measure reciprocate.

In another group one man kept a diary of his reactions. Here is his account of an experience in which he came really to accept his almost abject desire for love, a self-acceptance which marked the beginning of a very significant experience of change. He says (Hall, 1965):

During the break between the third and fourth sessions, I felt very droopy and tired. I had it in mind to take a nap, but instead I was almost compulsively going around to people starting a conversation. I had a begging kind of a feeling, like a very cowed little puppy hoping that he'll be patted but half afraid he'll be kicked. Finally, back in my room I lay down and began to know that I was sad. Several times I found myself wishing my roommate would come in and talk to me. Or, whenever someone walked by the door, I would come to attention inside, the way a dog pricks up his ears; and I would feel an immediate wish for that person to come in and talk to me. I realized my raw wish to receive kindness.

Another recorded excerpt, from an adolescent group, shows a combination of self-acceptance and self-exploration. Art had been talking about his "shell," and here he is beginning to work with the problem of accepting himself, and also the facade he ordinarily exhibits:

Art: I'm so darn used to living with the shell; it doesn't even bother me. I don't even know the real me. I think I've uh, well, I've pushed the shell more away here. When I'm out of my shell—only twice—once just a few minutes ago—I'm really me, I guess. But then I just sort of pull in the [latch] cord after me when I'm in my shell, and that's almost all the time. And I leave the [false] front standing outside when I'm back in the shell.

Facil.: And nobody's back in there with you?

Art (*crying*): Nobody else is in there with me, just me. I just pull everything into the shell and roll the shell up and shove it in my pocket. I take the shell, and the real me, and put it in my pocket where it's safe. I guess that's really the way I do it—I go into my shell and turn off the real world. And here: that's what I want to do here in this group, ya know, come out of my shell and actually throw it away.

Lois: You're making progress already. At least you can talk about it.

Facil.: Yeah. The thing that's going to be hardest is to stay out of the shell.

Art (*still crying*): Well, yeah, if I can keep talking about it, I can come out and stay out, but I'm gonna have to, ya know, protect me. It hurts; it's actually hurting to talk about it.

Still another person reporting shortly after his workshop experience said, "I came away from the workshop feeling much more deeply that 'It is all right to be me with all my strengths and weaknesses.' My wife has told me that I appear to be more authentic, more real, more genuine."

This feeling of greater realness and authenticity is a very common experience. It would appear that the individual is learning to accept and to *be* himself, and this is laying the foundation for change. He is closer to his own feelings, and hence they are no longer so rigidly organized and are more open to change.

The Cracking of Facades

As the sessions continue, so many things tend to occur together that it is difficult to know which to describe first. It should again be stressed that these different threads and stages interweave and overlap. One of these threads is the increasing impatience with defenses. As time goes on, the group finds it unbearable that any member should live behind a mask or a front. The polite words, the intellectual understanding of one another and of relationships, the smooth coin of tact and cover-up—amply satisfactory for interactions outside—are just not good enough. The expression of self by some members of the group has made it very clear that a deeper and more basic encounter is *possible*, and the group appears to strive, intuitively and unconsciously, toward this goal. Gently at times, almost savagely at others, the group *demands* that the individual be himself, that his current feelings not be hidden, that he remove the mask of ordinary social intercourse. In one group there was a highly intelligent and quite academic man who had been rather perceptive in his understanding of others but who had not revealed himself at all. The attitude of the group was finally expressed sharply by one member when he said, "Come out from behind that lectern, Doc. Stop giving us speeches. Take off your dark glasses. We want to know *you*."

In Synanon, the fascinating group so successfully involved in making persons out of drug addicts, this ripping away of facades is often very drastic. An excerpt from one of the "synanons," or group sessions, makes this clear (Casriel, 1963, p. 81):

> Joe (*speaking to Gina*): I wonder when you're going to stop sounding so good in synanons. Every synanon that I'm in with you, someone asks you a question, and you've got a beautiful book written. All made out about what went down and how you were wrong and how you realized you were wrong and all that kind of bullshit. When are you going to stop doing that? How do you feel about Art?
>
> Gina: I have nothing against Art.
>
> Will: You're a nut. Art hasn't got any damn sense. He's been in there, yelling at you and Moe, and you've got everything so cool.

Gina: No, I feel he's very insecure in a lot of ways but that has noth-
　　　ing to do with me. . . .
Joe: You act like you're so goddamn understanding.
Gina: I was *told* to act as if I understand.
Joe: Well, you're in a synanon now. You're not supposed to be acting
　　　like you're such a goddamn healthy person. Are you so well?
Gina: No.
Joe: Well why the hell don't you quit acting as if you were.

If I am indicating that the group at times is quite violent in tearing
down a facade or a defense, this would be accurate. On the other hand, it
can also be sensitive and gentle. The man who was accused of hiding
behind a lectern was deeply hurt by this attack, and over the lunch hour
looked very troubled, as though he might break into tears at any moment.
When the group reconvened, the members sensed this and treated him
very gently, enabling him to tell us his own tragic personal story, which
accounted for his aloofness and his intellectual and academic approach to
life.

The Individual Receives Feedback

In the process of this freely expressive interaction, the individual rapidly
acquires a great deal of data as to how he appears to others. The "hail-
fellow-well-met" discovers that others resent his exaggerated friendliness. The executive who weighs his words carefully and speaks with
heavy precision may find that others regard him as stuffy. A woman who
shows a somewhat excessive desire to be of help to others is told in no
uncertain terms that some group members do not want her for a mother.
All this can be decidedly upsetting, but as long as these various bits of
information are fed back in the context of caring which is developing in
the group, they seem highly constructive.

Feedback can at times be very warm and positive, as the following
recorded excerpt indicates:

Leo (*very softly and gently*): I've been struck with this ever since she
　　　talked about her waking in the night, that she has a very delicate
　　　sensitivity. (*Turning to Mary and speaking almost caressingly.*)
　　　And somehow I perceive—even looking at you or in your eyes
　　　—a very—almost like a gentle touch and from this gentle touch
　　　you can tell many—things—you sense in—this manner.
Fred: Leo, when you said that, that she has this kind of delicate

sensitivity, I just felt, *Lord yes!* Look at her eyes.
Leo: M-hm.

A much more extended instance of negative and positive feedback, triggering a significant new experience of self-understanding and encounter with the group, is taken from the diary of the young man mentioned before. He had been telling the group that he had no feeling for them, and felt they had no feeling for him (Hall, 1965):

Then, a girl lost patience with me and said she didn't feel she could give any more. She said I looked like a bottomless well, and she wondered how many times I had to be told that I *was* cared for. By this time I was feeling panicky, and I was saying to myself, "My God, can it be true that I can't be satisfied and that I'm somehow compelled to pester people for attention until I drive them away!" At this point while I was really worried, a nun in the group spoke up. She said that I had not alienated her with some negative things I had said to her. She said she liked me, and she couldn't understand why I couldn't see that. She said she felt concerned for me and wanted to help me. With that, something began to really dawn on me, and I voiced it somewhat like the following. "You mean you are all sitting there, feeling for me what I say I want you to feel, and that somewhere down inside me I'm stopping it from touching me?" I relaxed appreciably and began really to wonder why I had shut their caring out so much. I couldn't find the answer, and one woman said: "It looks like you are trying to stay continuously as deep in your feelings as you were this afternoon. It would make sense to me for you to draw back and assimilate it. Maybe if you don't push so hard, you can rest awhile and then move back into your feelings more naturally."
Her making the last suggestion really took effect. I saw the sense in it, and almost immediately I settled back very relaxed with something of a feeling of a bright, warm day dawning inside me. In addition to taking the pressure off of myself, however, I was for the first time really warmed by the friendly feelings which I felt they had for me. It is difficult to say why I felt liked only just then, but, as opposed to the earlier sessions, I really *believed* they cared for me. I never have fully understood why I stood their affection off for so long, but at that point I almost abruptly began to trust that they did care. The measure of the effectiveness of this change lies in what I said next.

I said, "Well, that really takes care of me. I'm really ready to listen to someone else now." I *meant* that, too.

Confrontation

There are times when the term "feedback" is far too mild to describe the interactions which take place, when it is better said that one individual *confronts* another, directly "leveling" with him. Such confrontations can be positive, but frequently they are decidedly negative, as the following example will make abundantly clear. In one of the last sessions of a group, Alice had made some quite vulgar and contemptuous remarks to John, who was entering religious work. The next morning, Norma, who had been a very quiet person in the group, took the floor:

> Norma (*loud sigh*): Well, I don't have *any* respect for you, Alice. *None*! (*Pause*.) There's about a hundred things going through my mind I want to say to you, and by God I hope I get through 'em all! First of all, if you wanted us to respect you, then why couldn't you respect *John's* feelings last night? Why have you been on him today? Hmm? Last night—couldn't you—couldn't you accept—*couldn't you* comprehend in any way at all that—that *he felt* his unworthiness in the service of God? Couldn't you accept this, or did you have to dig into it today to find something *else there*? And his respect for womanhood—he *loves* women—yes, he does, because he's a real person, but you—you're not a real woman—to me—and thank God, you're not my mother! ! ! ! I want to come over and beat the hell out of you ! ! ! I want to slap you across the mouth so hard and—oh, and you're so, you're many years above me—and I respect age, and I respect people who are older than me, *but I don't respect you, Alice. At all*! And I was so *hurt* and *confused* because you were making someone else feel *hurt* and *confused*. . . .

It may relieve the reader to know that these two women came to accept each other, not completely, but much more understandingly, before the end of the session. But this *was* a confrontation!

The Helping Relationship outside the Group Sessions

No account of the group process would, in my experience, be adequate if it did not make mention of the many ways in which group members are of assistance to one another. Not infrequently, one member of a group will spend hours listening and talking to another member who is undergoing a painful new perception of himself. Sometimes it is merely the offering of help which is therapeutic. I think of one man who was going through a very depressed period after having told us of the many tragedies in his life. He seemed quite clearly, from his remarks, to be contemplating suicide. I jotted down my room number (we were staying at a hotel) and told him to put it in his pocket and to call me anytime of day or night if he felt that it would help. He never called, but six months after the workshop was over he wrote to me telling me how much that act had meant to him and that he still had the slip of paper to remind him of it.

Let me give an example of the healing effect of the attitudes of group members both outside and inside the group meetings. This is taken from a letter written by a workshop member to the group one month after the group sessions. He speaks of the difficulties and depressing circumstances he has encountered during that month and adds:

> I have come to the conclusion that my experiences with you have profoundly affected me. I am truly grateful. This is different than personal therapy. None of you *had* to care about me. None of you had to seek me out and let me know of things you thought would help me. None of you had to let me know I was of help to you. Yet you did, and as a result it has far more meaning than anything I have so far experienced. When I feel the need to hold back and not live spontaneously, for whatever reasons, I remember that twelve persons, just like those before me now, said to let go and be congruent, to be myself, and, of all unbelievable things, they even loved me more for it. This has given me the *courage* to come out of myself many times since then. Often it seems my very doing of this helps the others to experience similar freedom.

The Basic Encounter

Running through some of the trends I have just been describing is the fact that individuals come into much closer and more direct contact with one another than is customary in ordinary life. This appears to be one of the most central, intense, and change-producing aspects of such a group experience. To illustrate what I mean, I would like to draw an example from a recent workshop group. A man tells through his tears, of the very tragic loss of his child, a grief which he is experiencing *fully*, for the first time, not holding back his feelings in any way. Another says to him, also with tears in his eyes, "I've never felt so close to another human being. I've never before felt a real physical hurt in me from the pain of another. I feel *completely* with you." This is a basic encounter.

Such I-Thou relationships (to use Buber's term) occur with some frequency in these group sessions and nearly always bring a moistness to the eyes of the participants.

One member, trying to sort out his experiences immediately after a workshop, speaks of the "commitment to relationship" which often developed on the part of two individuals, not necessarily individuals who had liked each other initially. He goes on to say:

> The incredible fact experienced over and over by members of the group was that when a negative feeling was fully expressed to another, the relationship grew and the negative feeling was replaced by a deep acceptance for the other.... Thus real change seemed to occur when feelings were experienced and expressed in the context of the relationship. "I can't *stand* the way you talk!" turned in to a real understanding and affection for you the *way* you talk.

This statement seems to capture some of the more complex meanings of the term "basic encounter."

The Expression of Positive Feelings and Closeness

As indicated in the last section, an inevitable part of the group process seems to be that when feelings are expressed and can be accepted in a relationship, a great deal of closeness and positive feelings result. Thus as the sessions proceed, there is an increasing feeling of warmth and group spirit and trust built, not out of positive attitudes only, but out of a realness which includes both positive and negative feeling. One member tried to capture this in writing very shortly after the workshop by saying that if he were trying to sum it up, "... it would have to do with what I call confirmation—a kind of confirmation of myself, of the uniqueness and universal qualities of men, a confirmation that when we can be human together something positive can emerge."

A particularly poignant expression of these positive attitudes was shown in the group where Norma confronted Alice with her bitterly angry feelings. Joan, the facilitator, was deeply upset and began to weep. The positive and healing attitudes of the group, for their own *leader*, are an unusual example of the closeness and personal quality of the relationships.

Joan (*crying*): I somehow feel that it's so *damned* easy for me to—to put myself *inside* of another person and I just guess I can feel that—for John and Alice and for you, Norma.

Alice: And it's *you* that's hurt.

Joan: Maybe I am taking some of that hurt. I guess I am. (*crying*.)

Alice: That's a wonderful gift. I wish I had it.

Joan: You have a lot of it.

Peter: In a way you bear the—I guess in a special way, because you're the—facilitator, ah, you've probably borne, ah, an extra heavy burden for all of us—and the burden that you, perhaps, you bear the heaviest is—we ask you—we ask one another; we grope to try to accept one another as we are, and—for each of us in various ways I guess we reach things and we say, *please* accept me. . . .

Some may be very critical of a "leader" so involved and so sensitive that she weeps at the tensions in the group which she has taken into herself. For me, it is simply another evidence that when people are real with each other, they have an astonishing ability to heal a person with a real and understanding love, whether that person is "participant" or "leader."

Behavior Changes in the Group

It would seem from observation that many changes in behavior occur in the group itself. Gestures change. The tone of voice changes, becoming sometimes stronger, sometimes softer, usually more spontaneous, less artificial, more feelingful. Individuals show an astonishing amount of thoughtfulness and helpfulness toward one another.

Our major concern, however, is with the behavior changes which occur following the group experience. It is this which constitutes the most significant question and on which we need much more study and research. One person gives a catalog of the changes which he sees in himself which may seem too "pat" but which is echoed in many other statements:

I am more open, spontaneous. I express myself more freely. I am more sympathetic, empathic, and tolerant. I am more confident. I am more religious in my own way. My relations with my family, friends, and coworkers are more honest, and I express my likes and dislikes and true feelings more openly. I admit ignorance more readily. I am more cheerful. I want to help others more.

Another says:

Since the workshop there has been a new relationship with my parents. It has been trying and hard. However, I have found a greater freedom in talking with them, especially my father. Steps have been made toward being closer to my mother than I have ever been in the last five years.

Another says:

It helped clarify my feelings about my work, gave me more enthusiasm for it, and made me more honest and cheerful with my coworkers and also more open when I was hostile. It made my relationship with my wife more open, deeper. We felt freer to talk about anything, and we felt confident that anything we talked about we could work through.

Sometimes the changes which are described are very subtle. "The primary change is the more positive view of my ability to allow myself to *hear*, and to become involved with someone else's 'silent scream.'"

At the risk of making the outcomes sound too good, I will add one more statement written shortly after a workshop by a mother. She says:

The immediate impact on my children was of interest to both me and my husband. I feel that having been so accepted and loved by a group of strangers was so supportive that when I returned home my love for the people closest to me was much more spontaneous. Also, the practice I had in accepting and loving others during the workshop was evident in my relationships with my close friends.

DISADVANTAGES AND RISKS

Thus far one might think that every aspect of the group process was positive. As far as the evidence at hand indicates, it appears that it nearly always is a positive process for a majority of the participants. There are, nevertheless, failures which result. Let me try to describe briefly some of the negative aspects of the group processes as they sometimes occur.

The most obvious deficiency of the intensive group experience is that frequently the behavior changes, if any, which occur, are not lasting. This is often recognized by the participants. One says, "I wish I had the ability to hold permanently the 'openness' I left the conference with." Another says, "I experienced a lot of acceptance, warmth, and love at the workshop. I find it hard to carry the ability to share this in the same way with people outside the workshop. I find it easier to slip back into my old unemotional role than to do the work necessary to open relationships."

Sometimes group members experience this phenomenon of "relapse" quite philosophically:

> The group experience is not a way of life but a reference point. My images of our group, even though I am unsure of some of their meanings, give me a comforting and useful perspective on my normal routine. They are like a mountain which I have climbed and enjoyed and to which I hope occasionally to return.

Some Data on Outcomes

What is the extent of this "slippage"? In the past year, I have administered follow-up questionnaires to 481 individuals who have been in groups I have organized or conducted. The information has been obtained from two to twelve months following the group experience, but the greatest number were followed up after a three- to six-month period.[4] Of these individuals, two (i.e., less than one-half of 1 percent) felt it had changed their behavior in ways they did not like. Fourteen percent felt the experience had made no perceptible change in their behavior. Another fourteen percent felt that it had changed their behavior but that this change had disappeared or left only a small residual positive effect. Fifty-seven percent felt it had made some negative changes along with the positive.

A second potential risk involved in the intensive group experience and one which is often mentioned in public discussion is the risk that the individual may become deeply involved in revealing himself and then be left with problems which are not worked through. There have been a number of reports of people who have felt, following an intensive group experience, that they must go to a therapist to work through the feelings which were opened up in the intensive experience of the workshop and which were left unresolved. It is obvious that, without knowing more about each individual situation, it is difficult to say whether this was a negative outcome or a partially or entirely positive one. There are also very occasional accounts, and I can testify to two in my own experience, where an individual has had a psychotic episode during or immediately following an intensive group experience. On the other side of the picture is the fact that individuals have also lived through what were clearly psychotic episodes, and lived through them very constructively, in the context of a basic encounter group. My own tentative clinical judgment would be that the more positively the group process has been proceeding, the less likely it is that any individual would be psychologically damaged through membership in the group. It is obvious, however, that this is a serious issue and that much more needs to be known.

Some of the tension which exists in workshop members as a result of this potential for damage was very well described by one member when he said, "I feel the workshop had some very precious moments for me when I felt very close indeed to particular persons. It had some frightening moments when its potency was very evident and I realized a particular person might be deeply hurt or greatly helped but I could not predict which."

Out of the 481 participants followed up by questionnaires, two felt that the overall impact of their intensive group experience was "mostly damaging." Six more said that it had been "more unhelpful than helpful." Twenty-one, or 4 percent, stated that it had been "mostly frustrating, annoying, or confusing." Three and one-half percent said that it had been neutral in its impact. Nineteen percent checked that it had been "more helpful than unhelpful," indicating some degree of ambivalence. But 30 percent saw it as "constructive in its results," and 45 percent checked it as a "deeply meaningful, positive experience."[5] Thus for three-fourths of the group, it was *very* helpful. These figures should help to set the problem in perspective. It is obviously a very serious matter if an intensive group experience is psychologically damaging to *anyone*. It seems clear, however, that such damage occurs only rarely, if we are to judge by the reaction of the participants.

Other Hazards of the Group Experience

There is another risk or deficiency in the basic encounter group. Until very recent years it has been unusual for a workshop to include both husband and wife. This can be a real problem if significant change has taken place in one spouse during or as a result of the workshop experience. One individual felt this risk clearly after attending a workshop.

He said, "I think there is a great danger to a marriage when one spouse attends a group. It is too hard for the other spouse to compete with the group individually and collectively." One of the frequent aftereffects of the intensive group experience is that it brings out into the open for discussion marital tensions which have been kept under cover.

Another risk which has sometimes been a cause of real concern in mixed intensive workshops is that very positive, warm, and loving feelings can develop between members of the encounter group, as has been evident from some of the preceding examples. Inevitably some of these feelings have a sexual component, and this can be a matter of great concern to the participants and a profound threat to their spouses if these feelings are not worked through satisfactorily in the workshop. Also the close and loving feelings which develop may become a source of threat and marital difficulty when a wife, for example, has not been present, but projects many fears about the loss of her spouse—whether well founded or not—onto the workshop experience.

A man who had been in a mixed group of men and women executives wrote to me a year later and mentioned the strain in his marriage which resulted from his association with Marge, a member of his basic encounter group:

> There was a problem about Marge. There had occurred a very warm feeling on my part for Marge, and great compassion, for I felt she was *very* lonely. I believe the warmth was sincerely reciprocal. At any rate she wrote me a long affectionate letter, which I let my wife read. I was *proud* that Marge could feel that way about *me*, [Because he had felt very worthless.] But my wife was alarmed, because she read a love affair into the words—at least a potential threat. I stopped writing to Marge, because I felt rather clandestine after that.
> My wife has since participated in an "encounter group" herself, and she now understands. I have resumed writing to Marge.

Obviously, not all such episodes would have such a harmonious ending.

It is of interest in this connection that there has been increasing experimentation in recent years with "couples workshops" and with workshops for industrial executives and their spouses.

Still another negative potential growing out of these groups has become evident in recent years. Some individuals who have participated in previous encounter groups may exert a stultifying influence on new workshops which they attend. They sometimes exhibit what I think of as the "old pro" phenomenon. They feel they have learned the "rules of the game," and they subtly or openly try to impose these rules on newcomers. Thus, instead of promoting true expressiveness and spontaneity, they endeavor to substitute new rules for old—to make members feel guilty if they are not expressing feelings, are reluctant to voice criticism or hostility, are talking about situations outside the group relationship, or are fearful of revealing themselves. These old pros seem to be attempting to substitute a new tyranny in interpersonal relationships in the place of older, conventional restrictions. To me this is a perversion of the true group process. We need to ask ourselves how this travesty on spontaneity comes about.

IMPLICATIONS

I have tried to describe both the positive and the negative aspects of this burgeoning new cultural development. I would like now to touch on its implications for our society.

In the first place, it is a highly potent experience and hence clearly deserving of scientific study. As a phenomenon it has been both praised and criticized, but few people who have participated would doubt that *something* significant happens in these groups. People do not react in a neutral fashion toward the intensive group experience. They regard it as either strikingly worthwhile or deeply questionable. All would agree, however, that it is *potent*. This fact makes it of particular interest to the behavioral sciences since science is usually advanced by studying potent and dynamic phenomena. This is one of the reasons why I personally am devoting more and more of my time to this whole enterprise. I feel that we can learn much about the ways in which constructive personality change comes about as we study this group process more deeply.

In a different dimension, the intensive group experience appears to be one cultural attempt to meet the isolation of contemporary life. The person who has experienced an I-Thou relationship, who has entered into the basic encounter, is no longer an isolated individual. One workshop member stated this in a deeply expressive way:

Workshops seem to be at least a partial answer to the loneliness of modern man and his search for new meanings for his life. In short, workshops seem very quickly to allow the individual to become that person he wants to be. The first few steps are taken there, in uncertainty, in fear, and in anxiety. We may or may not continue the journey. It is a gutsy way to live. You trade many, many loose ends for one big knot in the middle of your stomach. It sure as hell isn't easy, but it is a *life* at least—not a hollow imitation of life. It has fear as well as hope, sorrow as well as joy, but I daily offer it to more people in the hope that they will join me. . . . Out from a no-man's land of *fog* into the more violent atmosphere of extremes of thunder, hail, rain, and sunshine. It is worth the trip.

Another implication which is partially expressed in the foregoing statement is that it is an avenue to fulfillment. In a day when more income, a larger car, and a better washing machine seem scarcely to be satisfying the deepest needs of man, individuals are turning to the psychological world, groping for a greater degree of authenticity and fullfilment. One workshop member expressed this extremely vividly:

[It] has revealed a completely new dimension of life and has opened an infinite number of possibilities for me in my relationship to myself and to everyone dear to me. I feel truly alive and so grateful and joyful and hopeful and healthy and giddy and sparkly. I feel as though my eyes and ears and heart and guts have been opened to see and hear and love and feel more deeply, more widely, more intensely —this glorious, mixed-up, fabulous existence of ours. My whole body and each of its systems seems freer and healthier. I want to feel hot and cold, tired and rested, soft and hard, energetic and lazy. With persons everywhere, but especially my family, I have found a new freedom to explore and communicate. I know the change in me automatically brings a change in them. A whole new exciting relationship has started for me with my husband and with each of my children—a freedom to speak and to hear them speak.

Though one may wish to discount the enthusiasm of this statement, it describes an enrichment of life for which many are seeking.

Rehumanizing Human Relationships

This whole development seems to have special significance in a culture which appears to be bent upon dehumanizing the individual and dehumanizing our human relationships. Here is an important force in the opposite direction, working toward making relationships more meaningful and more personal, in the family, in education, in government, in administrative agencies, in industry.

An intensive group experience has an even more general philosophical implication. It is one expression of the existential point of view which is making itself so pervasively evident in art and literature and modern life. The implicit goal of the group process seems to be to live life fully in the here and now of the relationship. The parallel with an existential point of view is clear cut. I believe this has been amply evident in the illustrative material.

There is one final issue which is raised by this whole phenomenon: What is our view of the optimal person? What is the goal of personality development? Different ages and different cultures have given different answers to this question. It seems evident from our review of the group process that in a climate of freedom, group members move toward becoming more spontaneous, flexible, closely related to their feelings, open to their experience, and closer and more expressively intimate in their interpersonal relationships. If we value this type of person and this type of behavior, then clearly the group process is a valuable process. If, on the other hand, we place a value on the individual who is effective in suppressing his feelings, who operates from a firm set of principles, who does not trust his own reactions and experience but relies on authority, and who remains aloof in his interpersonal relationships, then we would regard the group process, as I have tried to describe it, as a dangerous force. Clearly there is room for a difference of opinion on this value question, and not everyone in our culture would give the same answer.

CONCLUSION

I have tried to give a naturalistic, observational picture of one of the most significant modern social inventions, the so-called intensive group experience, or basic encounter group. I have tried to indicate some of the common elements of the process which occur in the climate of freedom that is present in such a group. I have pointed out some of the risks and shortcomings of the group experience. I have tried to indicate some of the reasons why it deserves serious consideration, not only from a personal point of view, but also from a scientific and philosophical point of view. I also hope I have made it clear that this is an area in which an enormous amount of deeply perceptive study and research is needed.

NOTES

1. In the preparation of this paper I am deeply indebted to two people, experienced in work with groups, for their help: Jacques Hochmann, M.D., psychiatrist of Lyon, France, who has been working at WBSI on a U.S.P.H.S. International Post-doctoral Fellowship, and Ann Dreyfuss, M.A., my research assistant. I am grateful for their ideas, for their patient analysis of recorded group sessions, and for the opportunity to interact with two original and inquiring minds.

2. Jack and Lorraine Gibb have long been working on an analysis of trust development as the essential theory of group process. Others who have contributed significantly to the theory of group process are Chris Argyris, Kenneth Benne, Warren Bennis, Dorwin Cartwright, Matthew Miles, and Robert Blake. Samples of the thinking of all these and others may be found in three recent books: Bradford, Gibb, & Benne (1964); Bennis, Benne, & Chin (1961); and Bennis, Schein, Berlew, & Steele (1964). Thus, there are many promising leads for theory construction involving a considerable degree of abstraction. This chapter has a more elementary aim—a naturalistic descriptive account of the process.

   [See Chapter 17 of the present volume. In that discussion, Jack and Lorraine Gibb present a synopsis of their theory to which Rogers refers above. The chapters by Haigh (22), Thomas (23), and Clark (27) also deal with aspects of the basic encounter group.—Editor]

3. The term "facilitator" will be used throughout this paper, although sometimes he is referred to as "leader" or "trainer."

4. The 481 respondents constituted 82 percent of those to whom the questionnaire had been sent.

5. These figures add up to more than 100 percent since quite a number of the respondents checked more than one answer.

REFERENCES

Bennis, W. G., Benne, K. D., and Chin, R. (eds.) *The Planning of Change.* New York: Holt, Rinehart and Winston, 1961.

Bennis, W. G., Schein, E. H., Berlew, D. E., and Steele, F. I., (eds.). *Interpersonal Dynamics.* Homewood, Ill.: Dorsey, 1964.

Bradford, L., Gibb, J. R., and Benne, K. D. (eds.). *T-group Theory and Laboratory Method.* New York: Wiley, 1964.

Casriel, D., *So Fair a House.* Englewood Cliffs, N. J.: Prentice-Hall, 1963.

Gibb, J. R., Climate for trust formation. In L. Bradford, Gibb, J. R., and Benne, (eds.), *T-group Theory and Laboratory Method.* New York: Wiley, 1964.

Gordon, T., *Group-centered Leadership*. Boston: Houghton Mifflin, 1955.
Hall, G. F. A participant's experience in a basic encounter group. (Mimeographed) Western Behavioral Sciences Institute, 1965.

6
The Influence of Small Groups on Individual Behavior
Darwyn E. Linder

Almost all human behavior, attitudes, beliefs, and actions are influenced by social factors. Almost everything we do is in some way conditioned by the groups to which we belong or aspire, or by our expectations of the approval or disapproval to be gained from certain groups for the actions we take. Leon Festinger's theory of social comparison processes (Festinger, 1954) defined a continuum of the ways in which beliefs and attitudes could be verified. At one end of the continuum are those things that are verifiable by appeal to physical reality, and at the other end of the continuum are those beliefs and attitudes that are only verifiable, in Festinger's terms, against a social reality. Relatively few beliefs can be unambiguously checked against physical evidence, such things as the time of day, the weather conditions outside and whether or not my watch will break if I drop it on the floor are beliefs or questions that can be answered by appeals to physical evidence. But a great many of our beliefs in political, religious, and other matters are anchored in a social reality. They are verifiable only to the extent that other people whom we value hold those same beliefs. Attitudes that have less of a possibly true or false nature than beliefs about a deity or an economic system, attitudes about clothing and food for example, are even more firmly anchored in social reality. It is interesting then that the Asch experiment reported by Charles and Sara Kiesler pitted a judgment based on physical reality against a social reality created by the experimenter. Yielding to the unanimous majority in the Asch experiment has been called conformity. But conformity and social influence, a more acceptable term, are divided by a very faint line indeed, as the Kieslers point out. As the physical reality becomes less and less unambiguous, the influence of a competing social reality becomes greater and greater. When a physical test of a belief is ambiguous or impossible, it can only be supported by the concurrence of others. Conformity or social influence?

However, the conflict between a physical reality and a social reality is not that clear. Rather, in the absence of compelling evidence we are free to believe what we want to believe, we are free to select from many positions concerning any given issue because there usually are groups espousing any conceivable position. Thus, on any complex issue it would be conceivable for an individual to adopt virtually any position. Yet we almost always end up adopting a position that is defined by a group to which we belong or to which we aspire, a group that we identify with, or a group that has been called, more formally, a reference group. We usually share attitudes, values, and behaviors with the other members of a reference group, and in turn are influenced by, or conform to, the normative expectations of a reference group. These norms effect our manners, dress, speech, and many other aspects of behavior. There is for example, no physical law that says "harness boots, flared and faded Levis, and Army field jackets are a better costume than corduroy pants and alpaca sweaters." Yet for one sub-culture, or very large reference group, the boots, jeans, and field jackets are badges of identification and membership, and are *de rigueur*.

It is difficult indeed to locate any aspect of behavior that is free of reference group influence, that is totally determined individually. Within a given group a majority is usually a potent force, and will overcome a dissenting minority, defining what will be the normative behaviors and beliefs, and enforcing adherence to those norms. However, a very attractive idea even if initially held only by a minority can become the norm. Perhaps there has to be a readiness for change, as in men's fashion several years ago, or in the shift to the miniskirt. Perhaps if a minority is to be successful in changing a majority position, the majority must have a mistaken reading of the position that one should take to display behaviors and attitudes that are congruent with one's ideal self. Something like this seems to me to occur in encounter groups. Everyone likes to think that he is open in his interactions. Being open and honest is a valued characteristic, but upon entering a group, most individuals find a new definition of openness that is espoused by a small number of members, or perhaps initially only by the group facilitator. Having been made aware of this new definition, the individual then attempts to adjust his behavior so that it is again congruent with his self image of being an open, honest individual in interaction, and he adopts the behaviors that are recommended. Once this valued trait has been defined and the appropriate position along the dimension located, an individual then moves to that position, which in fact facilitates the development of a true basic encounter.

Even the conflict of the bystander at an emergency concerning whether or not to help is based in the pull and tug of different reference groups. There is a generalized norm of helping based in family, church, and American ideals, and yet there is a concern about looking foolish to the group of people who may witness one's intervention. It is true that the other bystanders at an emergency are only a weakly defined, poorly developed reference group, and yet this group and one's fears of looking silly in front of it do seem to affect the way people behave. It should be noted that bystanders are not always unresponsive. A study by Piliavin, Rodin, and Piliavin (1969) found that helping was unaffected by the size of the crowd and in most instances was almost immediate. In their study they staged an emergency in a natural setting, a New York subway. Regardless of the number of people in the subway car when a man apparently ill (one condition) or apparently drunk (another experimental condition) fell prone to the floor of the car, bystanders came to his assistance almost immediately. Why the behavior of bystanders in a New York subway should be so strikingly different from that reported by Latané and Darley is an open question. Perhaps one answer is that the victim in the subway car was immediately and visually present to the bystanders, while in the Latané and Darley experiments the victim has most often been in another room and his or her distress could only be heard and not seen. Whatever the eventual answer to these questions, it is clear that behavior in emergencies is affected by social factors.

It seems then that the vast majority of our actions and beliefs are shaped by the various groups to which we belong or aspire. I am reminded of the idea expressed by Cooley that human nature is shaped by primary groups. Those of us who cherish an image of ourselves as rugged individualists are often surprised to find, after honest examination, that very little of what we believe or what we do has not been influenced by what others have thought and what others may say about our behavior. It is a rare person who holds beliefs shared by no others, who has ideas no one else has ever had, or behaves as no one else does. Such persons are either called geniuses and are applauded, or insane and are incarcerated or scorned. Perhaps the most important factor determining how society will respond to such individuals is the number of others who are influenced to adopt these unique beliefs and behaviors. Group norms have enormous power to shape individual thought and action. Social psychologists have described many effects of that power but we have only begun to understand its sources. Perhaps human nature, as Cooley said, is shaped by primary groups, but I think that much of human behavior and many or almost all of our beliefs are shaped by our membership in or identification with the small and not so small groups in which we interact almost continuously.

REFERENCES

Festinger, L., A theory of social comparison processes. *Hum. Relat.*, 1954, 7, 117–140.

Piliavin, I. M., Rodin, J., and Piliavin, J. A., Good samaritanism: An underground phenomenon? *J. Personality and soc. Psychol.*, 1969, 13, 289–299.

Part 4
Interaction of Groups in Conflict

I

Interaction of Groups in Conflict

Darwyn E. Linder

I am quite certain that even if an objectively equitable distribution of wealth and material goods among humans could be achieved there would still be conflict between individuals and groups. When the distribution of resources is as inequitable as it is in our society and today's world, then conflict between groups is almost certain. It would be a mistake though to assume that all conflicts are based on competition for material goods. In the course of human history some of our bloodiest and costliest wars have been fought under the banners of conflicting ideologies rather than for purposes of acquiring land or resources. Some might argue that beneath the ideological conflict there is in all wars a competition for land or material goods. But attempting to discover primary causes of naturally occurring events is often a futile activity and I think that in most instances of real conflict and actual war both ideological differences and a desire to acquire more land or to control more natural resources contribute to the development of conflict.

The laboratory study of individuals and groups in conflict has focused mainly on competition for some sort of reward, whether it be points in a game, or money, or experimental credit. Much of the research has used the paradigm of game-based conflict discussed by Rapoport in his article presented earlier in the book. A number of investigators have taken this basic paradigm and created from it some realistic and very engaging games. One example is the trucking game devised by Deutsch and Krauss (1960). An elaborate gameboard was devised with electronic controls and two players would compete for points accumulated by moving a truck across a route on the board in minimum time. The conflict was provided by designing the board so that part of the route was shared by the two players but only one of them could occupy it at a given time. If the two players met on this part of the route, neither could pass the other and both would lose points by allowing time to elapse without making progress toward the end of the route. One of the interesting and controversial findings of the Deutsch and Krauss study was that when players were given the ability to erect barriers to one another's progress the level of outcomes that the players attained was less than when these barriers, or weapons, were not available. But these players were competing only for points. Other researchers, for instance Gallo (1966) have provided players with real and significant monetary incentives and found that the level of cooperation was greatly enhanced when such real incentives were used. Furthermore, Gallo found that the availability of threats and barriers did not diminish the outcomes attained by the players when they were competing for real money. This field of research, with its wide variety of possible parameters, the kind of incentive used, the payoff matrix, the characteristics of the players has become a subspecialty of its own and I shall not attempt to discuss all of the conflicting and sometimes confusing results that have been obtained.

While it is fairly easy to study competition for some sort of material incentive in the laboratory it is difficult to create ideological conflict. For this reason when psychologists attempt to understand ideological and political conflict in the real world, they are forced to make their generalizations from the kinds of conflict experiments that I have just discussed. Of course there have been a number of attempts at simulation of international conflict (for example, Guetzkow, *et al.*, 1963). In these studies individuals play the roles of heads of nations and are fed information concerning their resources, military strength, population, and alliances with other nations, along with other data. Their behavior as decision makers in this complex setting is then observed. It is a difficult step to generalize from this setting to the behavior of nations, since in most instances the behavior of a nation is not controlled by a single man, but rather by a complex set of ruling bodies. Perhaps some nations are directed by the will of a single, powerful dictator, but very rarely is a nation under the complete control of one man.

Given that it is difficult to generalize to international conflict from either laboratory studies of conflict and competition or simulations of international conflict, social scientists often must only observe the conflict and try to understand and predict modes of conflict resolution. In the first selection presented in this section James Laue discusses a model of the development and resolution of conflict that he applies to civil rights challenges by black Americans. However, his model, which assumes that a democratic process of change is available, is perhaps also applicable to the conflicts generated by student demands for greater power within universities and to conflicts generated by demands of women for rights and opportunities equal to those enjoyed by men.

In the last three selections presented in this section, Herbert York, Jerome Frank and Charles Osgood discuss aspects of international behavior related to weapons, war and the prevention of war. All three of these men were testifying before congressional committees as they made the comments reprinted here. I think it is a significant development that government is paying increasing attention to social scientists as they attempt to grapple with problems of international relations. As these writers point out, it would be silly to attempt a simple generalization from the behavior of individuals in psychological laboratories to the behavior of nations in conflict. And yet as they also and rightly point out the parallels are striking. If the conditions leading to conflict between nations have analogies in the psychological laboratory perhaps the modes of conflict resolution employed in laboratory studies will have analogies in the resolution of conflicts between nations.

REFERENCES

Deutsch, M. and Krauss, R. M. The effect of threat on interpersonal bargaining. *Journal of Abnormal and Social Psychology*, 1960, *61*, 181–189.

Gallo, P. S. Effects of increased incentives upon the use of threat in bargaining. *Journal of Personality and Social Psychology*, 1966, *4*, 14–20.

Guetzkow, H., Alger, C. F., Brady, R. A., Noel, R. C., and Snyder, R. C. *Simulation in International Relations*. Englewood Cliffs, N.J.: Prentice-Hall, 1963.

2
Power, Conflict, and Social Change

James H. Laue

Viewing *power* as the *control over decisions*, and *social change* as the continuous process of *redistribution of power* within social systems, this paper examines the role of conflict in the extensive changes in American racial patterns in the last ten years. It develops a framework to help explain what has happened, and raises questions about the nature and directions of racial change today and in the next few years. The model[1] is intended to have general applicability to processes of change through conflict.[2]

I have seen communities go through a common sequence of stages in working out desegregation and elimination of certain discriminatory practices in response to challenges from minority groups. The phase-structure of social change presented here was developed in response to the data from my research on the direct action movement of the early 1960's in more than one hundred southern communities, with particular emphasis on the sit-ins and Freedom Rides.[3] In every community, the pattern seemed to be the same: challenge by the minority group, a period of overt community conflict cresting in a crisis, the drawing of hitherto uninvolved elements of white power into negotiation, and the working out of some change.

MINORITIES AND POWER

The model is called the 7 C's. It is an attempt to systematize the process which I saw occurring in city after city as desegregation was achieved. It starts with the assumption implied at the beginning of the paper, that significant social change takes place when new combinations of community power groups emerge to force an alteration in the perceived self-interest of the powerful and, therefore, a change in their priorities for actions. Direct action achieved success as a technique for forcing certain

Power, Conflict, and Social Change by James H. Laue is reprinted from Louis M. Masotti and Don R. Bowen (eds.), *Riots and Rebellion: Civil Violence in the Urban Community* (1968), pp. 85–96, by permission of the publisher, Sage Publications, Inc., Beverly Hills, California.

concessions because it developed a new source of power within groups which did not have sufficient amounts of the normal sources of power-for-change in a democratic system. Lacking sufficient political and economic power, Negroes used the only form remaining to them—their bodies. Through the testing and refining of direct action techniques (literally "putting your body on the line"), the movement developed negotiable forms of power. In turn, legislation and other action stimulated by the civil rights movement have begun to equip Negroes more adequately with the standard forms of political and economic power.

In explaining how redistribution of community power occurs through the 7 C's phase-structure, I begin with an eighth C: Competition. Competition is a constant in all social interaction. All the stages of the model are varying forms of the competitive process. Competition is the process whereby persons quietly oppose one another in seeking the scarce rewards they have learned to want. It is, in this statement, close to what Sumner meant by "antagonistic cooperation."[4] It is a natural, ever-present condition of all social interaction, and the starting point for any analysis of social change. The holders of power in all social systems try to suppress the notion that certain types of competition exist. The American race-related version, once restricted to the south but now heard increasingly in northern cities in only slightly altered language, is "our colored people are (or were) happy."

THE 7 C's

The 7C's—the stages communities have transacted in working out change in racial patterns—are:

1. Challenge

2. Conflict

3. Crisis

4. Confrontation

5. Communication

6. Compromise

7. Change

1. *Challenge* is the open and dramatic presentation of demands and grievances by the minority, including the range from single specific

grievances to an attack on the whole pattern of systematic discrimination in a community. The challenge is usually a last resort after less public approaches (educational and legal, for instance) have failed to bring significant communication or change. The classic example is the sit-in. Other are marches, picketing, or other well publicized challenges to the status quo, such as lawsuits or boycotts.

2. *Conflict* is intensified competition of which a substantial proportion of the community is now aware. An accumulation of challenges brings ever-present competition to the surface, and it breaks through into overt conflict. Traditional mechanisms of social control are no longer able to manage the increasing frequency of challenges.

3. *Crisis* exists when elites with the power to change the discriminatory patterns challenged *define* the situation as severe enough to demand immediate action and rapid resolution. They have, that is, changed their perception of their own self-interest and what it will take to maintain and expand it. When the powerful decide to act, the crisis has been achieved. Crisis thus is a subjective power-term, determined by the plans and actions of the powerful, rather than by the objective conditions of the situation. Some of the conditions which have persuaded the powerful to make the crisis-definition are demonstrations, boycotts, economic loss, damage to the city's image, a court decision on desegregation, violence—or the seriously anticipated threat of any of the above. Once the crisis-definition is mad, for whatever reasons, the meeting of at least some of the demands presented in the Challenge is inevitable, and the process usually hurries through the final stages to Change.

4. *Confrontation* takes place when the decision-makers being challenged recognize that the minority group has legitimate demands which can no longer be explained away, but which must be dealt with. If there is a stage in the process in which normative awareness develops on the part of the powerful, that is it. Awarness of the moral legitimacy of demands results from the harder realities of economic and political awareness learned in the previous stage. At least it may be said that the challenge-targets are more suggestible and more receptive to previously rejected change proposals and persons.

5. *Communication* is direct, face-to-face negotiation between the challengers and the dominant group(s), each now bargaining from a position of power, Post-crisis communication is always more frank and goal-directed than pre-crisis communication, for the powerful have been

forced to drop defenses and take positive steps to remedy problems of which everyone is now consciously aware. The newfound power of the challengers consists of threats (to create further crises if certain demands are not met) and promises (*not* to create crises if demands *are* met).

6. *Compromise* is a result of the bargaining which takes place in stage 5, and usually requires the enlistment (often covert) of community power resources beyond the parties in the Communication process. There are victories and concessions for all communicating parties, with each faction usually asking for more than it expects to gain, in preparation for the anticipated giving-in of the Compromise stage.

7. *Change* is, by definition, the achievement by the protesters of at least some of the goals set forth in the Challenge.

OTHER DIMENSIONS OF THE MODEL

There are several qualifications and subsidiary processes regarding the operation of this system. First, the model as outlined here recognizes that there are many centers and sources of power in communities and nations, and that the 7 C's process therefore operates simultaneously at many levels. Community power structure is not seen as monolithic, but rather as a series of interacting and interlocking systems—which means that the conflict process may operate within and between systems as well as in relation to the total community. It is macro as well as micro.

Second, the system *cycles*—that is, it runs its course on different issues over and over again in communities, with the stage 7 resolution of one conflict situation becoming the plateau upon which new challenges arise. A good example is Nashville, which in the years from 1960 through 1963 went through virtually the same process of appeal, Negro demonstration, white violence, boycott, arrests, community concern, and change on four different desegregation issues: lunch counters, theaters, retail employment, and the better restaurants. The emergence of the early stages does not always mean the cycle will run its course, however. It may get bogged down at any stage, then remain latent until sufficient challenges are taken up again. This was the case with Albany, Georgia, in 1961 and 1962, when the process never got past the conflict stage despite white retail losses of more than sixty percent. Local white influentials refused to make the crisis-definition, and eventually the movement lost momentum.

Lateral communication operates when non-conflict cities move to make change because of conflict and crisis in other communities. An avoidance model quickly develops. In Carolina and Virginia cities, significant changes which had been the object of protest for many months came about in a matter of days in mid-1963, because Birmingham was on. A typical northern example came from Philadelphia in August, 1967, largely as a result of the message from Detroit. The city's business leaders discovered 1200 jobs "for the idle poor" in response to the Mayor's "call for help in easing ghetto tensions" and his statement that such hiring is "not now a matter of charity, but an investment in our community."[5]

Short-circuiting is the process whereby communities move directly from stage 1 or 2 to stage 5 or 6. They have recognized, based on previous local experience or contemporary lateral communication, that the change being demanded by the challengers is inevitable, and that it is in the self-interest of the powerful to move directly to Communication (stage 5) or to the sixth stage of active re-ordering of priorities and enlistment of other community resources for change. A dramatic southern example is the immediate compliance of Albany, Georgia, officials with the 1964 Civil Rights Act, telling newsmen, "Of course we're going to obey the law. We don't want Martin Luther King coming down here again."[6] Short-circuiting of the change process also will be one result, I believe, of the current public and private sector activities responsive to the summer's urban racial violence.

The other side of the short-circuiting process, however, is the *neutralization of crisis*. Crisis tolerances change as communities learn to combat direct action and other forms of challenges. In most cities in the early 1960's, sit-ins were enough to stimulate a crisis-definition, but today they are dealt with as a matter of course and are generally not effective as a change technique. A surprising exception took place in early June, 1967, in Boston, however, when policemen tried to disperse a group of welfare mothers sitting and lying-in overnight in a public building, and triggered two days of violent conflict between Negroes and the police.

From the viewpoint of systemic integration, it can be added that the operation of the 7 C's is, in the long run, a healthy process. Although conflict is disruptive in the short run, it serves to bring systemic stresses to the surface and forces communities to confront them and deal with them forthrightly, as Lewis Coser and others have pointed out.[7] Conflict is not the cause of social system stresses—rather it is a symptom, a process whereby the stresses may be transformed for remedial action. Andrew Young of the Southern Christian Leadership Conference has summed it up best in lay terms. "The movement did not 'cause' problems in Selma, as Sheriff Jim Clark and others claimed," Young says. "It just brought them to the surface where they could be dealt with. Sheriff Clark has been beating black heads in the back of the jail on Saturday night for years, and we're only saying to him that if he still wants to beat heads he'll have to do it on Main Street at noon in front of CBS, NBC, and ABC television cameras."

CASES IN POINT, SOUTH AND NORTH

There are other examples from hundreds of communities of how conflict-produced crises have forced White Power to enable changes in racial patterns, a few of which may be mentioned here. Desegregation of lunch counters took place in more than two hundred southern cities within a year after the sit-in movement began in February, 1960. The Freedom Rides took place in May of 1961, Alabama whites provided the violent counterpoint, the federal government intervened—and by November a Federal Communications Commissions order was issued (and enforced) banning discrimination in interstate transportation facilities.

Atlanta and Birmingham offer other instructive empirical cases. The different crisis-tolerances in these cities is directly reflected in the ease with which change takes place, and the extent of the change. In Atlanta, a few sit-ins and arrests, SNCC picketing and Klan counter-picketing were enough to mobilize the necessary power centers for change. But in Birmingham it took Bull Connor, police dogs, fire hoses, 3500 arrests, and pictures transmitted all over the nation and world before the "Committee of 100" got itself organized to make changes it had been capable of making all along.

It has worked in the North, too. In 1967 in Cleveland, Sealtest short-circuited the 7 C'S by responding to the threat of a boycott with a $300,000 program for job training and community development in the Hough ghetto—a program it had been capable of delivering for some time. In Chicago, the Daley machine responded to SCLC's challenges in 1966 by giving minor concessions at the first push on housing inspection and enforcement and other targets. The Chicago Metropolitan Council for Open Cities, which is now working actively with the endorsement of corporate, labor, religious, and political elites, came into being after a summer of Negro open-housing demonstrations and violent white responses. The Council was, in effect, a trade for King's agreeing not to lead a massive march into Cicero.

At a national level, the Civil Rights Act of 1964 and the Voting Rights Act of 1965 are direct results of the operation of the 7 C's process. After three years of direct action throughout the South, Birmingham produced a crisis-definition in the national administration in May of 1963. President Kennedy proposed the Act within a month, communicated on nationwide television using everpresent but previously unused Biblical and Constitutional value statements, and the Administration fought the bill through the compromise process of the Congress to enactment and the beginning of the change process within a year. The phase-structure of passage of the 1965 Voting Rights Act was much the same: the beating at the Selma bridge in March of 1965, a dramatic film clip on national television the next night, mobilization of national support by the movement, President Johnson going before the Congress and national prime-time television several weeks later to request legislation and say "We shall overcome," the passage of the Act four months later in July, and the registration of more than 1.5 million new southern Negro voters within the next two years.

BUT DOES IT STILL WORK?

But a look at Congress, the urban violence, and the poll data on white attitudes today makes me seriously ask, "Do the 7 C's still work?" The last part of the paper is directed toward that question, based on an analysis of the changing conditions of racial conflict we have experienced and may expect in the next few years. This concluding section offers few answers but raises many questions bearing on the viability of the 7 C's model in the North in 1968 and beyond.

I question whether the model has long-range applicability as the racial focus moves urban and North because of two conditions which must be met if a social system is to achieve change through conflict:

1. The 7 C's can only operate in a social system in which the superordinate power *permits* conflict as a way of doing change. The 7 C's would not have worked in Nazi Germany; rather a kind of short-circuiting from Challenge (1) to repressive Change (7) would have taken place.

2. It appears that the superordinate power must not only permit conflict, but must, in fact, approve of the goals of the protesters.

What operated in the South, then, was a concessions model in which Negroes challenged politically expendable cities, counties, and states, while the federal government permitted the conflict process to run its course through to change, and tacitly (and often openly) supported the goals of the protesters as being consistent with basic American values. The permissive superordinate power was the federal government, supported by the mass media and the white liberal-labor coalition.

But now it is the superordinate power itself which is under attack. The targets now are the federal government, the large northern cities (with their nonexpendable Democratic machines), housing codes, the real estate industry—in short, the whole middle-class establishment, including people who write articles like this and people who read them. It was easy for the superordinate power in its various forms to support conflict in Alabama and Mississippi: the moral issues were seemingly clear, the devils were readily available in brutal sheriffs and unattractive politicians, and it was far away. But the same persons, newspapers, private organizations, and government officials who endorsed the movement's implicit use of the 7 C's process in the South, now confuse demonstrations with riots and label southern protest techniques turned northward as ill-considered and irresponsible.

An important theoretical question, then, is whether the American black movement needs and can find a higher superordinate power to legitimate and support its activities. Contacts of civil right groups with revolutionaries and established governments in Africa and Latin America have been increasing in the last year. SCLC is beginning to convert its program to an international base, as presaged by the late Dr. Martin Luther King's anti-war activity and the continuing work of some SCLC staff members in Africa. And the movement has long considered soliciting United Nations support in the struggle against American racism.

In the light of these recent shifts in targets and allies—and of the urban racial violence of the past four summers—an even more important question is "Under what conditions will the crisis-definition become repressive?" In the current statement of the 7 C's, the crisis-definition is essentially oriented to democratizing change. It assumes, within the context of a sympathetic superordinate power, that crisis always moves the targets of the challenge toward actions supporting desegregation and equal opportunity.

In addition to specifying the conditions under which the crisis-definition becomes repressive, we need to develop an alternate version of the stages following crisis.

Political and military reactions to the 1967 urban summer violence lead some to speculate that political leadership at both local and national levels is closer to a repressive crisis-definition in relation to an American minority group than at any time since the Japanese "relocation" in World War II.

"Don't reward the rioters" sentiment is high among whites, and black ghettos are full of rumors that the concentration camps are ready— and the wry comment that ghettos are too ecologically strategic for the Man to bomb the people.

The rise of black nationalism confirms the hostility of white leaders: "Look at all we have done for them in the last few years, and now they're saying maybe they don't even want integration!" To the consternation of whites, the slain Malcolm X is coming to be the same kind of hero for many black ghetto people that the slain John Kennedy is for many white liberals.

Despite the intensifying confrontation between white sentiment for law-and-order and black sentiment for change, there are some tentative signs that the 7 C's are operating for change on schedule, at least at the national level:

¶ Vice-President Humphrey called for an urban Marshall Plan in a Detroit speech in August, 1967—a concept developed and popularized by Whitney Young, Bayard Rustin, Martin Luther King, Roy Wilkins, and others more than two years ago, but rejected by the Administration.

¶ The President made strong value statements about poverty, discrimination, and other structural conditions of urban ghettos in his televised address to the nation in response to the riots, in addition to strong remarks about law and order.

¶ The Urban Coalition was formed by New York Mayor Lindsay, David Rockefeller, the U.S. Conference of Mayors, and others on July 31, 1967. It has begun a national political mobilization to get Congress moving on urban legislation, urged the nation not to "penalize the majority because of resentment of the criminal acts of a tiny fraction," and has "called upon the nation and the Congress to reorder our national priorities, with a commitment of national resources equal to the dimensions of the problems we face."[8]

¶ Both the late Senator Robert Kennedy and Vice-President Humphrey have in recent movements put the issue in basic value terms in speeches about Negro alienation and identity, Kennedy saying that the ghetto poor have been denied "the most fundamental of human needs—the need for identity, for recognition as a citizen and as a man."

¶ The New Detroit Committee formed after the 1967 disorder and composed of board chairmen and presidents of the automobile industry and the most powerful local retail businesses, has mobilized significant political and economic power for change in a short time. They have actively and personally lobbied for statewide open-housing legislation with the Michigan Legislature and, from August, 1967, to February, 1968, opened up 50,000 jobs in Detroit—half of them going to Negroes. Corporations like Chrysler and Michigan Bell have placed employment offices in Detroit ghettos, and are exercising new flexibility regarding educational backgrounds and arrest records of prospective employees.[9]

But in the face of these positive change-oriented responses, we must raise the question of how long the essentially expressive violence of the summer outbursts will be tolerated by the national political system. We can predict with some degree of confidence that the system will soon develop repressive crisis-responses if the violence moves from the expressive level to the strategic or political. And with somewhat less certainty, I suggest that city and national administration leaders will not long permit the kind of massive applications of nonviolent direct action techniques to northern urban systems of government, transportation, and commerce that SCLC led in Washington, D.C., in the spring and summer of 1968.

THE THEORETICAL TASKS AHEAD

I look forward to the unfolding of events in the next few years as they inform the unfolding of this particular change model. In summary, I believe that the next tasks in the theory's development are:

1. Develop a typology of the antecedent conditions which can predict whether the crisis-definition will be *democratic* or *repressive*, and develop an alternate version of the stages that follow a repressive crisis-definition.

2. Determine the social structural prerequisites for movement of the process from phase to phase.[10]

3. Develop a model to sort out the interaction patterns and interchanges within and between systems in conflict, with special attention to repressive and counterrevolutionary variables.

4. Develop a hierarchy of negotiable issues—and of meaningful concessions available to urban white power—as a guide to prediction of racial conflict and change patterns in the next few years.

If negotiable issues between urban blacks and whites can be found, then the 7 C's process will continue to operate in the urban North as satisfying concessions are elicited. If not—if the superordinate powers under attack move steadily toward repressive crisis-definitions—then the kind of conflict theory discussed here will seem pale in the face of the realities of violent change to come.

NOTES

1. This paper's outline of the change-through-conflict process is consciously called a "model" rather than a "theory" because, at this level of its development, it provides only a set of sequential categories for understanding the process—not structural determinants for explanation and prediction.

2. Other change processes involving lesser degrees of conflict include drift and rational means-ends chains (planned change through legislation or moderate private social reform measures).

3. Data throughout this paper are drawn largely from my doctoral dissertation, "Direct Action and Desegregation: Toward a Theory of the Rationalization of Protest" (Harvard University, 1966) and from written and personal sources available to me in the course of my work in the Community Relations Service from 1965 to 1969.

4. William Graham Sumner, *Folkways* (N.Y.: Dover, 1959; originally published in 1906), pp. 16–18.

5. United Press International, August 19, 1967.

6. Associated Press, July 3, 1964.

7. Lewis Coser, *The Functions of Social Change* (N.Y.: Free Press, 1965), and *Continuities in the Study of Social Conflict* (N.Y.: Free Press, 1967); Kenneth E. Boulding, *Conflict and Defense* (N.Y.: Harper and Row, 1962); and Thomas Schelling, *The Strategy of Conflict* (Cambridge: Harvard Univ. Press, 1960).

8. *New York Times*, August 1, 1967.

9. Report of the New Detroit Committee, January 29, 1968.

10. This task, begun in my dissertation, is being expanded in *Black Protest: Toward a Theory of Movements*, with Martin Oppenheimer, in preparation for Blaisdell and Company.

3
ABM, MIRV, and the Arms Race

Herbert. F. York

In 1955, about a year after the United States started development of its first intercontinental ballistic missile (ICBM), the Army asked the Bell Telephone Laboratories to make a study of the feasibility of developing an anti-ballistic missile (ABM). The problem was then thought of as being simply how to hit a "bullet with a bullet," or, more accurately, how to intercept large, simple, incoming warheads one at a time. The Bell Laboratories concluded that the technological state of the art in radar, electronic computing, nuclear explosives, and rocketry had reached a point such that is was indeed feasible to build an ABM with that simple objective. As a result, the Nike Zeus project was started late in 1956.

Very soon after, it was recognized that the defense problem might well be complicated by various hypothetical "penetration aids" available to the offense. The Office of the Secretary of Defense set up a committee to review the matter. In early 1958 that committee pointed out the feasibility of greatly complicating the missile defense problem by using decoys, chaff, tank fragments, reduced radar reflectivity, nuclear blackout, and—last but by no means least—multiple warheads.

At first, the designers of our offensive missiles did not take missile defense very seriously. By 1960, however, technical progress in our own Nike Zeus program, plus accumulating evidence of a major Soviet effort in the ABM field, forced the developers of our ICBM's and Polaris missiles to take this possibility into account. These weapons designers

Reprinted by permission from *Science*, July 17, 1970, Vol. 169, pages 257–260. Copyright 1970 by the American Association for the Advancement of Science.

accepted the challenge, and they initiated a number of programs to exploit the possibilities enumerated above. Thus began the technological contest between missile defense and missile offense which continues to the present and which was discussed before the Senate in considerable detail last year.

CYCLE OF ACTION AND REACTION

For our purposes here today, the most important result of this contest was the emergence of the multiple warhead idea as the most promising of all the various "penetration aid" concepts. At first, the idea involved a shotgun technique in which a group of warheads plus some lightweight decoys were to be launched along several different paths all leading to a common target area. But shortly after, methods for aiming each of the individual warheads at separate targets were invented. There were three reasons for this extension of the original idea: (i) it provided additional flexibility for the offense, (ii) it made the defense problem still harder, and (iii) it was more complicated and expensive, and thus provided the weapons engineers and scientists with a still better means of displaying their technological virtuosity. This extension of the original idea is, of course, the now well-known MIRV, an acronym standing for multiple independently targetable reentry vehicles. It is, I think, most important to note that these early developments of MIRV and ABM were not primarily the result of any careful operations analysis of the problem or of anything which might be described as a "provocation" by the other side. Rather, they were largely the result of a continuously reciprocating process consisting of a technological challenge put out by the designers of our own defense and accepted by the designers of our own offense, then followed by a similar challenge and response sequence in the reverse direction. In this fashion, our ABM development program made very substantial progress during the early 1960's.

Concurrent with this internal contest, the Soviets were making progress on their own. As early as 1962, Premier Khrushchev and Defense Minister Malinovsky boasted about how they had solved the missile defense problem. By 1965, Soviet progress in development and deployment of an ABM had proceeded to the point where we felt compelled to react. As a result, we decided to deploy MIRV as the one certain means of assuring penetration of Soviet defenses and thus maintaining the credibility of our deterrent.

What was the result of this cycle of action and reaction? Last year, in the course of the national ABM debate, it was said that the Soviets had deployed about 70 ABM interceptors, all of them around Moscow. This year it was announced that the United States was going ahead with its plans to deploy MIRV's on our Minute Men and on our submarine-launched Poseidon missiles. Using figures generated by the Senate Foreign Relations Committee last year, we see that the result of this U.S. reaction will be a net increase of around 5000 in the number of warheads aimed at Russia. If every one of those Soviet interceptors was successful in the event of an attack (and I have substantial doubt that they would be), they could cope with just 70 of those additional 5000 warheads. The deployment of the Moscow ABM must rank as one of history's most counterproductive moves. It also shows more clearly than any speculative analysis how, despite its defensive nature, the ABM can be a powerfully accelerating element in the nuclear arms race.

But that's not the whole story. The Soviets have proceeded with a multiple warhead development of their own. Their program apparently is a number of years behind ours. It was probably stimulated by our program, and their technologists probably used the same justifications for it that ours did. The device they are currently testing is the payload package for the large SS-9 missile. It is said to contain three separate warheads of five megatons each. The present device may not be a true MIRV, but there is no doubt they could develop one soon.

After making a number of estimates and projections concerning the accuracy, the reliability, and the current deployment and rate of buildup of such SS-9 missiles, our defense officials concluded last year that the threat posed by this Soviet MIRV required us to deploy the Safeguard ABM system to defend our Minute Man force. We thus see that the whole process has made one full turn around the spiral: Soviet ABM led to U.S. MIRV; U.S. MIRV led to Soviet MIRV; Soviet MIRV leads to U.S. ABM.

Last year, some of those who spoke in favor of the Safeguard System described the Soviet MIRV development as being especially dangerous and foreboding because it seemed to them that its only rational purpose was to destroy our Minute Men before they could be launched. They further speculated that, if this were so, the Soviet MIRV indicated preparation for a possible preemptive strike against us. These same people argued, by contrast, that our own MIRV development was clearly benign, since its main purpose was to maintain the credibility of our deterrent in the face of a hypothetical extensive Soviet ABM, and that, in any event, our MIRV was clearly not a "missile killer."

The main argument in support of this supposed difference between the purposes of the U.S. and Soviet MIRV's involves the large difference in their explosive power. The Soviet SS-9 MIRV is said to have an estimated yield of 5 megatons. This yield is 25 times the yield usually quoted for one of the individual warheads in the U.S. Minute Man MIRV; it is 100 times the common estimate of the yield of a single Poseidon MIRV warhead. These large differences in yield are doubtless real, and they are important, but they are not by any means the whole story. The killing power of a warhead against a hard target, such as a missile silo, depends much more critically on accuracy than on yield. In fact, a factor of 3 in accuracy makes up for a factor of 25 in yield, and a factor of 4.6 in accuracy makes up for a factor of 100 in yield. To be more specific, a Minute Man MIRV warhead having a yield of 200 kilotons and an accuracy[1] of about $\frac{1}{8}$ nautical mile (accuracy of about 232 meters) has a 95 percent chance of destroying a so-called "300 psi" target (300 pounds per square inch is a typical estimate of the strength or hardness of a missile silo). Similarly, a Poseidon MIRV warhead having a yield of 50 kilotons and an accuracy of about $\frac{1}{16}$ mile (nautical) has the same probability of destroying a missile silo.

And what are the prospects for attaining such accuracies? The accuracy of real operational missiles is classified, but in last year's debates a figure of about $\frac{1}{4}$ mile for accuracies of U.S. missiles was commonly used. That is quite different from $\frac{1}{8}$ or $\frac{1}{16}$ mile, but what is the record of progress in improving accuracy? In 1944, the German V-2 missile, which used a primitive version of the guidance system the present-day Minute Man and Poseidon use, achieved an accuracy of about 4 miles in a range of about 200 miles. Ten years later, when the decision to build the U.S. ICBM was made, an accuracy of 5 miles in a range of 5000 miles was estimated to be both possible and sufficient. That was a 20-fold improvement in the ratio of accuracy to range. Now we talk about $\frac{1}{4}$ mile accuracy at the same range, so in an additional 15 years we have achieved another 20-fold improvement. Altogether, that makes a 400-fold improvement in only 25 years. Any conservative Soviet planner considering these figures would have to conclude that, in a relatively short time, U.S. technology could improve missile accuracy by another factor of 2 or 4 and thus convert not only the Minute Man MIRV but even the Poseidon MIRV into a missile-silo destroyer.

We have seen that the SS-9 MIRV is causing our Defense Department to fear for the viability of our deterrent and to react strongly for that reason. In the context of the present international situation, and in the absence of any real progress in arms control, the Soviets must be expected to react to our MIRV in some similarly fear-inspired way.

ABM and MIRV are thus inseparable; each one requires and inspires the other. Separately or in combination, they create uncertainty in each of the nuclear powers about the capability and even the intentions of the other. These uncertainties eventually lead in turn to fear, overreaction, and further increases in the number and types of all kinds of weapons, defensive as well as offensive.

THE "LAUNCH-ON-WARNING" DOCTRINE

What about the future? In the absence of international arms control agreements, what can we expect? Predictions are, of course, very uncertain, but one can single out some likely possibilities.

The ABM is a low-confidence system. The expressions of confidence in the system made by those who supported it last year are bound to give way to a more realistic appraisal by the time the system is deployed. When that happens, the defense establishment will turn, in accordance with the precepts of "worst plausible case" analysis, to other methods of insuring the survival of the Minute Man. Of the various possibilities, the surest, quickest, and cheapest is simply to adopt the "launch-on-warning" doctrine. This doctrine involves (i) detecting the fact that a launch of enemy missiles has occurred; (ii) analyzing the information in order to determine whether the launch endangers our missile forces; and (iii) if it does, launching our missiles toward their targets before the incoming warheads can catch them in their silos and destroy them. This method of coping with the problem has been in people's minds since the beginning of the missile program.

In the early 1950's we anticipated that the early warning systems then foreseen would provide about 15 minutes' notice before enemy warheads landed. For that reason, the original Atlas was designed to be launched within less than 15 minutes after receipt of orders for launch. One of the major reasons for switching, in the early 1960's, to the Titan II, with its storable propellants, and the Minute Man, with its solid propellants, was that the time from the "go signal" to the actual launch could be made still shorter.

Many of the people who have proposed this solution to the problem are thoughtful and moderate, but, even so, I find this resolution of the dilemma to be completely unsatisfactory. The time in which the decision to launch must be made varies from just a few minutes to perhaps 20 minutes, depending on the nature of the attack and on the details of our warning system, our communication system, and our command and control system. This time is so short that the decision to launch our missiles must be made either by a computer, by a "pre-programmed" President, or by some "pre-programmed" delegate of the President. There will be no time to stop and think about what the signals mean or to check to see whether they might somehow be false alarms. The decision will have to be made on the basis of electronic signals electronically analyzed, in accordance with a plan worked out long before by apolitical analysts in an antiseptic and unreal atmosphere. In effect, not even the President, let alone the Congress, would really be a party to the ultimate decision to end civilization.

If launching *our* missiles on electronic warning does not seem so bad, then consider the situation the other way around. Our current technical developments—specifically, the greater accuracy and reliability of our missiles, MIRV and ABM—are pushing the Soviets in the same direction. Further, in their case a far larger fraction of the deterrent is provided by fixed land-based forces than in ours, and so they have an even greater need to find a truly reliable means of protecting their deterrent from a preemptive attack by us. If we continue with our MIRV developments, and thus force the Soviets to go to a launch-on-warning system, can we rely on them to invent and institute adequate controls? Do they have the necessary level of sophistication to solve the contradiction inherent in the need for a "hair trigger" (so that their system will respond in time) and a "stiff trigger" (so that they will not fire accidentally)? How good are their computers at recognizing false alarms? How good is the command and control system for the Polaris-type submarine fleet they are now rapidly, if belatedly, building? Will it be "fail-safe"?

It cannot be emphasized too strongly that unfavorable answers to these questions about *their* capability will mean diminished national security for *us*. Yet there is no way for us to assure favorable answers. The only way we can avoid the danger to our security inherent in these questions is by eliminating the need to ask them. Strategic weapons systems on both sides must be designed so that no premium is put on a preemptive attack, and so that neither side is forced to adopt the kind of "hair trigger" epitomized in the launch-on-warning concept.

Fortunately for us, the Soviets have also expressed concern about this problem. In words very similar to those used by witnesses before our Senate last spring, Foreign Minister Gromyko last summer said[1]:

[There] is another matter that cannot be ignored. . . . It is linked to a considerable extent to the fact that the command and control systems for arms are becoming increasibly autonomous, if one can put it this way, from the people who create them. Human capacity to hear and see are incapable of reacting to modern speeds. The human brain is no longer capable of assessing at sufficient speed the results of the multitude of instruments. The decisions made by man depend in the last analysis on the conclusions provided by computers. Governments must do everything possible to be able to determine the development of events and not to find themselves in the role of captive of events.

STEADY DECREASE IN NATIONAL SECURITY

The nuclear arms race has led to a situation that at once is absurd and poses a dilemma. Ever since the end of World War II, the military power of the United States has been steadily increasing, while at the same time our national security has been rapidly and inexorably decreasing. The same thing is happening to the Soviet Union.

At the end of World War II, the United States was still invulnerable to a direct attack by a foreign power. In 1949, the development of the atomic bomb by the Soviet Union ended that ideal state of affairs, perhaps forever.

By the early 1950's, the U.S.S.R., on the basis of its own unilateral decision to accept the inevitable retaliation, could have launched an attack on the United States with bombers carrying fission bombs. Most of these bombers would have penetrated our defense, and the American casualties could have numbered in the tens of millions.

During the late 1950's and early 1960's, first thermonuclear bombs and then intercontinental missiles became part of the equation. As a result, by 1970 the U.S.S.R., again on the basis of its own unilateral decision to accept the inevitable retaliation, could launch an attack that could produce 100 million or more American casualties.

This steady decrease in national security does not result from inaction on the part of responsible U.S. military and civilian authorities. It is the inevitable consequence of the arms race and the systematic exploitation of the fruits of modern science and technology by the United States and the U.S.S.R. Our attempts to deploy bomber defenses during the 1950's and 1960's did not substantially modify this picture, and

ABM deployment will, I believe, have an even smaller direct impact on the number of casualties we might suffer in a future attack.

EFFECTS ON STRATEGIC ARMS LIMITATION TALKS

Nearly everyone now recognizes the futility of the arms race, and nearly everyone now realizes that still more of the same baroque military technology is not going to provide a solution to the dilemma of the steady decrease in our national security that has accompanied the increase in our military power. The SALT talks are one hopeful result of the widening recognition of the absolute necessity of finding some other approach to the problem, and finding it soon.

So, how do ABM (and MIRV) affect these talks? We must consider both of these elements of the arms race, since they are really inseparable. ABM automatically leads to MIRV, and vice versa. There are at least two major effects.

First of all, ABM has both a multiplying and a ratchet effect on the arms race; its deployment produces a stepwise, irreversible increase in the number of offensive missiles required. It does not matter whether the deployment is Chinese-oriented or Soviet-oriented. Consider a Chinese-oriented ABM. People who propose such a system imagine the Chinese blackmailing us with just a few (50 to 100) ICBM's by threatening to destroy some small but vital part of the United States. Since the defensive coverage of an ABM interceptor is small as compared to the dimensions of the United States, since Hawaii and Alaska must be defended, and since the offense in this special and peculiar case could concentrate all of its missiles on just one small area of the United States, we would need many times as many ABM's as the Chinese have missiles. If they have no penetration aids, we might get by with only 24 times as many interceptors as they have missiles; however, if they do have good decoys or multiple warheads, a cautious U.S. defense planner would call for a great many more. Thus, a really serious Chinese-oriented ABM system requires many thousands of U.S. ABM interceptors. Now reverse this and ask what the Soviets would have to do in the face of such a Chinese-oriented U.S. ABM deployment. In their case we do not imagine them as merely blackmailing us by threatening to destroy a few cities. Rather, we imagine them as trying to deter us, as we try to deter them.

According to the current fashion in strategic analysis, in order to achieve deterrence it is necessary to have an offensive force which, after weathering a surprise attack, can still retaliate and destroy a large fraction of the enemy's population and industrial base, and as much of his offensive force as may still remain in silos and on bases. In order for the Soviets to be able to do that, they must be able to penetrate *all* parts of our ABM shield with whatever force they might have left after a first attack by us. And to guarantee that outcome, a conservative Soviet planner would have to call for many more total Soviet offensive warheads than there were total U.S. interceptors. Thus, an ABM designed to cope with blackmail by 50 to 100 Chinese missiles can produce a multiplying and a ratchet effect requiring a total Soviet warhead inventory much larger than the more than 1000 warheads they now possess. Clearly, in such an event we cannot hope to achieve any meaningful strategic arms limitation.

A second way in which ABM and MIRV affect the possibility of a successful outcome of the SALT talks is through the uncertainties they introduce into the strategic equation. The main uncertainty connected with ABM is the one that has been so persistently raised for more than a decade: How well will it work? The main uncertainty connected with MIRV has to do with the impossibility of knowing how many warheads were actually poised for launch. As is well known, we are fairly confident about our ability to know how many missiles the Soviets have, but, as others have pointed out, it is quite another matter to know how many MIRV warheads each missile carries.

At present, then, each of us, the United States and the U.S.S.R., is fairly confident in his predictions about the results of a hypothetical nuclear exchange, and each is confident that he has a force adequate to deter the other. With ABM and MIRV, this confidence will be greatly weakened, and neither of us will be sure of what we could do to the other, and of what he could do to us. Unfortunately, experience has clearly shown that such gross uncertainties produce an atmosphere in which arms control agreements are practically impossible. For example, for more than a decade, similar uncertainties about detecting underground explosions, combined with wild speculations about the kinds of developments which might flow from a secret series of underground tests, have inhibited any progress toward eliminating such tests and thus achieving a complete nuclear test ban. In the same way, the uncertainties inevitably associated with ABM and MIRV will lead us into a similar morass, and no progress will be possible in the extremely vital area of strategic arms limitations.

In summary, the steady progress of the arms race has led to an equally steady and seemingly inexorable decrease in our national security and safety. Today, the strategic balance is such that strategic arms limitation agreements, which could bring an end to the nuclear arms race, seem possible. ABM and MIRV threaten to upset this balance in a way which will make such agreements impossible, or at least extremely difficult. ABM and MIRV are inseparable; each inspires and requires the other. They must be stopped before it is too late, if we are to avoid another increase in the magnitude of the nuclear holocaust we all face.

REFERENCE AND NOTE

1. An "accuracy of x nautical miles" means that, if a large sample of missiles were fired at a single target, then half of them would fall within a distance of x nautical miles from the target. This measure of accuracy is usually referred to as CEP, or "circular error probable."
2. Report to the Supreme Soviet of the U.S.S.R., 10 July 1969.

5
Statement on Psychological Aspects of International Relations

Jerome D. Frank

DR. FRANK. Thank you, Senator Fulbright.
I should like to express my gratitude for being offered the unusual opportunity of appearing before this committee. As a psychiatrist and psychologist, my field of interest is the study of normal and maladjusted people and treatment of the latter in individual interviews and small groups. Since at first glance these activities seem to have nothing to do with international relations, a word of explanation may be in order.

RELATIONSHIP OF GROUP OR INDIVIDUAL BEHAVIOR TO NATIONS

No psychiatrist or psychologist would be so rash as to claim that one can make solid or positive inferences about the behavior of nations from

From Statement on psychological aspects of international relations before a hearing of the Committee on Foreign Relations, United States Senate, May 25, 1966, pp. 9–16.

that of individuals. Obviously a host of new and important factors come into play in passing from the individual to the national level. National policies, however, are made by decision-makers acting individually or as members of committees, so that insights gained by observation of persons in private and group interviews may not be without relevance. In fact, it is startling how often similarities between the behavior of nations and individuals seem to emerge when one starts to look for them. Calling attention to some of these similarities may raise questions that policymakers would wish to consider in their deliberations.

It should be made explicit that my observations will deal only with the motives and behavior of normal people. As in the rest of medicine, one learns about health through studying illness. Persons with problems reveal processes that operate in everyone but are often obscured in persons who are functioning well.

For the first time in history all nations are faced with the possibility of sudden annihilation. This forces them to reexamine traditional ways of conducting their affairs and to devise the new ways of dealing with each other that are more appropriate to the conditions of life today. Such an undertaking requires examination of the greatest possible range of information and ideas from all fields of knowledge that might possibly have something to offer. I believe that the study of human nature is such a field.

The views I shall express are my personal opinions and not necessarily those of any organization to which I belong.

BELIEFS AND EXPECTATIONS DETERMINE THOUGHT AND BEHAVIOR

The role of psychological factors in international conflict has not gone unnoticed by national leaders. For example, Gen. Douglas MacArthur, addressing the American Legion in 1955, said:

> The present tensions with their threat of national annihilation are kept alive by two great illusions. The one, a complete belief on the part of the Soviet world that the capitalist countries are preparing to attack it; that sooner or later we intend to strike. And the other, a complete belief on the part of the capitalist countries that the Soviets are preparing to attack us; that, sooner or later, they intend to strike.
> Both are wrong—

He continues—

Each side, so far as the masses are concerned, is equally desirous of peace. For either side, war with the other would mean nothing but disaster. Both equally dread it. But the constant acceleration of preparation may well, without specific intent, ultimately produce a spontaneous combustion.

General MacArthur calls attention to an important psychological principle that appears highly relevant to international affairs—namely, that a person's beliefs and expectations largely determine how he thinks and behaves. Since members of the same society tend to share the same beliefs, this principle becomes important in understanding how nations see and behave toward each other.

In order to survive, every person has to organize the flood of experiences pouring in on him to enable him to predict what the effects of his behavior will be upon both things and other people. This organizing process starts as soon as he is born, and is guided by his experiences with his family and other people in his society. The expectations thus created filter and arrange incoming information.

We are not aware that our expectations are constantly shaping our picture of the world because the process goes on outside of consciousness. To take a simple example, a psychologist had Mexican and American schoolteachers look into a device that showed a different picture to each eye at the same time. A picture of a baseball player was presented to one eye and a picture of a bullfighter to the other. An overwhelming proportion of the Mexicans "saw" the bullfighter; an overwhelming proportion of the Americans saw the baseball player. What they saw was largely determined by whether they were Mexicans or Americans.

A person's group membership also influences what he hears and remembers. Back in 1941 some Republicans and Democrats were asked to listen to a speech containing equal numbers of statements for and against the New Deal. A little while later they were asked what it contained. The Republicans said it was a speech denouncing the New Deal and remembered quotations, supporting their position. The Democrats said it favored the New Deal and recalled quotations supporting this view.

The pictures of the world formed by the expectations of members of every society and nation resemble each other in many ways but differ in others—and each believes its own to be true, just as true as that the sun will rise tomorrow.

THE "SELF-FULFILLING PROPHECY"

When nations are in conflict, the images of each other that they form regularly take on the same features. Each adversary sees itself as peacefully inclined and the other as aggressive.

Contributing to the formation of this "mirror image" of the enemy is a psychological process termed "psycho-logic"—the continual effort to make one's world-view emotionally consistent even if it is not logically consistent. Thus, once nations find themselves in a position of mutual antagonism, each interprets all actions of the other as based on bad motives, just as its own acts always spring from good ones. This has several unfortunate consequences.

The view that another nation's acts always have hostile motives may create a self-fulfilling prophecy. This term refers to the fact that sometimes a person's expectations cause him to do things that make his expectations come true. A striking domestic example occurred in 1929 at the start of the depression. Many depositors in solvent banks expected them to fail. They therefore hastened to withdraw their deposits, thereby bringing about the very bank failures they feared.

The classic example of the self-fulfilling prophecy in international relations is an arms race. Each side anticipates an attack by the other. In response to this expectation, each arms itself, thereby convincing the other that its fears are justified, leading to another round of arms increases.

When nations are heavily armed and mutually fearful, this kind of conflict spiral can lead to war with breathtaking speed, as occurred immediately preceding the outbreak of the first world war. Detailed analysis of thousands of state papers produced in the weeks following the assassination of Archduke Ferdinand at Sarajevo has revealed that the leaders of each of the great powers saw themselves as offering friendship but receiving hostility. That is, each selectively emphasized the other's hostile gestures and discounted their friendly ones. These mutual distortions led to reciprocal acts that in a few weeks culminated in a general war from which Europe has never really recovered.

SHAPING OF JUDGMENT BY EXPECTATION

Once nations are actually fighting, similar acts are viewed as evil when committed by the enemy and morally neutral when performed by us. An unpleasant example of this double standard of morality is the concept of atrocities. All modern wars involve the killing of noncombatants. In the course of time certain traditional forms of killing gradually come to be recognized as legitimate. Other forms, that sooner or later appear in any war, are regarded as legitimate or unavoidable by the side that resorts to them, and as atrocious by the other. Each side then uses the atrocities committed by the other to confirm its harsh view of the enemy and justify its own acts. Thus in the first world war the German General von Hausen saw nothing wrong in shooting down Belgian civilian hostages because the Belgian Government "approved perfidious street fighting, contrary to international law." In Vietnam, each side is outraged by the "atrocities" of which each accuses the other. We dwell on the assassination and tortures committed by the Vietcong. Communist leaders castigate Americans for using "the most cruel and barbaric means of annihilating people," by which they mean new antipersonnel weapons, chemical destruction of crops, and napalm, made possible by our more advanced technology. As we see it, we resort to these measures reluctantly and only out of necessity. In this way, we preserve our own self-image as a humane, compassionate people.

The image of the enemy as evil, finally, acts to block acceptance of his genuine conciliatory moves. Since he is, by definition, implacably hostile, an apparently friendly gesture tends to be seen either as evidence of his weakening, or as an effort to create dissension within our own ranks. The usual response to such a move, therefore, is angry rejection coupled with reassertion of one's undiminished determination to continue the fight. A recent example was Peking's rejecting as "frauds," to use their word, American offers to let our scientists and scholars visit China and Chinese ones visit the United States and Senator Mansfield's proposal for an Asian conference.

Psychological dynamisms like the mirror image of the enemy, the double standard of morality and the self-fulfilling prophecy operate in all nations at war and impede efforts to restore peace. The Vietnam war has an additional tension-producing feature—a strong ideological component. To understand what this implies it is necessary to consider briefly the psychological functions of ideologies.

THE NEED FOR IDEOLOGIES

A psychologically crucial part of the reality world of any group is its beliefs about the meaning of existence. Every person has to shield himself somehow from the unendurable realization that his individual life is a very transitory and insignificant event in an ongoing universe. He does this by embracing an ideology or religion that links his life to some larger, more enduring purpose. For many this is an abstraction like God or democracy or communism. A shared ideology is vital not only to the individual but to his group as well, since the common philosophy of life binds the members together. Therefore, for many persons surrendering the belief that gives meaning to their lives and links them to their group would be intolerable—it would represent a kind of psychological death harder to contemplate than biological death.

The existence of a group that holds an ideology differing from our own creates anxiety. Why? Because the very fact that they maintain different beliefs implies that ours might be wrong. The sense of mutual threat is intensified if each of the rival ideologies requires its adherents to convert or destroy believers in the other. In the past this has been true of Islam and Christianity, of Catholicism and Protestantism. It used to be true of communism and free enterprise, and probably still is in the minds of old line Chinese Communists.

Humans, like all living creatures, are incited to violence by threats to their survival. We differ from all other creatures primarily in our power to symbolize, so that we respond with violence not only to actual provocations like direct threats to life or property, but to psychological ones like threats to our ideology or self-esteem.

IDEOLOGICAL CHARACTER OF THE VIETNAMESE WAR

In the Vietnam war, psychological issues have become very important. From a strictly materialistic standpoint, the territory of Vietnam is of limited strategic importance to us, and the Vietcong would be much better off economically if they peacefully acquiesced to our presence. But we see behind the struggle over territory such psychological issues as whether our will or that of China is stronger, whether other nations can trust our commitments, and, above all, whose view of the world will eventually prevail.

Judging from their statements, our adversaries see themselves as fighting against neocolonialism—a concept loaded with psychological overtones—and also, for some, to further the ideology of communism.

Thus the Vietnam war has assumed an ideological character similar to the holy wars of former times, and this has ominous implications.

People who are fighting for their ideals seldom if ever can be forced into surrendering by punishment. One can control behavior by punishment, as every parent knows. But whether punishment changes the child's basic attitude or not, depends mainly on whether he believes it to be deserved. If he does, he feels guilty for having transgressed and renounces the bad behavior indefinitely. If he feels the punishment to be unjust, he will stop misbehaving to be sure, but only while the punisher can observe him. The first time he believes he can get away with it, he will resume his misdeeds. At the same time, the punishment increases his resentment and rebelliousness, provoking him to more mischief. Children who have been harshly punished are more prone to become delinquents than those who have been disciplined in gentler ways.

Nations at war, if they could be said to resemble children at all, clearly would be like the ones who believe the punishment to be unjust. Since they see themselves as righteous, punishment by their opponents, far from making them contrite, is bitterly resented. While a defeated nation may be forced to accept the victor's terms, it typically bides its time until it can get revenge. This seems to be one of the reasons why one war so often leads to another, as in the cycle of wars between France and Germany between 1870 and 1940.

Insofar as the Vietnam war resembles a holy war, punishment would seem to have particularly little likelihood of success. To suffer and die for a holy cause is highly virtuous, and one hopes to convert others through the example of one's own sacrifice. The notion that one can cause people to abandon their ideologies by inflicting pain on them should have died in Rome with the Christian martyrs. In contrast to wars fought for tangible spoils ideological wars have no natural end point. As a result, in the past they have characteristically been stopped only by exhaustion of both sides after tremendous carnage, with the survivors still clinging to their respective beliefs. Today, with weapons of unlimited destructive power lurking in the wings, such wars threaten to expand until they destroy civilization.

INCENTIVES AND MEANS FOR SURVIVAL AND COOPERATION

These are some of the dark aspects of the picture as a psychologist sees it. Fortunately, the same conditions of life that have created new dangers have also created new incentives and means for overcoming them. From a

psychological standpoint, the central longterm task is to learn to understand and deal with people of other nations on their own terms. The new
incentives are, on the one hand, the threat of mutual annihilation if
nations do not mend their ways and, on the other, the enormous gains in
human welfare nations could achieve by working together. As President
Johnson has said:

> The most exciting horizons are in the life of man himself—
> and what we can do to improve it. We can eliminate poverty. We
> can cure man's ills, extend man's life, and raise man's hopes.

The new means for promoting international cooperation are supplied by gigantic advances in communication and transportation like
Telstar and jet transports. Psychologists, psychiatrists, and others have
accumulated considerable information as to how to foster mutually helpful communication among citizens of different nations and avoid the
pitfalls involved, but it would go too far afield to review their findings
here.

ENFORCED COOPERATION AS A MEANS OF REDUCING
ANTAGONISM

Modern science has created new means of reducing international tension,
however, that deserves a word of comment. Many scientific projects that
have only recently become feasible require international cooperation
to obtain their full benefits. Examples are weather control and space
exploration. An experiment done in a boys' camp some years ago suggests
that activities requiring cooperation between hostile groups have a
powerful effect in reducing mutual antagonism. In this experiment, boys
who were initially strangers to each other were formed into two groups.
Then the groups were made enemies through athletic competitions. In
time, they became like two hostile nations. The members of each group
chose their friends only from among themselves, looked down on members of the other, and the two groups fought at every opportunity. Once
when a member of one tried to act as a peacemaker, he was promptly
ostracized by his fellows. Simply bringing the two groups together did
nothing to reduce their mutual antagonism. However, when the camp
director surreptitiously arranged matters so that both groups had to
cooperate, mutual hostility rapidly diminished. For example, he secretly

arranged for the camp water supply to be interrupted, and the whole camp had to get out and repair it. The truck carrying food for an overnight hike unaccountably ran into a ditch and stalled, and all the boys had to get on the towrope to pull it out. It took a series of such events to break down the hostility between the two groups, but friendly relations were eventually completely restored.

I would hesitate to generalize from 11-year-old boys to nations in conflict were it not for certain obvious parallels. In a sense the nations of the world today are in the same predicament as the boys in the camp. They will have to cooperate in order to survive. Moreover, working together toward common goals seems also to be effective on the international scene. For example, cooperation of many nations in the Antarctic to gain valuable information about the earth's surface that no one of them could acquire alone led to its complete demilitarization and a treaty which has given no trouble at all.

The development of the Mekong River delta is a similar undertaking. On a larger scale, President Johnson's recent initiatives toward keeping the moon and planets open for international scientific cooperation on the model of Antarctica are most encouraging. Just as everybody would lose in a nuclear war, in this type of project everybody gains.

BUILDING BRIDGES TO MAINLAND CHINA

But this is for the future. A pressing, immediate task is to build bridges—to borrow Secretary McNamara's phrase—between mainland China and the United States. This requires overcoming formidable barriers on both sides. It takes considerable courage to try to make contact with a distrusted adversary, because this exposes one to dangers not only from him but from one's own side as well. The peacemaker's own group are apt to accuse him of disloyalty, while the opponent may try to take advantage of his good will to dupe him or ferret out secrets.

The first step, and probably psychologically the most difficult one, would be for the United States to be willing to reexamine its own image of China. We know that they misjudge our intentions. Can we be sure that we are not to some extent misjudging theirs? We would have to open our minds to the possibility that their bluster is motivated in large part by fear of our intentions toward them. This view gains plausibility from the illuminating review of the history of the relations of China with the Western powers presented at recent hearings of this committee.

The problem of establishing communication with China and North Vietnam involves overcoming intense mutual mistrust. Here, perhaps what psychiatrists have learned about establishing communication with a frightened, angry, and suspicious person may have some relevance. The first step, we have found, is simply to show a persistent willingness to listen to such a person and to refuse to be discouraged by his rebuffs. You studiously avoid provoking him. At the same time you firmly defend yourself against physical attack but you ignore merely verbal abuse.

In approaching a deeply suspicious person, it does not pay to be too friendly. Since he is convinced that you mean him no good, he is prone to misinterpret an overly friendly manner as an effort to put something over on him. So a firm, reserved but not unfriendly manner makes more headway than effusiveness. With persistence in this approach, in time he may come to believe that your professed desire to understand and help him may not be entirely insincere, and the first steps toward useful communication have been made.

Assuming that we are willing to broaden communication with China in an effort to reduce mutual tension, a similar strategy may be appropriate. Our recent proposals may be a beginning. They have met the expected angry rejection, but this should not discourage us from continuing. In view of China's historic sense of humiliation, perhaps we should be prepared to go even further and accept some symbolic humiliation at their hands. If, as is generally anticipated, they scornfully reject the first invitation to join the U.N., perhaps our best strategy would be to urge that the invitation be repeated until it looks as if, by accepting it they are doing the rest of the world a favor, rather than the reverse.

Sometimes it helps to let a frightened, suspicious person overhear you discussing him with someone else. This permits him to listen without having to acknowledge that he is doing so and does not put him under any pressure to respond. That is, it leaves the initiative with him. For these reasons, permitting him to eavesdrop may be less apt to arouse his anxiety and suspicion than a direct attempt to influence him. To make a long jump, the public discussion of our Vietnam and China policies now going on in the United States, which is being overheard by those nations and the rest of the world, may have similar values. Of course, it does carry the danger of reinforcing the adversary's mistaken belief that our determination to resist will weaken if they persist long enough.

But the demonstration that important American policymakers and segments of the public are actively trying to understand our adversaries' view of the world and are searching for ways to improve relations with them might be a better way of relieving their fears concerning our intentions than attempts to reassure them directly.

NECESSITY FOR WORLDWIDE MUTUAL UNDERSTANDING

To conclude, in this shrinking, interdependent world, living daily under the threat of destruction, all nations must eventually learn to understand each other's point of view. They must learn to accept and live with their differences, while searching for and exploiting shared beliefs and goals. This is necessary for the creation of a stable world order that will exclude war as a way of settling international conflicts. I have tried to suggest a few of the psychological aspects of this staggering task, which may indeed prove to be beyond human capabilities. If nations fail to master it, the days of civilization are probably numbered. If they succeed, the potentials for human welfare will have no bounds.

The Chairman.   Thank you very much, Dr. Frank. I think that is a very interesting statement.
Dr. Osgood, would you proceed with your statement before the questions.

Dr. Osgood.   Yes, sir.

The Chairman.   You may proceed.

6
Statement on Psychological Aspects
of International Relations

Charles E. Osgood

Dr. Osgood.   I would like to thank the members of this committee for the opportunity to express some of my thoughts about this very important problem.

I also would like to say that the ideas expressed in my statement are my own and do not necessarily represent those of any institution to which I may belong.

Like many other people in this country today, I have been trying to put our present crises into perspective, trying as best I can to understand them as part of a larger scheme of things. For there will be more Vietnams, more Dominican Republics, more African Congos, for as far into the future as we can see. Rebellions, revolutions, and so-called "wars of national liberation" are stimulated, in considerable part, by a tide of rising expectations among "have-not" peoples, a tide which we have done perhaps the most to create. The simultaneous development of nuclear weapons technology, however, has placed severe restrictions upon how we can deal with such conflicts. The fundamental problem, as I see it, for Americans is this: How can a "have" nation like the United States use its immense wealth and military power for what it defines as benevolent ends?

Both escalation strategists (the so-called hawks) and deescalation strategists (the so-called doves) are well aware of the constraints imposed by the nuclear age. Both agree that political objectives must be severely limited and that the steps taken to achieve them must be prudently graduated. But here agreement ends: each sees the other as espousing a course that must lead inevitably to the surrender of legitimate national goals. These competing strategists come to ultimate confrontation within the mind of one man, our President, Lyndon B. Johnson. I do not believe he has fully committed himself to either policy approach, but rather is

From Statement on psychological aspects of international relations before a hearing of the Committee on Foreign Relations, United States Senate, May 25, 1966, pp. 16–23.

probing and testing the feasibilities and consequences of each. Since I am a psychologist by training and by outlook, I shall stress the psychological facets of these strategies. However, let me confess at the outset that it is hard for me to draw any sharp line between what is really psychological and what is really political in this particular matter.

CALCULATED ESCALATION AND CALCULATED DEESCALATION

Calculated escalation as a political strategy has been described as "a competition in resolve" and as "a competition in risktaking." As in the game of chicken between teenagers on our highways, it is assumed that two opponents will differ in the level of tension they can tolerate, either for psychological (political) reasons or for reasons of relative military capability, or both. The initiator gradually increases the level of force being applied, in calculated steps, hoping to reach a level at which the opponent is no longer willing to take risks before the initiator reaches his own risk ceiling. A victory is achieved when the opponent concedes the political objective of the initiator.

Calculated escalation has four very significant features. First the steps are unilaterally initiated; we do not negotiate with the North Vietnamese about increasing the tempo of our bombing or moving it closer to Hanoi—we just do it unilaterally.

Second, each step in escalation propels the opponent into reciprocating, if he can, with more aggressive steps of his own. To the extent that the escalation is calculated and can be controlled, the steps by both sides are carefully graduated. But military escalation is deliberately tension increasing.

If we change this last feature, shift it from tension increasing to tension decreasing, we have the essence of a strategy of calculated deescalation. It is one in which nation A devises patterns of small steps, well within its limits of security, intended to reduce tensions and designed to induce reciprocating steps from nation B. If such unilateral initiatives are persistently applied, and reciprocation is obtained, then the margin for risk taking is widened and somewhat larger steps of the same sort can be taken. Both sides, in effect, begin backing down the escalation ladder. The intended direct effect is damping of mutual tensions and lessened chances of expanded conflict; the intended psychological side effect is increased mutual confidence and trust. This strategy does assume some rationality on the part of the components; it probably would not work against another Hitler. But by virtue of its carefully graduated nature, it allows us to find out if we are in fact dealing with a rational opponent.

This strategy includes the "stick" as well as the "carrot." Sufficient nuclear and graded conventional forces are retained to insure that we can resist military escalation by others. If any opponent misinterprets our tension-reducing moves as signs of weakness, and makes an aggressive probe to test his interpretation—as the Soviets did in Cuba—then we shift promptly to the "stick"; we resist firmly, yet calculatedly, using precisely that level of force estimated to restore the status quo. As a matter of fact, such probes, and their consequences, provide the most effective learning experiences for both sides. The three years following the Cuban missile crisis were characterized by reciprocative tension-reducing moves between the United States and the U.S.S.R., and there was a noticeable warming of relations. The Soviets even coined their own name for this. They called it the policy of mutual example.

CAN ESCALATION AND DEESCALATION BE MIXED?

Now, can escalation and deescalation strategies be "mixed" in the sense that military men speak of the best "mix" of weapons systems? Is it possible to escalate the intensity of attack upon an opponent with one hand while simultaneously holding out an olive branch in the other? I do not believe this is psychologically feasible. The reactions to one treatment conflict directly with reactions to the other—aggressive impulses versus conciliatory impulses. An opponent can be bombed into surrender, or even into nonexistence, but he cannot be bombed into honest negotiations.

My colleagues in experimental psychology would recognize what I have described as a strategy of calculated deescalation as being similar to the familiar process which they call shaping behavior in the laboratory. The giving of rewards and punishments is made to depend precisely upon what the subject has just done; in this way he is encouraged to learn which reactions to which properties of complex situations lead him to success.

In other words, the purpose of such "shaping" is to make one form of behavior dependent upon one set of circumstances and another form of behavior dependent upon a different set of circumstances. My colleagues would also recognize calculated escalation as an attempt to "shape" the behavior of an opponent. But I think they would question a strategy which provides only negative instances, a strategy that offers only punishments, a strategy that offers no cues for when to behave one way rather than another.

I am not suggesting that principles of individual behavior can be applied to the behavior of nations in any direct, simple-minded fashion. What I am trying to suggest is that such principles may provide us with hunches about internation behavior that can be tested against experience in the larger arena.

No one in his right mind wants a full-scale nuclear war. Therefore escalation as a strategy comes down to knowing when and how to get off the escalator. But it is always the opponent who is expected to back down. At each rung on the escalation ladder, the initiator offers both the threat of further escalation, if further provoked, and promise of cessation, if appeased. Do both of these "messages" get through with equal clarity? Psychologically, I believe, the answer must be "No." In any conflict situation, it is easier to believe an opponent's aggressive statements (such as "we will bury you") than his conciliatory statments. Threats are consistent with what one expects from an enemy; promises are inconsistent. In communication under conflict conditions, therefore, there is a constant bias of credibility which favors further escalation and hinders deescalation.

In the game of chicken as practiced by some of our teenagers, there is a premium upon convincing the fellow in the other car that your are violently hostile and irrational, and even that you have thrown away your steering wheel. Why? To maintain the credibility that you will not be the one to swerve to safety as your cars drive at each other down the center of the road. Needless to say, if both drivers throw away their steering wheels, neither has much chance of survival.

There are two kinds of credibility, however. Credibility type I is the implacably hostile image: A behaves in such a way as to convince B that he is likely to attack regardless of what B does. A behaves unpredictably, does not practice what he preaches, and in general keeps B uncertain and anxious. This is the kind of credibility created by rival gangs in our city slums. Credibility type II is the firm but potentially cooperative image. A behaves in such a way as to convince B that he will only attack if B breaks certain clearly prescribed rules. He creates the impression of rationality by behaving predictably, by making his words and deeds consistent with each other, and generally by trying to make B feel less threatened. This is the kind of credibility a wise father tries to create, the kind of credibility police officers have found most effective in deterring criminal behavior. A powerful nation can behave either way, but I submit that only the second type of credibility is consistent with long-term survival in a nuclear age.

THE IMPULSE TOWARD ESCALATION

If the United States is, indeed, experimenting with calculated escalation as a strategy for dealing with "Wars of national liberation," then I think that we are in danger of swallowing a baited hook. For 20 years this nation has been building up the mightiest military force that has ever been seen on the face of the earth. Yet, for most of these years, our leadership has made us sit on our arms—almost literally—and for some people this is frustrating if not downright humiliating posture. The strategy of calculated escalation offers a rationalization for the use of force, indeed, gives it a hard, scholarly legitimacy. This is the bait—the temptation to use the military power we obviously have. What is the hook?

The hook is psychological. It may be true that, physically, escalators can run down just as easily as up, but, psychologically it is much easier to keep on going up than to stop, reverse, and back down. Each increase in tension makes it more difficult to achieve the accurate communication and the shared understandings that are necessary for deescalation of tensions. Internally, particularly, I think, in a democracy, a sense of commitment is created which makes backing down extremely difficult politically. Externally, escalation up to some point produces hardening rather than softening in the opponent's resolve, and this critical point is very difficult to predict. Psychologically, one can become glued to an escalator only too easily. This is the hook.

Individuals learn from experience. I think nations learn from experience, too—particularly from crisis experience. Each crisis is like one trial in a long series of trials, extending backward into our past and forward into our future. Success of escalation in one crisis, even if only in military form, makes the choice of this strategy even more probable in the next crisis. Just as an individual human being can become fixed on a maladjustive form of behavior—a compulsion, an obsession—so may a nation become fixed upon a kind of international behavior which is essentially maladjustive and contrary to its own real interests and values.

The paths of history are strewn with the relics of such nations. Is it possible to get off an escalator once you are caught on it?

DEESCALATION AS APPLIED TO COMMUNIST CHINA

Many people think that deescalation strategy can be successfully applied only where some degree of good will already exists. This is definitely not the case. All that is required is a sufficient amount of rational self-interest on both sides. Another psychological phenomenon is relevant here. If a person is constrained, either by his own self-interest or by external pressures, to keep on behaving as if he favored another and agreed with him—when in fact he does not—then what psychologists call cognitive dissonance is created. This is conflict between what one believes and how one behaves. Something must give, and, if the pressures toward continuing cooperation are strong, it is usually beliefs and feelings about the other person that change.

I think the same thing applies to nations, or rather to people within nations, and their perceptions of each other. If they can be constrained by reason of their self-interest to repeatedly behave toward each other in ways that are inconsistent with their hostility and distrust, then pressures are set up for modifying these mutual perceptions. In other words, a continuing pattern of reciprocating acts of a tension-reducing nature can literally create some mutual good will where very little or none of it existed to begin with. I think we experienced this psychological side effect in our relations with the Soviet Union over the past 3 years. Recent events are reversing this trend, however.

The debate over our future policy toward Communist China has already begun. Many Americans have deep resistance to even considering deescalation of tensions with respect to the Chinese. There are at least two psychological factors here. One is the assumption that the primary motive behind Chinese policy toward the United States is aggression, and that they are kept from it only by their fear of our military power. Let me suggest, as another possibility, that their primary motivation may actually be fear, and that they act aggressively because of this fear. China is relatively weak militarily—certainly when our nuclear arsenal is taken in the balance. In much the same way that some fish puff themselves up into a threatening ball of spines when a feared predator is encountered, so may a fearful nation bluster and growl in the hope of warding off a more powerful competitor. But note that China's blustering words have not been matched in her deeds. We Americans, knowing that we are really peaceful in intent, projecting this knowledge into the minds of others, and assuming that they also know that we are really peaceful in intent, find it very difficult to believe that people in any other nation could actually fear us. But they can.

The other source of resistance is the assumption that "what is good for them must be bad for us." This is another example of what Dr. Frank has called 'psycho-logic''—the attempt to force a complex real world with its varying shades of gray into absolute and simple blacks and whites. Quite to the contrary, I would submit, that what is good for the Chinese— in health, in economic well-being, in education, and in security from external threat—may also be good for us in the long run. As has proven true for the Soviets, the more one has to lose, the less he is willing to risk losing it. In the broadest sense, then, this would be effective deterrence against future Chinese aggression.

NECESSITY FOR PERSPECTIVE IN THE NUCLEAR AGE

Developing and applying policies that are appropriate to the time in which we live requires depth of perspective. One ingredient is understanding our own goals as a society. We are pretty clear about what we are against—communism—but we are not so clear about what we are for. I believe most Americans would agree on at least the following goals:

First, we want to survive, with as much of happiness, health, and the other good things of life as we can muster for ourselves and for those who come with us. I put this primitive value first, because without life there is very little we can do about anything else. Second, we want to preserve our way of life—basically, one in which the individual has a relatively large share of freedom of choice as compared with the State which governs him. Third, we want to extend to others what we see as a good and secure life— not by force but by the power of example. No nation in history has ever given so freely, if not always wisely, to others, and our President has repeatedly indicated his desire to improve the conditions of other humans on this teeming planet.

Another ingredient of perspective is understanding how the advent of nuclear technology has changed the rules of international relations. It is one of the paradoxes of the nuclear age that, the more military power a nation has, the more restrained it must be in its use of that power. To use an analogy, in a canoe, it is more dangerous for a big man to throw his weight around than for a little man to do so. In other words, the very nature of nuclear weapons has forced a strict limitation on political objectives in conflict situations and a strict control over the military means of obtaining these objectives. To return to my analogy, the problem is for a big man to learn how to handle a canoe without capsizing it in the process.

Yet another ingredient of perspective is understanding ourselves. We forget too easily, I think, that human civilization is a fragile thing, still in its infancy as the clock of the universe measures things. Our written history goes back only about 5000 years; go back another mere hundred thousand or so and you will find us huddled in caves and gnawing on raw bones. It is not surprising, then, that our ways of thinking have not kept up with our facility with tools. This gap—between our understanding and control of things and our understanding and control of ourselves—is the crux of our problem as a species as we enter the nuclear age.

In preserving a system of beliefs—an ideology, if you will—which simplifies and renders comprehensible a very complicated real world, human beings are prone to accept evidence which is consistent with the system and reject evidence which is not, to assume that others share their world view and then punish them if they do not behave accordingly, to attribute good motives to themselves and evil motives to their opponents, even for exactly the same behavior. Such mental processes have served to create bogeymen with inhuman powers out of opponents in every human conflict. The only protection against the effects of these emotional ways of thinking is awareness that we are susceptible to them by virtue of being merely human.

UNITED STATES POLICIES IN A REVOLUTIONARY WORLD

I should like to stress the fact that such ways of thinking are central, not peripheral, to problems of foreign policy. Over the past few decades we have created a bogey out of communism and have endowed it with assumed properties and powers that tend to obscure its true nature and render us less effective in dealing with it than we could be. By reacting to each new crisis as if we were in fact faced by a monolithic, unmodifiable and implacably hostile world communism, we tend to create the very kind of opponent we assume to exist. This is a self-fulfilling prophecy but it is also self-defeating. I think we make the Communist world more monolithic, more implacably hostile and more unmodifiable by the very way we respond to its challenges. Communism is an alien and unacceptable way of life for Americans and we are justified in competing with it vigorously across the world. But we should be competing with the real thing, intelligently, not against a phantom created in part by the workings of our own minds. I think we should realize that the real war, the real war against communism, as a way of life, must ultimately be won in men's minds, not on the battlefield.

Rome wasn't built in a day, and neither will be security for a free world. As participants in a young and bustling society, most Americans tend to be impatient. We have a tradition of progress through tackling problems head on; we have the power and feel a tremendous urge to use it to get things done.

But we cannot expect peoples everywhere to make "a great leap forward" into democracy the moment they are secure from internal or external oppression. It may even be necessary for underpowered countries to go through some period of tightly centralized control, in order to create the minimum conditions for a more democratic way of life later—freedom from perpetual hunger, freedom from perpetual ignorance, and freedom from perpetual fear. If this is true, then I think the best way a powerful democratic nation like the United States can wage the real war against communism as a way of life is to help people move through and out of this stage as rapidly as possible. This means helping to create, even in Communist countries, those additional conditions which make their political system first awkward, then irritating, and eventually intolerable. Quite unintentionally, simply by being an envied model of success in this world, we have been applying pressures throughout the world, and we have been inducing vast changes. But the changes in societies I am talking about require generations, and that is why, I think, we need a great deal of patience.

6
The Resolution of Intergroup and International Conflict
Darwyn E. Linder

James Laue has provided a useful general model that describes the development and resolution of conflict in certain kinds of situations. But only if the opposing groups are in communication with one another and the superordinate group is willing to reallocate some power and resources in response to demands by the subordinate group does this model of the conflict situation seem to apply. It is, of course, not an explanatory account but it is useful in the sense that one can predict the course of conflict and conflict resolution in these kinds of settings. For example, the conflict between women's rights groups and the male dominated power structure of our society can be seen to follow the outline provided by Laue. Of course there is never a perfectly clean and orderly progression from the Step 1 of challenge to Step 7 of change. In most real instances several of these processes are going on at the same time. It is clear that the women's liberation movement has issued a challenge, but it appears that the processes of conflict, crisis and confrontation are all going on at the current time. Perhaps the entire seven-step process is occurring at one time with the different steps related to different issues as each separate issue finds its way through the sequence. For example, changes have already occurred in the wage structure so that women are approaching the goal of equal pay for equal work, and at the same time new challenges are being offered by women attempting to secure equal opportunity in new areas of the job market. In many ways demands by students to share in the decision making power of university administrations can be seen to follow this same 7 C's process. Raymond Mack (1970) recommends the mode of change within universities that Laue has outlined. That is, he recommends sharing decision making power with students, and both communication and compromise as the way to achieve change and to reunite the university so that instead of dealing with internal conflict it may deal with problems of our society.

But the kind of conflict described by Laue and characterized by women's liberation and student power movements is not the deadly conflict that engulfs nations in war and often threatens the continued existence of mankind on this planet. In the kinds of conflict we have been discussing there are democratic processes of change that may be used and there exist channels of communication so that negotiation and compromise can occur. In international conflict effective means of communication are very often absent and there is no established process by which compromise and change may occur. Instead, nations attempt to understand the actions of their opponents and respond to one another on the basis of that understanding. But that understanding is often imperfect and the attributions that a nation makes concerning the motives of its opponent are very often those that imply the most dire of future actions. Herbert York's discussion of ABM and MIRV is an excellent case in point. In the development of weapon systems the nation that observes an opponent making an advance is almost forced to assume that the opponent intends to use the new technology. What follows is an international analogue to the games Anatol Rapoport has used to study conflict in dyads. The nation that has observed the development of a new weapon system by an opponent must decide between two classes of response, whether to develop a weapon system that would nullify this new threat or whether to make what could be called a cooperative response and decide not to develop the new technology. As in the cases of dyads, making the cooperative move leaves a nation open to exploitation because the cooperative gesture necessitates neglecting or abandoning an adequate defense. In the instance of international conflict the possibilities for exploitation can be of the most serious kind.

The potential costs, then, of making a cooperative move in an arms race are extremely high, especially when one nation has no confidence that the opponent will also remain cooperative rather than exploitative, and thus an arms race escalates. The reasoned response by a nation to the development of a new weapon by an opponent is to develop the means of nullifying that weapon, whether it be a defensive deployment such as ABM or an offensive development such as MIRV. Of course this oversimplifies the international situation and is a drastically simplified picture of the U.S.–Soviet arms race. Yet it seems clear that when an opponent's motives have been judged to be of the most sinister kind, a nation can only reply to a threatening gesture with a posture, either offensive or defensive, that nullifies the new threat. Escalation comes about because once the threat of a new offensive development has been nullified, the former threatener is now in danger of being outrun by his opponent and must attempt another advance to regain his position of superiority.

Jerome Frank and Charles Osgood, in their testimony before the

Senate Committee on Foreign Relations, offered some suggestions, based on their knowledge and research as psychologists, for the means of breaking out of this spiralling arms race and for beginning to de-escalate the conflict between nations. Their suggestions were mainly concerned with communicating motives and intentions, first by reversing the escalation process in a series of small steps of de-escalation which Charles Osgood in other writings (Osgood, 1962) has called a system for the graduated reduction of international tension. The second means of helping to reduce conflict between nations is as Jerome Frank pointed out, to open mutual channels of communication and to provide superordinate goals for which nations might strive in concert rather than in conflict. Their testimony was taken in May of 1966. Now, in 1972, more than six years later, perhaps we can discern a trend toward the resolution of international conflict by noting that some of the things that they recommended have come to pass. The People's Republic of China has now been accepted into the United Nations, the American presence in Southeast Asia is being de-escalated, at least the ground forces have been diminished, and President Nixon has visited both Moscow and Peking, achieving significant advances toward mutual understanding. If Frank and Osgood were correct in their assertions that such processes of de-escalation and better communication would reduce the level of international conflict, then perhaps we may indeed be hopeful that nations will find a way to resolve their differences, whether they be ideological or material, without resort to warfare.

REFERENCES

Mack, R. W., Ideology versus intellect: The Vietnamization of the university. *Social Problems*, 1970, *18*, 137–144.
Osgood, C. E., *An Alternative to War or Surrender*. Urbana: University of Illinois Press, 1962.

Indexes

Author Index

A complete citation of a work is given on a page listed in italics.

Alger, C. F., *245*

Anderson, C. S., *58*

Anson, P. F., *12*

Argyle, M., 84, 95, *102*, 105, 109, 113, *116*, 119, *121*

Aronson, E., 28, *31*, 35, *40*, *41*, 79, *83*

Asch, S., 174, *176*, 188, 189, 237

Atkinson, J. W., 8, *12*

Back, K., *13*, 32, *42*, 78, *83*

Backman, C. W., 32, *41*, *42*

Baer, D. M., 1, *4*

Bakan, D., *13*

Baker, H. J., *13*

Banks, F., *59*

Barber, B., *60*

Barker, R. G., 105, 106, 114, *116*

Bates, A., *59*

Beier, E. G., 164, *167*

Bell, R. P., *61*

Beller, E. K., *13*

Benne, K., *236*

Bennis, W., *236*

Bergin, A. E., 159, *166*

Berne, E., 21, *23*, 166, 167

Berscheid, E., 29, *31*, 80, *83*

Birdwhistell, R., 84, *86*, 94, *102*, 117, *121*

Blood, R., 44, *58*

Blumberg, L., *61*

Bonney, M. E., 32, *41*

Boulding, K. E., *256*

Bradford, L., *236*

Brady, R. A., *245*

Burdick, H., 8, *14*

Burgess, E. W., *58*, *86*

Burt, C., *13*

Buss, A. H., 148, *150*

Byrne, D., 29, *31*, 33, *41*

Cartwright, D. C., *13*, 175, 176, 236

Casriel, D., 222, *236*

Child, I. L., *15*

Chinn, R., *236*

Christensen, H., 43, *58*

Coombs, R. H., *58*

Cope, V., *41*

Coser, L., 250, *256*

Crook, J. H., *103*

Darley, J. M., 29, *31*, *209*

Davis, F., 104, *116*

Davis, K. E., 71, 73, 76, *78*, 169, *170*
Dean, D., *13*
Dean, J., 84, *85*, 95, *102*, 105, 109, 113, *116*, 119, *121*
Delora, J., *58*
De Tocqueville, *181*
Deutsch, M., 243, 244, *245*
Dinitz, S., *59*
Dornbusch, S. M., 104, *116*
Draguet, R., *13*
Dreyer, A. S., *13*
Duff, D. F., 95, *103*
Duncan, S., 85, *86*

Ehrlich, D., *13*
Ehrmann, W., *58*, *60*
Ekman, P., 84, *86*, 105, *116*
Ellis, A., 161, 162, *166*
Ellison, B., *102*
Exline, R., *14*, 84, *86*, 105, 109, 110, *116*

Faris, R. E. L., *13*
Fast, J., 85, *86*
Festinger, L., 5, 6, 7, *13*, *14*, 27, *31*, 32, *42*, 195, 237, *240*
Finneran, M., *13*
Florquist, C. C., 71, 73, 76, *78*, 169, *170*
Floyd, J., 28, *31*
Folsom, J. K., *57*
Frank, J., 245, 283, 287, *288*
French, E., 8, *14*
Friessen, W. V., *86*

Gallo, P. S., 244, *245*
Gerard, H., *13*, *42*
Gergen, K. J., 65, 77, *78*, 169, *170*
Gewitz, J. L., 1, *4*, *14*
Gibb, J. R., 217, *236*
Gibby, R. G., *14*

Gilchrist, J. C., *14*
Goffman, E., 84, *86*, 103, 104, 105, 115, *116*
Goldman, M., *14*
Goldstein, S. P., 160, 164, *166*
Gonick, M., *116*
Goode, W. J., *59*
Goodman, N., 104, *116*
Gordon, A. I., *59*
Gordon, T., *237*
Guetzkow, H., 244, *245*
Gullahorn, J. T., 32, *42*
Gumpert, P., 169, *170*

Haeberle, A., *14*
Hailman, J. P., *102*
Haley, J., *167*
Hall, E. T., 84, 85, *86*, 100, *103*, 119, *121*
Hall, G. F., 220, 224, *237*
Halpern, H. M., 163, *167*
Harlow, H. F., 21, 22, *23*, 173, *176*
Harlow, M., 21, 22, *23*, 173, *176*
Hastorf, A. H., 104, *116*
Havens, E., 44, 45, *58*
Heinzelman, F., *15*
Heller, K., 160, 164, *166*
Hess, E. H., 3, *4*, 22, *23*, 118, *121*
Hillmer, M. L., 32, *42*
Himes, J. S., *58*
Hoffman, P. J., *14*
Hollander, E. P., *195*
Hollingshead, A. B., 43, *58*, *59*
Homans, G., 32, *42*
Hooker, H. F., *14*
Hoppe, F., *14*
Horowitz, M. J., *14*, 95, *103*
Horwitz, M., *14*,
Howard, G. E., 177

Inbau, F. E., *102*
Itard, J. M., 3, *4*
Iverson, M. A., 32, *42*

Jackson, J. M., 32, *42*
Jacobs, H., 92, *102*
James, J. W., *102*
Jones, E. E., 30, *31*, 65, 69, *77*, *78*, 81, 104, *116*, 169, *170*
Jones, R. G., 65, 69, *77*, *78*

Katzogg, E. T., *15*
Kelley, H. H., 33, *42*, 78, 79, *83*, 104, *116*, 162, *167*, 169, *170*
Kelly, G., 161, 162, *166*
Kendall, P., 32, *42*
Kendon, A., 118, *121*
Kierkegaard, S., 123, *150*
King, M. G., *102*
Kleck, R., 104, 105, 106, 112, *116*
Klopfer, P., *102*
Krauss, R., 243, 244, *245*

Laski, H. J., 146, *150*
Latané, B., *209*
Laue, J., 245, 286
Lawrence, D. H., *14*
Lear, J., 92, *102*
LeBon, G., 173, *176*
Lee, F., *14*
Leipold, W. E., 94, 95, *102*
Lemann, T. B., 32, *42*
Leslie, C. R., *59*, *61*
Levine, G., 44, 45, 52, 54, *58*, *60*, *61*
Levy, J., *14*
Levin, H., *15*
Lewin, K., 174, 175, *176*
Linder, D. E., 35, 40, *41*, *83*
Lipman, A., 99, *103*
Lippit, R., 174, *176*
Lobel, L. S., *60*
Lorenz, K., 22, *23*

McBride, G., 95, *102*
Maccoby, E., *15*
McCormic, T. C., *58*

McDonough, J. J., 147
McGinnis, R., *59*
Mack, R., 286, *288*
Marquis, D. G., *16*
Mathewson, G. C., *42*
Mehrabian, A., *121*
Meyerson, L., *116*
Milgram, S., 122, 148, *150*, 168
Miller, N. E., *150*
Mills, J., *41*
Moreno, J. L., 162, *167*
Murphy, G., *14*
Murphy, L., *14*

Newcomb, T., 5, *13*, *14*, 32, *42*, 78, *83*
Noel, R. C., *245*
Nowles, V., *15*

Ono, H., 104, 114, *116*
Oppenheimer, M., *257*
Osgood, C., 245, 287, *288*

Park, R. E., *86*
Pasamanick, B., *59*
Pepitone, A., 5, *13*
Piliavin, I. M., 239, *240*
Piliavin, J. A., 239, *240*
Precker, J. A., 32, *42*

Rappaport, A., 122, *151*, 168, 243, 287
Ray, E., 38, *42*
Ray, J. D., *59*
Ray, M. H., 105, 106, 114, *116*
Reid, J. E., *102*
Reiss, I., 29, *60*, 79
Rhamey, R., 33, *41*
Richardson, A. H., *59*, *61*
Richardson, H. M., 32, *42*
Richardson, S. A., 104, *116*
Riecken, H. W., 7, *13*, *195*
Rodin, J., *209*, 239, *240*

Rogers, C., 161, *166*, 176
Rogers, E., 44, 45, *58*
Rosenow, C., *14*
Ruchmick, C. A., *14*

Sampson, E. E., 21, 23
Schacter, S., 7, 8, *13*, *14*, *15*, 20, 32, *42*, *195*
Scheidlinger, S., *15*
Schein, E. H., *236*
Schelling, T., *256*
Schlosberg, H., *16*
Schonbach, P., 10, *15*
Scott, J. P., 132, 147, *150*
Sears, P. S., *15*
Sears, R. R., *15*
Seaton, R., *103*
Sechrest, L. B., 160, 164, *166*
Secord, P. F., 32, *41*, *42*
Shapiro, D., 32, *42*
Sherif, M., 174, *176*
Slawson, J., *15*
Sletto, R. F., *15*
Smith, E. A., *59*
Smith, W., 44, *58*, *59*
Snyder, R. C., *245*
Soloman, R. L., 32, *42*
Sommer, R., 84, *86*, 91, *103*, 119, 120
Spinoza, B., 38, *42*
Spitz, R. A., 21, 23
Stagner, R., *15*
Steele, F. I., *236*
Stevenson, H. W., 20, *23*
Stieper, D. R., *15*
Stotland, E., 32, *42*
Stratton, L. O., 95, *103*
Sullivan, H., *16*, 20, 22, 163
Sumner, W. G., 247, *256*
Sundal, A.P., *58*
Sussmann, L., 44, 45, 52, 54, *58*, 60, 61

Sussman, M., *59*

Taylor, J. A., *15*
Thibaut, J. W., *13*, *15*, 33, *42*, 78, 79, *83*, 104, *116*, 162, *167*, 169, *170*
Thurstone, L. L., *15*
Thurstone, T. G., *15*
Tinbergen, N., 98, *103*
Torrance, E. P., *15*
Trager, G., 85, *86*
Triplett, N., 173, 174, *176*

Usdane, W. M., 104, *116*

Waller, W., 43, 44, 45, 46, 51, 53, 57, *58*
Wallin, P., *58*
Walster, E., 80, *83*
Walters, R. H., 38, *42*
Weissberg, A., *15*
White, R. K., 174, *176*
White, R. W., 39, *42*
Whiting, J. W. M., *15*
Whyte, A. H., *14*
Wiener, D. N., *15*
Willerman, B., 28, *31*
Williams, J. L., 94, *102*
Williams, M., *121*
Willis, R. H., *195*
Winch, R. F., 29, *31*, 32, *42*, *59*
Winters, L. C., 84, *86*, 105, *116*
Witty, P. A., *15*
Woodworth, R. S., *15*, *16*
Wright, B., *116*
Wrightsman, L., *16*

Young, P. T., *16*

Zander, A., *13*, 175, *176*

Subject Index

A—B variable, (in psychotherapy), 159, 165
Addams, J., 178
Affiliation, 8, 21
Affiliative behavior, 5, 8
Affiliative needs, 4
Aggression, 144, 282, 283
Altruism, 196
Anxiety, 21
Anxiety reduction, 38, 40
Arrival distance, 100
Argyris, C., 236
Asocial responses, 164
Attraction, 34, 81, 83, 122
Autistic conspiracy, 64, 65

Blake, R., 236
Body language, 117
Bystander intervention, 174

Campus social class, 54, 55
Carson, R., 122, 169
Clarke, B., 61
Class-dating theory, 46
Class endogamous marriages, 46
Cognitive field, 130
Cohesiveness, 27

Communication, 83, 84, 121, 153, 248, 249, 250, 280, 281, 287, 288
Communism, 272, 283, 284, 285
Comparison level for alternatives, 163
Competition, 243, 244, 247, 278
Competitive-materialistic, 44, 56
Complementarity of need, 29, 32
Compliance, 62, 184
Comprehension, 87
Conflict, 137, 138, 152, 207, 243, 244, 245, 246, 248, 249, 250, 253, 269, 273, 278, 280, 282, 284, 286, 288
Conformity, 65, 67, 68, 69, 70-73, 75, 76, 81, 148, 173, 182, 183, 184, 189, 191, 237
Cooley, C. H., 173, 239, 240
Cooperation, 20, 152, 156, 157
Counter-attitudinal advocacy, 162
Critical period, 22
Cultural truisms, 190

Daley, R., 251
Dalliance relationship, 43, 46, 51
Darwin, C., 195

Davis, W., 61
De-individuation, 6
Dependence-confirming tactic, 62
Desegregation, 246, 248, 249, 251, 253
Dietrich, R., 61
Dreyfuss, A., 236
Dyad, 27, 78, 105, 159, 168, 169, 170, 287
Dyadic interaction, 30, 122, 123, 152, 168, 170

Effectance, 39
Elges, E., 147
Elms, A., 147
Encounter group, 85, 175, 210, 212, 227, 231, 235, 238
Endogamy, 57
Eye contact, 109, 110, 113, 117, 118, 119, 120

Facial expression, 119
Feral children, 2
Flattery, 62

Gain-loss phenomenon, 34, 38, 40, 79
Gerritz, K., 209
Gestalt therapy, 85, 211
Grant, E., 98, 99
Gregariousness, 7, 23
Group dynamics, 175, 176
Group mind hypothesis, 173
Group pressure, 195
Group therapy, 175, 211

Hedonic effects, 163
Hochmann, J., M.D., 236
Humphrey, H. H., 254
Hutchinson, P., 61

Imprinting, 3, 22
Individual distance, 91, 94

Ingratiation, 61, 62, 64, 65, 67, 68, 69, 73, 77, 81
Instinct, 1, 2, 3, 21, 23
Integration, 250
Interminable therapy, 166
Interpersonal attraction, 31, 37

Johnson, L. B., 252, 277

Kennedy, J. F., 252, 254
Kennedy, R. F., 254
Kinestic behavior, 84
King, M. L., 251

Level of intimacy, 120
Leventhal, H., 150
Lindsay, J., 254
Loneliness, 17, 18, 19, 22
Love, 16, 17, 81

MacArthur, D., 267
Malcolm X, 254
Marceau, M., 121
Miles, M., 236
Milgram, Sasha, 147
Miller, J., 147
Motoric activity, 111
Motoric inhibition, 114
Murata, T., 147
Mutual dependence, 62

Nixon, R., 288
Nonverbal behavior, 85, 114, 117, 118, 120, 121
Norms, 120, 238, 240

Obedience, 123-125, 127, 130, 133, 140, 141, 167

Panic, 197, 199
Paralinguistic behavior, 85
Parental social class, 54, 55
Passive inhibition, 132

Personality traits, 47, 120, 193
Physical stigma, 103, 112, 113, 114, 115, 120
Physionomy, 120
Portable territory, 92
Prestige, 44, 45, 52, 53
Preadolescence, 16, 18, 19, 22
Primary groups, 177, 179, 180, 181, 239, 250
Primary reinforcement, 1, 2
Private acceptance (type of conformity), 184
Propinquity, 32, 57
Proxemics, 84
Proximity, 132, 149
Psychotherapy, 159
Punishment, 23, 125, 126
Pupil dilation, 118

Rational-emotional therapy, 162
Reference group, 238
Reinforcement, 1, 23, 38
Richardson, L. F., 158
Rockefeller, D., 254
Ross, L., 209
Russo, N., 96, 99, 101, 120

Secondary reinforcement, 1, 2
Self-evaluation, 6
Settled distance, 100

Simmel, G., 117
Simulated conflict, 152
Social class homogamy, 45
Social comparison processes, 6, 237
Social inhibition, 199
Social isolation, 9, 10, 20
Social motivation, 21, 22
Social reality, 237
Spatial invasion, 93, 101, 119
Stier, S., 147
Sullivan, H. S., 20, 22, 163

Tension, 135, 136, 137, 138, 140, 141, 231, 232, 273, 275, 278, 281, 282
T-group, 175, 210, 211
Therapeutic paradox, 163
Tit-for-tat strategy, 156
Transference reaction, 164
Trucking game, 243

Westermarck, E., 177
Whitman, W., 4
Williams, J. T., 147

York, H., 245, 287

Zimbardo, P., 167, 168

ABCDEFGH79876543